RITUAL AND

COGNITIVE SCIENCE OF RELIGION SERIES

Series Editors: HARVEY WHITEHOUSE
and LUTHER H. MARTIN

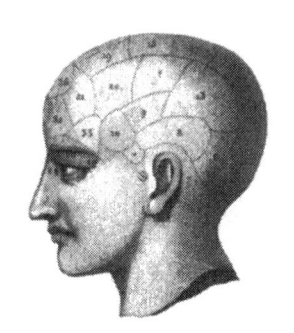

The Cognitive Science of Religion Series publishes research into the cognitive foundations of religious thinking and behavior and their consequences for social morphology. The emphasis of the series is on scientific approaches to the study of religion within the framework of the cognitive sciences, including experimental, clinical, or laboratory studies, but works drawing upon ethnographic, linguistic, archaeological, or historical research are welcome, as are critical appraisals of research in these areas. In addition to providing a forum for presenting new empirical evidence and major theoretical innovations, the series publishes concise overviews of issues in the field suitable for students and general readers. This series is published in cooperation with the Institute for Cognition and Culture at Queen's University Belfast.

TITLES IN THE SERIES:

Modes of Religiosity
A Cognitive Theory of Religious Transmission
By Harvey Whitehouse

Magic, Miracles, and Religion
A Scientist's Perspective
By Ilkka Pyysiäinen

Why Would Anyone Believe in God?
By Justin L. Barrett

Ritual and Memory
Toward a Comparative Anthropology of Religion
Edited by Harvey Whitehouse and James Laidlaw

Theorizing Religions Past
Archaeology, History, and Cognition
Edited by Harvey Whitehouse and
Luther H. Martin

How the Bible Works
An Anthropological Study of Evangelical Biblicism
By Brian E. Malley

FORTHCOMING TITLES:

Mind and Religion
Psychological and Cognitive Foundations of Religion
Edited by Harvey Whitehouse and
Robert N. McCauley

The Evolution of Religion
By Harvey Whitehouse

God from the Machine
By William Sims Bainbridge

RITUAL AND MEMORY

Toward a Comparative
Anthropology of Religion

EDITED BY
HARVEY WHITEHOUSE
AND JAMES LAIDLAW

ALTAMIRA PRESS
A Division of Rowman & Littlefield Publishers, Inc.
Walnut Creek • Lanham • New York • Toronto • Oxford

ALTAMIRA PRESS
A division of Rowman & Littlefield Publishers, Inc.
1630 North Main Street, #367
Walnut Creek, CA 94596
www.altamirapress.com

Rowman & Littlefield Publishers, Inc.
A wholly owned subsidiary of The Rowman & Littlefield Publishing Group, Inc.
4501 Forbes Boulevard, Suite 200
Lanham, MD 20706

PO Box 317
Oxford
OX2 9RU, UK

Copyright © 2004 by AltaMira Press

All rights reserved. No part of this publication may be reproduced, stored in a retrieval system, or transmitted in any form or by any means, electronic, mechanical, photocopying, recording, or otherwise, without the prior permission of the publisher.

British Library Cataloguing in Publication Information Available

Library of Congress Cataloging-in-Publication Data

Ritual and memory : toward a comparative anthropology of religion / edited by Harvey Whitehouse and James Laidlaw.
  p. cm. — (Cognitive science of religion series)
Based on 3 conferences held 2001–2003.
Includes bibliographical references and index.
ISBN 0-7591-0616-9 (cloth : alk. paper) — ISBN 0-7591-0617-7 (pbk. : alk. paper)
1. Ethnology—Religious aspects—Congresses. 2. Religion—Philosophy—Congresses. 3. Whitehouse, Harvey—Congresses. I. Whitehouse, Harvey. II. Laidlaw, James. III. Series.

BL256.R59 2004
306.6—dc22   2004001231

Printed in the United States of America

Dedicated to the Memory of Ernest Gellner

CONTENTS

Preface ix

Introduction   JAMES LAIDLAW   1

CHAPTER 1
Divergent Modes of Religiosity in West Africa   J. D. Y. PEEL   11

CHAPTER 2
Modes of Religiosity and the Legacy of Ernest Gellner   DAVID SHANKLAND   31

CHAPTER 3
Is Image to Doctrine as Speech to Writing? Modes of Communication and the Origins of Religion   JACK GOODY   49

CHAPTER 4
Ritual and Deference   MAURICE BLOCH   65

CHAPTER 5
The Doctrinal Mode and Evangelical Christianity in the United States   BRIAN MALLEY   79

CHAPTER 6
Embedded Modes of Religiosity in Indic Renouncer Religions   JAMES LAIDLAW   89

CHAPTER 7

Conceptualizing from Within: Divergent Religious Modes from Asian Modernist Perspectives   SUSAN BAYLY   111

CHAPTER 8

Late Medieval Christianity, Balinese Hinduism, and the Doctrinal Mode of Religiosity   LEO HOWE   135

CHAPTER 9

Religious Doctrine or Experience: A Matter of Seeing, Learning, or Doing   GILBERT LEWIS   155

CHAPTER 10

Universalistic Orientations of an Imagistic Mode of Religiosity: The Case of the West African Poro Cult   CHRISTIAN K. HØJBJERG   173

CHAPTER 11

Toward a Comparative Anthropology of Religion   HARVEY WHITEHOUSE   187

Index   207

About the Contributors   217

Preface

THIS BOOK IS BASED UPON the papers presented, largely by anthropologists, at an international conference on "modes of religiosity" at King's College, Cambridge, in December 2001. The Cambridge conference was the first of three. The second was held at the University of Vermont in August 2002, at which an international group of archaeologists, classicists, historians, and historians of religion assessed the predictions of the modes theory against a wide range of data, and whose findings are published in this series as *Theorizing Religions Past: Archaeology, History, and Cognition* (Whitehouse and Martin 2004). The third conference was held at Emory University in August 2003, at which an international group of cognitive scientists discussed the psychological foundations of religiosity and their implications for the modes theory. The resulting book, *Mind and Religion: Psychological and Cognitive Foundations of Religion*, will be published in this series next year (Whitehouse and McCauley, forthcoming). We are grateful to the British Academy for providing a Networks Grant that made all three of the conferences possible, and for awarding a two-year Research Readership to Whitehouse, during which most of his contributions to the writing and editing of this volume were made. We are also grateful to King's College, Cambridge, for the generous provision of outstanding facilities and technical support throughout the 2001 meetings.

Harvey Whitehouse
James Laidlaw

Introduction

JAMES LAIDLAW

IN THIS VOLUME A SINGULARLY ambitious theory—one that seeks to identify and explain universal features of religion—is subjected to a determinedly searching critical examination. The theory in question should be of very general interest. It claims, in brief, that there exist two contrasting styles of religious life. These two "modes of religiosity" are characterized by quite different kinds of rituals and ceremonies; different kinds of ideas, leaders, and forms of religious authority; and different sizes and types of groups and institutions. The kaleidoscopic and apparently irreducible variety of religions we find throughout human history and in different parts of the world may, according to this theory, be explained in terms of interactions between these two universal forms. And the existence of these two "modes" can in turn be explained as the consequence of universal features of the human mind, specifically two distinct mechanisms of long-term memory, which stand respectively at the center of each of the two modes of religiosity.

This "modes of religiosity" theory has been put forward by Harvey Whitehouse, in a number of publications beginning in 1992. The most comprehensive published statement, at the time of writing, is the 2000 book, *Arguments and Icons*, and this is the version that was under discussion at a conference, held in King's College, Cambridge, in December 2001, where this volume began. This conference, which was a gathering principally of anthropologists but included also historians of religion, cognitive scientists, and philosophers, was part of a larger project, with funding from the British Academy,[1] that included another gathering of historians of religion and archaeologists held the following year, in Vermont, and of cognitive scientists the year after that, at Emory University in Atlanta. The purpose of the project as a whole is to test, interrogate, refine, amend, and seek to establish the usefulness and the limits of the "modes of religiosity" theory, and in particular to respond to the fact that while the theory is framed so as to apply, its author hopes, to all religions everywhere, it was developed on the basis of ethnographical research on a couple of modern religious movements in the Eastern New Britain region of Papua New Guinea (Whitehouse 1995).

The question of the relation between the determined particularity of ethnographical research and the generality of theoretical claims that emerge from such research is of course a perennial one in anthropology, and also in allied disciplines in the human sciences. The Cambridge conference and this volume have sought to address this question in a practical manner. Contributors do not share the same methodology or intellectual style, either with Whitehouse or with each other, as will be evident from the chapters that follow. They differ, pertinently, in their enthusiasm for cognitive science and their evaluation of the hopes of those, like Whitehouse, who argue that it provides the basis for a fundamental and productive reformulation of core anthropological concepts, notably "culture." The majority of contributors are robustly skeptical about such claims. But they do not simply reject them, as do many in anthropology, on the grounds that there is something somehow morally or politically objectionable about any attempts to use scientific knowledge to throw light on human social and cultural life, including religion. For those who hold this position, and those in general for whom "reductionism," "essentialism," "positivism," "scientism," "objectivism," and (apparently a wild-card this, but a much-used one and also relevant) "binarism" are all more or less interchangeably terms of general disapprobation, their objections would not be met, but would indeed be more likely to be further aroused, by any apparent success in the application of the ideas to detailed ethnographic and historical cases. The contributors to this volume do agree, at least, in rejecting this kind of objection. They welcome the fact that Whitehouse's theory is framed in such a way as to invite empirical test and challenge, by attempting to make clear what would count as refutation.

The contributors also share a positive commitment to a broadly comparative project for anthropology, as demonstrated by the fact that many of them have carried out research in more than one cultural area. Within British social anthropology, this has been an important tradition, and it is one respect in which the fact that the conference was held in Cambridge, where this tradition has been notably strong, is reflected in the character of the volume. So even those contributors who argue that Whitehouse's hypotheses need to be fairly radically reformulated, or are more limited in application than Whitehouse has hoped, welcome the fact that they are formulated in ways that encourage and facilitate comparison. The idea of an interrelated complex of features of a "mode" of religiosity—relating type of memory, features of rituals, and political form—has proved to be a perspicuous new framework for ethnographic interpretation, as is demonstrated by the insights which many of our contributors have found in bringing the theory to bear on their own ethnographic areas. So even the most skeptical agree that if, in the end, the theory as a whole and the dichotomous model it gives rise to do not survive empirical challenge, they will in the meantime have provided a productive comparative framework for the anthropology of religion.

Whitehouse's theory, while undoubtedly original in several respects, does not emerge from a vacuum. The general framework is clearly a descendant of the comparative religious sociology of Max Weber, and the reformulation of that work in the writings of Ernest Gellner. This fact is reflected in several of the contributions to the volume. And Whitehouse's use of cognitive studies of memory is part of a more general rapprochement between anthropology—or at any rate a small but growing number of prominent figures with it—and cognitive and evolutionary science.

The theory seeks to explain "some of the varied ways in which religious commitments are experienced, organized, transmitted, and politicized" and seeks to do so "in terms of underlying cognitive mechanisms" (Whitehouse 2002: 293). In common with Dan Sperber (1996), Scott Atran (2002), Maurice Bloch (1998), Pascal Boyer (2001), McCauley and Lawson (2002), and others (e.g., Barkow et al. 1998), Whitehouse invokes a broadly selectionist model of the transmission of cultural representations. New ideas arise all the time. Only those that are successfully transmitted between individuals and retained and recalled by them over time become parts of "culture." Ideas that are not readily communicated or recalled are likely to die out. Various "cognitive mechanisms" are involved in the transmission and recall of ideas, and the activation of these mechanisms biases cultural selection in a variety of ways. Each mechanism will, comparatively speaking, favor some kinds of representations over others. Thus the kinds of ideas human cultures can consist of will be affected by the forms of transmission and memory that human communities have available to them.

This much is common currency among authors working in cognitive science and evolutionary psychology. At its simplest, Whitehouse's theory fits within this general enterprise, as a set of hypotheses about the effects on the parts of "culture" we identify as "religion" of two specific "cognitive mechanisms," the forms of long-term explicit memory identified by cognitive psychologists respectively as semantic and episodic (or autobiographical) memory. Semantic memory refers to mental representations of a general, propositional nature. "For instance, the knowledge I have concerning road signs, the history of anthropological theory, how to behave in a restaurant, and what happens in the story of Little Red Riding Hood, are all expressions of my semantic memory" (Whitehouse 2000: 5). By contrast episodic or autobiographical memory, as these terms imply, is mental representations of specific events that have been personally experienced and are remembered, insofar as they are remembered, as distinct episodes.

Whitehouse's theory begins from the intuition that the distinction between these two forms of memory corresponds to the binary distinctions drawn by a whole variety of authors, from Weber to Gellner among others, who have attempted to generalize about religion. The reason for this, Whitehouse suggests, is that reliance on one rather than the other of these two forms of memory in the transmission of ritual actions has far-reaching consequences for the content of religious ideas, the way they are organized, and the kinds of sociopolitical groups that espouse them. In sum, to each of these two forms of memory corresponds a whole complex of features that together define a style of religious life, what Whitehouse calls a "mode of religiosity." These two modes are identifiably different in terms of the kinds of religious life they result in: the style, tone, and ethos of their characteristic rites and practices. The "doctrinal" mode, which relies on semantic memory, is more sober, organized, and verbal; the "imagistic" mode, which relies on episodic memory, is more emotional and personal, and ideas are conveyed nonverbally to a much greater degree.

Normally, these mechanisms of semantic and episodic memory are processually connected. For instance, I have a general set of representations of what happens when one has a haircut, and this is a result, over time, of the experiences I have had and remembered of specific haircuts I have had. Most of those events, as distinct singular events, I have forgotten. The episodic or autobiographical memories I had of these have been assimilated into my semantic memory, the "schema" I have of what happens, in general, in a haircut. As singular events, I remember only a little of the most recent haircuts I have had, and I may remember a few episodes from longer ago when something that happened was particularly unusual or shocking. Episodic long-term memory is mostly concerned with unique and notable events. In particular, the phenomenon of "flashbulb memory" is thought to result in particularly vivid and detailed memories of specific unique episodes that were especially surprising or shocking at the time: the "Where were you when Kennedy was shot?" phenomenon. Such memories may remain vivid and detailed—whether they are accurate or remain the same is a different set of questions—for the rest of one's life, and they may retain much of the emotional force of the original experience. It is this, according to Whitehouse, that the imagistic mode particularly exploits.

While the doctrinal mode is characterized by frequent repetition of religious doctrine in verbal form, which feeds into semantic memory, the imagistic mode is organized around infrequent dramatic and shocking events—such as traumatic initiation ceremonies—that give rise to flashbulb memories of baffling experiences that those involved may come to understand, insofar as they do, only after prolonged reflection over the course of their lives. Frequent repetition in the doctrinal mode of routinized rehearsals of details of religious doctrine, in regular liturgical ceremonies with sermons, well-known hymns, readings, and familiar and habitual bodily movements, contribute to well-formed schemas of semantic memory. Practitioners of a religion with routinized liturgical rites may come to know the central dogmas of their religion implicitly, almost indeed unconsciously, so routinized does their participation become, but they may have absolutely no memory of when or with whom they learned them. This is the basis for widespread but impersonal solidarity among those who share the same body of doctrine. By contrast, those who have gone through a unique, traumatic experience together are likely to have in common the vivid, detailed, emotionally charged episodic memories of the event, including precise recall of others who were present at the time. This can be the basis of a different kind of solidarity, intense and personal but limited to far fewer people.

These two kinds of solidarity in turn give rise to different kinds of religious leaders and different kinds of coherence in the ideas their members share. In the doctrinal mode, the dispersed nature of the group and the need for frequent verbal rehearsal of doctrine both tend to lead to the emergence of religious leaders whose authority rests on expertise in doctrine. They may be educated, articulate, variously inspired or inspiring, and they will tend to be concerned with policing doctrinal orthodoxy, since their own position and authority depend on this. This encourages and gives powerful survival value to organizational centralization. These features—centralization, identifiable leaders, and consciously maintained orthodoxy—all facilitate spread of the religion through large and widespread populations.

In the imagistic mode, by contrast, the episodic memories people have of very infrequently performed rituals are a poor basis for verbally transmitted information to become shared. Instead, these traumatic and mysterious memories become a reference point for individual reflection on the possible meaning of the events that gave rise to them. Such reflection, often experienced as divine revelation or personal inspiration, leads people to draw their own associations between the images and symbolism involved in the rites. There is very little basis for these meanings to become shared. Even the experience later in life of organizing similar rites—such as for the initiation of the next generation—requires a measure of agreement about what is done and almost none about its meaning. Thus even within the small and intensely cohesive groups formed by shared traumatic experience, there remains wide diversity and very little agreement on religious ideas. Indeed, the experiences and memories may be so traumatic and disturbing that there is very little discussion of them, and so there is almost no occasion to come to an agreement on the shared meaning. In these circumstances, such leadership as may arise will be weakly placed to shape and police any systematic body of shared belief, or to organize and direct any program of action based on shared belief. The combination of the personalized intensity of local solidarity and this lack of dynamic leadership means that cults in the imagistic mode are unlikely to spread very far or fast. Where they do spread, this occurs by neighboring groups adopting for themselves some version of their infrequent emotional rites, rather than accepting a body of doctrine. The groups will tend to remain separate. All religious traditions, Whitehouse concedes, will have elements of both of these models in them (2000: 11). All will involve some use of both semantic and episodic memory, for example. All will have some routine and some infrequent and emotionally stimulating events. But the connections between the elements of these models—form of memory, frequency and style of event or ritual, and form of social association and solidarity—are mutually reinforcing. So there is a powerful tendency pulling toward one or the other of these poles. Any particular tradition, in a particular time and place, will tend to form into a version of one or the other of these "modes." Each can be represented diagrammatically as a set of interconnected features.

The contrast between the two modes may be further represented by means of a series of twelve variables. The first five of these, which according to Whitehouse have causal primacy, are what he calls psychological features. They are primary because "they are founded in the material conditions of brain activity—expressed in the form of memory effects" (Whitehouse 2002: 308). The remaining variables are sociopolitical features, features of the groups that form respectively in the two modes.

The claims Whitehouse makes about these two modes, and their explanatory importance in relation to the human experience of religion, are large. First of all,

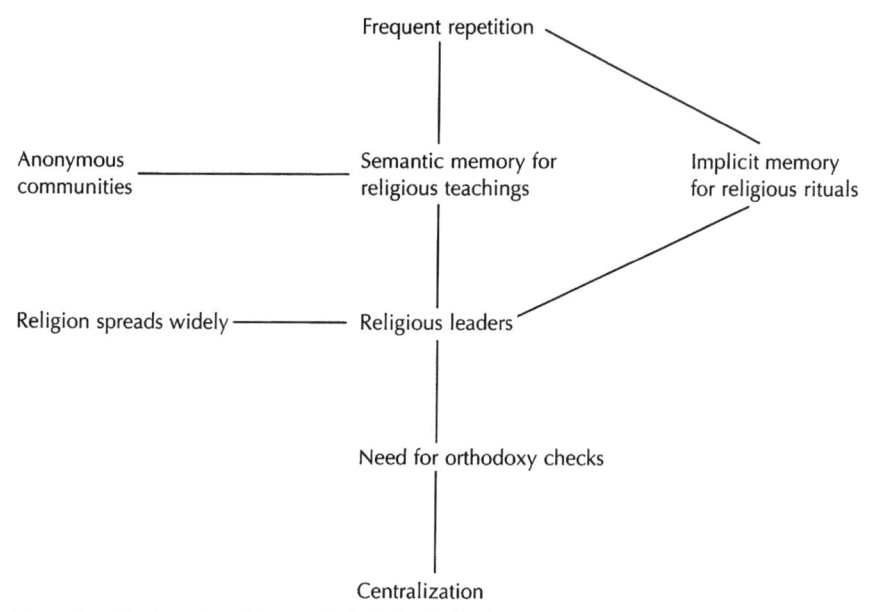

Figure 1. The Doctrinal Mode of Religiosity (Whitehouse 2002: 297)

```
                    Infrequent repetition          High arousal
                            |                           |
                            |                           |
                            |                        Intense
                            |                        cohesion
                            |                           |
                            |                           |
                    Episodic memory ─────────────── Localized/
                            |                        exclusive
                            |                       communities
                            |                           |
                            |                           |
                    Spontaneous          Diversity of
                    exegetical (SER)     religious representtions
                            |          /
                            |        /
  Lack of ──────── Lack of dynamic ──────────────── Hard to spread
  orthodoxy        leadership
                            |
                            |
                            |
                    Lack of centralization
```
Figure 2. The Imagistic Mode of Religiosity (Whitehouse 2002: 303)

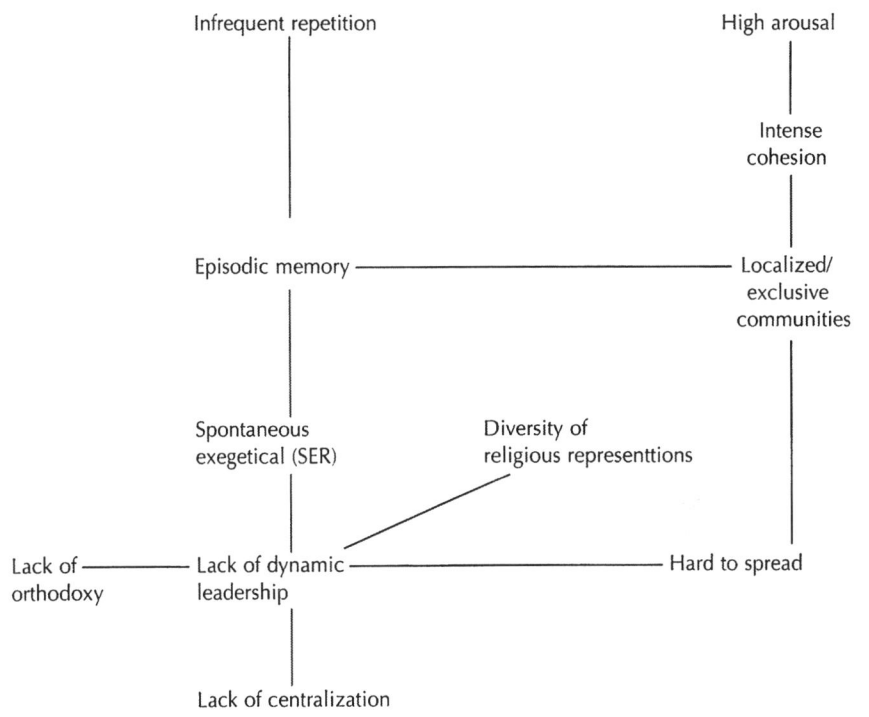

VARIABLE	DOCTRINAL	IMAGISTIC
	Psychological Features	
1. Transmissive frequency	High	Low
2. Level of arousal	Low	High
3. Principal memory system	Semantic schemas, implicit scripts	Episodic/flashbulb memory
4. Ritual meaning	Learned/acquired	Internally generated
5. Techniques of revelation	Rhetoric, logical integration, narrative	Iconicity, multivocality and multivalence
	Sociopolitical Features	
6. Social cohesion	Diffuse	Intense
7. Leadership	Dynamic	Passive/absent
8. Inclusivity/exclusivity	Inclusive	Exclusive
9. Spread	Rapid, efficient	Slow, inefficient
10. Scale	Large-scale	Small-scale
11. Degree of uniformity	High	Low
12. Structure	Centralized	Noncentralized

Figure 3. Modes of Religiosity Contrasted (Whitehouse 2002: 309)

they are ubiquitous. He suggests that the imagistic mode can be discerned behind surviving visual imagery from the Upper Paleolithic, and has been part of human religious life ever since. The doctrinal mode is more recent, having apparently first become established in Mesopotamia after 6000 BC. Nowadays, interaction between the two modes lies at the core of emerging patterns of religious dynamics throughout most of the world's traditions (Whitehouse 2000: chapter 8).

Secondly, they are always and everywhere distinct. So powerful are the causal links connecting the features of each of the two modes that although they are almost invariably both found, at least intermittently, in every society, they do not ever merge or fuse. The tendency for religious phenomena to coalesce into one or the other of these modes, and the fact that the features of them are in many ways diametrically opposed, leads Whitehouse to describe them as "divergent." The diversity of empirically observable forms of religion and patterns of change in different societies are produced not by mixtures, in varying degrees, of the two modes, but instead by complex patterns of interaction between them. They will always remain recognizably distinct, both to indigenous practitioners and to outside observers.

Almost all of the main hypotheses and generalizations in this theory are challenged at some point in the course of the volume: from the causal priority of psychological over sociopolitical features, through the characterization of the two modes, to the extent to which they are "divergent" and therefore empirically exhaustive and exclusive. These challenges have not, of course, resulted in a new unanimity. But they have resulted in significant clarification and revision to the theory, as will be evident to readers of Whitehouse's chapter at the end of the volume. Here we find, for example, an explicit restriction of the scope of the two modes. Many of the most widespread phenomena of human religious life—ideas of gods, ghosts, and so forth—are to be explained in different ways, which resemble ideas put forward by Boyer (1994), Sperber (1996), and others. This leads in turn to significant reformulation of the ways and extent to which the two modes may be thought to be "divergent" and what kind of predictions this yields for the forms of religious life we may expect to be possible.

The interest of the volume lies not only in the fact that these revisions seem in themselves to be advances—significant improvements to the heuristic and interpretive as well as the putative explanatory value of the theory—but also in the fact that they are illustrations of the process of anthropological inquiry at work. We see generalizing theory being confronted with a wide range of ethnographical, including historical, data, and we see not only the way theory enlivens ethnography and inspires interpretation, but also the way ethnography requires and compels revision to theory.

Note

1. The British Academy Networks grant that enabled this project to get off the ground was subsequently augmented by substantial additional funding from the Templeton Foundation and the Emory University Conferences Subvention Fund. The Cambridge conference was also supported by the King's College Research Centre.

References

Atran, Scott. 2002. *In Gods We Trust*. New York: Oxford University Press.
Barkow, Jerome H., et al., eds. 1998. *The Adapted Mind*. New York: Oxford University Press.
Bloch, Maurice. 1998. *How We Think They Think*. Boulder, Colo.: Westview.
Boyer, Pascal. 1994. *The Naturalness of Religious Ideas*. Berkeley: University of California Press.
———. 2001. *Religion Explained*. London: Heineman.
McCauley, Robert N., and E. Thomas Lawson. 2002. *Bringing Ritual to Mind*. Cambridge: Cambridge University Press.
Sperber, Dan. 1996. *Explaining Culture*. Oxford: Blackwell.
Whitehouse, Harvey. 1992. "Memorable Religions: Transmission, Codification, and Change in Divergent Melanesian Contexts." In *Man* (NS) 27: 777–97.
———. 1995. *Inside the Cult*. Oxford: Clarendon Press.
———. 2000. *Arguments and Icons: Divergent Modes of Religiosity*. Oxford: Clarendon Press.
———. 2002. "Modes of Religiosity." *Method and Theory in the Study of Religion* 14: 293–315.

Divergent Modes of Religiosity in West Africa   I

J. D. Y. PEEL

THE INTELLECTUAL AMBITION of Harvey Whitehouse's project on "divergent modes of religiosity" (hereafter DMR) compels respect: no less than to develop a general theory of religion. Though there have recently been some others (Rappaport 1999, Boyer 2001), what makes Whitehouse's project somewhat different is that it has grown out of ethnography of a particular region—Melanesia. It is a region marked by a religious scene of remarkable diversity, where the confrontation between local tradition and missionary Christianity has not only produced a range of movements drawing on each, but has forced the contrast between different kinds of religion to the center of analytic attention. The tension between anthropology's ambition to develop theory of a general, even universal, scope and its main research practice of regionally based ethnography is, of course, very much what drives it as a discipline. Yet if the history of anthropology shows anything, it is that its high ambition to be a "science of man" or a "natural science of society" has continually faltered in the face of the problems of regional and historical specificity that ethnography creates. While it is true that ethnographic research has sometimes been inspired by theoretical concerns of high generality, these theories have repeatedly become merely models, that is, conceptual instruments for the more precise description and analysis of particular cases. The subject has tended to be "centrifugal," in that theories are evaluated on the grounds of whether they are "useful," or have "heuristic value" in relation to the problems created by particular local (or at the most regional) studies. Whitehouse's aim is "centripetal," in that it seeks to draw on local studies to test and refine the theory.

As Whitehouse points out (2000: 3–4), his distinction between "imagistic" and "doctrinal" modes of religiosity has a definite affinity with many of the other dichotomous contrasts that have been proposed in the sociology of religion, from

Max Weber and Emile Durkheim onward. While these authors' ambition to make arguments about the overall character of religious variation and change pushes them toward multivalence, the central focus of these dichotomies has usually been on the content of the religions: what they are "about" or their orientation to life and the world. Thus Ruth Benedict's contrast of Apollonian and Dionysian religions studies the ethos that they express and promote; while Victor Turner and other anthropologists of Africa have distinguished between cults that are primarily oriented to ancestors or "forces of society" or to deities/spirits of the land or "forces of nature." Of course, such variations in content will tend to be linked to other attributes, such as how religions are organized or their range or scale, but it is the linkage of such features with content that has tended to be the crucial issue both for sociological arguments about the functional importance of various features of religion and for historical arguments about the impact of particular religions on the direction of social change.

The distinctiveness of Whitehouse's approach shows up most instructively when we contrast it with Weber's, since there is much overlap in their content. Weber's sociology of religion pivoted on a distinction between "traditional," "primitive," or "small-scale" religions and "world" religions. Though this might seem to imply a primary concern with the effects of scale, Weber was essentially concerned with differences in their soteriological content: with whether salvation is a material, this-worldly matter or whether it has other-worldly objectives, as is the case with world religions; with the various directions that the search for salvation may take; with the affinities between different notions of salvation and the orientations of particular status groups; and with the consequences of these cultural choices for other areas of life. For several decades now the most impressive work in the Weberian tradition, which covers much of the same subject matter (and a lot more besides) as Whitehouse's *Arguments and Icons* (2000), has been Bryan Wilson's *Magic and the Millennium* (1973). Its comparative analysis of movements in Africa, North America, Melanesia, and elsewhere is based on a sevenfold typology of their "responses to the world." The sheer empirical variety and complexity of religious phenomena that led Wilson (as it would surely have led Weber) to this diversification of the original Troeltschean two-term typology of "sect" vs. "church" is for Whitehouse a means to the more strenuous testing and refinement of his dichotomous typology and its theoretical underpinning. Wilson points out that sociologists of religious movements have been largely preoccupied by the issues of doctrine, organization, and the relations between them (and that often in ways shaped by their Christian antecedents). For Whitehouse it is neither the "content" of doctrine (or as he prefers, revelation) nor organization that is the pivot of his typology, but the way in which the core revelation of a movement is encoded and transmitted. "Mode of religiosity" is perhaps too general and all-embracing a term for this. For the theory of DMR is not concerned with what experiences or circumstances produce particular revelations, and it treats organizational forms as outcomes, or at most as corollaries, of modes of religiosity, rather than an independent variable. Its framework is Darwinian, since it is about what religions have to do/be in order to survive and perpetuate themselves, and its premises are drawn from cognitive psychology.

Any revelation's accurate transmission over time depends upon the mechanisms of memory that it can call upon. Again, the emphasis of the theory of DMR is not on how the *content* of memory may be influenced by external forces, but on the effects of different *forms* of memory (Whitehouse 2000: 5). These are of two kinds: "episodic memory," which is of particular personal experiences, and "semantic memory," which is of the generalized knowledge, whether practical or theoretical, that people acquire or have been taught as members of a community. Corresponding to these are two ideal-typical "modes of religiosity": an imagistic mode, where adherents' grasp of their religion is encoded in personal recollections of relevant experiences, particularly of an emotionally arousing kind, such as of a terrifying initiation or a dramatic conversion; and a "doctrinal" mode, where it derives from such means as sermons, catechizing, and rituals of a more routine kind. From an evolutionary viewpoint, each mode has its own limitations. The imagistic mode, since it depends on the recall of exceptional, irregular, and personally variable experiences, tends to generate cults that are limited to small local communities and are susceptible to constant modification. The standardized and constantly repeated forms of the doctrinal mode do facilitate its spread to populations of varying local circumstances and ensure a relatively faithful transmission of its revelation. The main problem faced by the doctrinal mode is that repetition creates boredom and so reduces the motivation of participants. Any religion that managed to combine appropriate elements from both modes would find the prospects for its transmission and spread greatly enhanced.

As already noted, the first impetus to the theory of DMR came from trying to make sense of the religious diversity of Melanesia, where the initiation rites of peoples like the Orokaiva or the Baktaman suggested the imagistic mode, and the very different face of mission Christianity the doctrinal mode. Whitehouse insists that, though the two modes are only tendencies and that most actual traditions contain elements of both, the strength of their respective internal logics means that in practice Melanesian traditions "gravitate strongly" to one or the other, or if toward both, they do so "within readily distinguishable domains of operation." The evolutionary framework of his argument enjoins us to look less at what gives rise to either mode in general and more to what enhances the survival prospects of particular cults or religions. Yet the question of origins is pertinent to the general argument in one respect. It seems highly likely that the imagistic mode is more ancient, possibly going back to the Upper Paleolithic era, and that the doctrinal mode, since it depends so much on codification by means of writing, came much later. So it is not surprising that Durkheim, when he came to characterize the forms of religion in general, drew his example from a Stone Age religion of a markedly imagistic kind. Whitehouse is led to comment that Durkheim overgeneralized, ignoring the different way in which the doctrinal mode operated. But it is less the deutero-Durkheim of *The Elementary Forms* than the proto-Durkheim of *The Division of Labour* (1964 [1892]: 226–229) who comes closest to the matter. For having first proposed that there are two forms of social solidarity, mechanical (deriving from *conscience collective*) and organic (deriving from the division of labor), of which the former progressively gives way to the latter as society becomes modern, Durkheim turns round to argue that *conscience collective* nevertheless remains basic to the very existence of society. So too, it seems, with modes of religiosity: though the doctrinal is more characteristic of modern and world religions, they cannot altogether dispense with the imagistic. For the vitality of any religion must depend on its adherents feeling that their doctrines articulate the past occurrence, and the possible reoccurrence, of some more-than-ordinary contact between the human and the divine, which calls for the imagistic mode. Weber made the same point with his argument that an access of charisma was the foundation of all religions, however much it is later institutionalized.

A theory such as DMR is one of those middle-range theories that social scientists have often asked for, mediating between highly abstract propositions drawn from cognitive psychology and ethnographic-cum-historical material of great empirical richness. So there are two broad approaches toward applying it. One would use a particular body of empirical data to test and refine the relations postulated between the variables of the theory at the abstract level; the other would apply a more pragmatic test and ask how far the theory enhances our understanding of a particular body of regional data. Here I shall take the latter approach, and especially with respect to what seems a crucial possibility suggested by the DMR theory: how the two modes may be combined or integrated in particular cults, religions, or local systems of religious provision.

As an ethnographic region, West Africa has some similarities to Melanesia. It too is an area of diverse local religions that over the past century and a half has witnessed extensive activity by Christian missions and large-scale conversion to them against a background of sweeping social change induced by colonialism. The cultural gap between the two kinds of religion, the pressures of colonialism, and the desire of Christian converts to seek power according to their own understandings gave rise, as in Melanesia, to movements of substantially Christian idiom, initiated by charismatic local leaders, that have variously been termed syncretist, prophetist, millenarian, and so forth. These similarities have often led to the inclusion of *ordinary pilgrims*

movements from West Africa and Melanesia within the same comparative and analytic frame. Yet in other respects the West African setting is very different. Most of its communities were traditionally far larger, including precolonial kingdoms with complex political hierarchies, large settlements with developed class and occupational structures, markets, and long-distance trade. Consequently many indigenous religions and cults were much more extensive in scope and scale than in Melanesia, and there was the centuries-old existence of Islam—itself testimony to the region's extensive links with the outside world—which interacted in complex ways with indigenous cults, and in some areas both anticipated and complicated the encounter between them and Christianity.

The DMR dichotomy evokes several of those current in the West African literature, so the question is whether it offers a more precise and profound characterization of differences already and independently recognized as real and significant. But here a caution needs to be registered: A theoretically cogent dichotomy is a powerful cognitive magnet, tending to draw other, related distinctions into itself. Then dichotomies get "stacked up" on top of one another, so that significant differences of emphasis get elided, or reduced to aspects or implications of the master dichotomy. Two dichotomies in particular have been much used in studies of religion in West Africa. The first is between traditional (or "primal," theologically PC for "primitive") and world religions, or preliterate religions and religions of the book, which is much the same distinction empirically but is viewed from a different angle. There is a more theorized version in Horton's contrast between microcosmic and macrocosmic cults, which embodies a crucial shift of emphasis, since it expressly allows for representations of the macrocosm to occur within the idiom of traditional religion. Second, with regard to traditional religion, anthropologists have drawn various closely related contrasts between two kinds of cult found widely in indigenous African societies: ancestors vs. deities, spirits of society vs. spirits of nature, political vs. fertility rituals. In all these cases distinctions that are manifest in empirical or synthetic form may be reworked analytically, so as to highlight aspects considered to be of particular theoretical relevance.

So how may either of these distinctions (traditional vs. world religions, ancestor vs. nature cults) be aligned with the DMR dichotomy of the imagistic vs. the doctrinal? It is obvious how the former may, but its relationship to the latter is not so clear. The argument to follow rests on the assumption that the imagistic mode is primary (both in the sense that it emerged first and that it remains basic to the appeal of religion) and the doctrinal mode came later. The semantic memories sustained by the doctrinal mode are the generalized codification of what is taken from the original episodic memories—that is, memories of those individuals who experienced divine revelation and communicated it to their fellows—on which all religious establishments and many social orders depend. It explores first how the ground for the doctrinal mode was prepared within the traditional religions of West Africa, later to be realized in a fairly pure form in the Evangelical Christianity brought by the missionaries in the nineteenth century; and secondly how the imagistic mode has been reconstituted within the "born-again" Christianity that is the dominant manifestation in West Africa today.

For our present purposes what most crucially distinguishes cults of the ancestors and of the earth or natural spirits is that the former are highly embedded socially, often to the point of being hardly more than the ritual aspect of the lineage structure that they regulate. Their membership is ascriptive and closed, while the latter tend to be free-standing religious institutions that have to take deliberate steps to reproduce themselves, for their memberships are open and fluctuating. Many ancestor cults, indeed, seem almost to stand outside the imagistic/doctrinal contrast, needing neither "doctrine" nor high-arousal experiences to motivate their practices, but merely the habitus of quotidian relations with elders and the spontaneous remembrance of them after their decease, autobiographical memory gradually blending into semantic (Kopytoff 1971). So it is understandable that ancestral cults in Africa tend to be poorly supplied with such mnemonic devices as myths or images. It is significant that in the Yoruba case, it is in the cult of a lineage's and town's *collective* ancestors called Egungun (as also with royal ancestors of importance to the community at large) that iconic representation bulks larger, with specialized priesthoods, annual festivals, and, in general, some degree of assimilation to the other kind of cult, of *orisa* or spirits of nature (Peel 2000: 93–97).

Though associated with natural features or substances, the *orisa* were imagined as personalized deities, many of them with specialized functions or pronounced personal characteristics. Since, unlike ancestors, the *orisa* cults did not ride on other institutions, they needed to develop specific ways to ensure their survival: They had to motivate their adherents—which meant above all to provide cogent evidence of the presence and power of their god—and they had to offer an adequate rationale of the ritual and behavioral requirements of the cult. In respect to the former, their dominant mode was strongly imagistic: If an individual had not been dedicated at birth, it was often an acute personal crisis interpreted by the diviner as a call from the *orisa* that first drew members into the cult; *orisa* on occasion possessed their most active adepts and priests, who temporarily became their vessels and might offer further revelations; the cult members met regularly to renew their special relationship with the *orisa* through shared sacrifice; at annual festivals, accompanied by drumming and dancing, praise-singing, and public parade of their images, links between the community and the *orisa* were confirmed. All this was highly performative—devotees were said to manifest their *orisa*'s active power by "playing" or enacting them (Barber 1981, Drewal 1992)—and often created (or were associated with) states of high arousal.

There was a doctrinal aspect, too. Partly it was implicit in the epithets of the praise-poetry and in the symbols and images of the *orisa*—the red-and-white clay beads on the forehead of the *Orisa Oko* devotee, the thunderbolt-axe of Sango, Obatala's white cloth—because such served as mnemonic pegs for stories (*itan*) about their origins and attributes. Cult knowledge was esoteric, and authority within any social unit—whether cult, craft, lineage, or town—went with mastery of relevant *itan*. So access to knowledge was both highly stratified—priests and adepts having a "deeper" knowledge than ordinary adherents, and they than outsiders—and segmented into parcels not shared by everyone. But there was a body of generally knowledgeable people in the *babalawo* ("fathers of mystery"), practitioners of the system of divination known as Ifa. The corpus of Ifa divination verses was the largest archive of myth and cosmology available to the Yoruba, and (since most people consulted *babalawo* occasionally and heard some of these verses) was probably the most widely available source of general religious knowledge.

Taken as a whole, Yoruba *orisa* cults were remarkably effective in staving off the two threats to survival which, according to the DMR theory, all cults face. The major cults, at least, were able to generate enough motivational interest—partly through their attachment to the major crises in human lives, which created a high level of personal identification with them, and partly through their own vivid presentation of *orisa*-power at festivals, through possession, etc.—as well as sufficient understanding of their theory and practice to achieve both wide geographical spread (extending in some cases well beyond the Yoruba-speaking area) and impressive stability over time. (See Barnes 1997 on Ogun, god of iron; or Murphy and Sanford 2001 on the river-goddess, Osun.) In this achievement of spatial and temporal extension, they may be contrasted with the nonlineage cults among peoples such as the Akan and the Kongo, whose spiritual forces—respectively, *abosom* or "deities" and *minkisi* or "fetishes"—not only lacked the personality and cult organization of the major *orisa* but, apparently like many traditional cults in Melanesia, showed a cyclical pattern in their rise and fall, as old ones lost their appeal and new crises led to the emergence of new ones (De Craemer, Vansina, and Fox 1976; McGaffey 1983). Cults established in conditions of social crisis and/or high emotional arousal seem to have lacked either the doctrinal elaboration or the social infrastructure to keep them perduringly in existence, though the cultural conditions for later revivals of similar movements remained in place.

The historical terrain that embraces both indigenous and world religions is likely to prove especially fruitful for examining the interplay of the two modes of religiosity, for there are movements that reach out either way: anticipations of the doctrinal within religious systems predominantly imagistic in character, and movements to recover the power of the imagistic by those placed within strongly doctrinal settings like missionary Christianity. Of the former, an excellent example is provided by the Yoruba divination cult of Ifa, which was held to be the special province of a particular deity, Orunmila. It was not the only system of divination, for the priests of other deities gave oracular guidance, too, typically through some form of trance or possession. Ifa, however, did not rely on its practitioners (*babalawo*) being possessed by their *orisa*, but on their mastery of a technique, which entailed their capacity to remember a vast corpus of verses. The babalawo began by manipulating a handful of palm-nuts to produce one of 256 (16 × 16) configurations (*odu*), to each of which corresponded a sequence of verses that described mythical precedents; these were then recited by the *babalawo*, and the client selected one that spoke to his situation. The source of the problem and the steps to be taken to resolve it, by a specified sacrifice to a particular *orisa*, would then be clarified by casting lots in response to the client's questions. Though Orunmila thus sustained the system of *orisa* cults as a whole (which indeed he belonged to), he also represented himself as somewhat above and outside it, as the sole channel of wisdom from the Supreme Being, Olodumare, who was the source of the Ifa verses. And as if to underscore this autonomy from the rest of the *orisa*, Ifa sometimes advised its clients that the answer to their problem was to become Muslim or Christian, that is to worship God directly, rather than through the *orisa*.

It is thus not surprising that missionaries accorded considerable respect to *babalawo*, who were ready dialecticians and their most astute critics, but also very ready to learn from them (Peel 1990). This affinity was widely perceived and even extended, in a triangle of mutuality, to Muslim *alufa*, the spokesman of the other world religion competing for Yoruba favor. The marks indicating the selected *odu* that the *babalawo* drew in the sacred powder on his ritual tray were widely interpreted by Yoruba pagans as a kind of literacy *avant la lettre*, and the reception of both Koran and Bible was conditioned by what was required of Ifa verses: to predict and to solve problems. In fact this degree of preadaptation to some of the features of the doctrinal mode may well have been written into Ifa from its origin, for it appears that the "16-options" systems of divination, found widely throughout sub-Saharan Africa and Madagascar, all ultimately derive from Islamic sources (Binsbergen 1996; Brenner 2000). A Yoruba clergyman and cultural nationalist, E. M. Lijadu, even went so far as to argue that in Orunmila, his pagan compatriots actually had some foretaste of the saving grace of Jesus Christ, and that Christianity was the fulfillment of Ifa (Peel 1993).

Yet though Ifa was the most doctrinal of the *orisa* cults and provided a doctrinal component to the system as a whole; though it became the most pan-Yoruba of all cults, and spread far beyond the Yoruba-speaking region, east to the lower Niger and west to the Volta region (Maupoil 1943); though its practitioners were able to enter into a serious engagement with Muslim and Christian clergy, it still fell short of being a full-blown realization of the doctrinal mode. First, it remained dependent on oral modes of transmission. Hence, though it was considered sacrilegious to add to or subtract from the corpus, and steps were taken (by such means as the stringent training of neophytes and Ifa-recitation competitions between experienced *babalawo*) to prevent these, there was almost certainly a slippage of content as well as some regional variation in the corpus. Second, since Ifa was a pragmatic and client-centered system of oracular consultation, and not a congregational religion, it worked in practice to embrace a multitude of individual perspectives (albeit within a common framework of cosmology and ritual practice) rather than impose any kind of collective ideology—hence, indeed, its openness to Islam and Christianity. Third, it enshrined the principle of secrecy, for only the *babalawo* knew how to access secrets or hidden things (*awo*). Secrecy is bound to undermine the diffusion of that standardized common understanding of religious knowledge that is at the heart of the doctrinal mode.

By contrast, missionary Christianity was in the strongest sense a religion of the book, its converts initially known in Yoruba as *onibuku* ("book-people"); in place of the pragmatic and personalized advice of Ifa were universal ethical injunctions, and it was vital that the Word of God should be made openly available in the language of the people (Peel 2000: 223–25). The other religion of the book, Islam, well ensconced by the mid-nineteenth century, had already been modified by the demands of Yoruba culture. The not-to-be-translated Koran lent itself to esoteric and magical uses, and quite a lot of the doctrinal/imagistic distinction seems to appear in the contrast between two faces of Yoruba Islam: the one communal and egalitarian, associated with public worship, Koranic exegesis and sermons, and learning to recite the Koran; the other individualist and hierarchical, when people consulted *alufa* for Koranic charms or sought access to esoteric power through *shaikhs* or *sharifs*. While there are difficulties in simply labeling the latter "popular" or heterodox—since it always drew in learned Muslims and had deep roots in the mainstream—there is no doubt that it could attract the criticism of preachers for encouraging wrong attitudes and is the target of contemporary reformism. Yet it provided a way to meet some basic Yoruba demands on religion which missionary Christianity found difficult to match. This was a primary stimulus to the independent religious movements and churches, which burgeoned in the early decades of the twentieth century.

Here we come to the reassertion of imagistic practices within African Christianity, as against the anticipation of doctrinal ones within traditional religion. African independent churches (or AICs) have given great scope for typology (Turner 1967). While most classifications were derived from labels used by the churches themselves—such as Ethiopian/Zionist in South Africa (Sundkler 1948) or African/Aladura in Nigeria (Webster 1964)—they have given rise to binary typologies of a more analytic character. So, for example, Fernandez (1964) constructed four types based on two cross-cutting continua: one (nativistic/acculturated) dealing with the movement's primary cultural orientation and the other (expressive/instrumental) having to do with the manner of its response to the colonial situation. Neither of these has much to do with the imagistic/doctrinal contrast. Yet the DMR theory does seem, in retrospect, to be pertinent both to certain empirical contrasts made in my study *Aladura* (Peel 1968) and to the searching critique of its approach expressed by Fernandez in an influential general review of the field (1978).

The Aladura are a cluster of churches founded by African religious innovators, who triggered a series of "revivals"—involving healing through sanctified water, witchcraft confession, mass destruction of idols, and some millennial preaching—between 1918 and the mid-1930s. Their basic aim was to make the power of prayer (*adura*, hence their name) more fully available than it was in the older Protestant missions for such this-worldly objectives as health, fertility, protection against witchcraft and danger, guidance, prosperity, and success—in sum, that state of all-around well-being that the Yoruba call *alafia*. While Aladura's theological content is strongly Christian, its ritual forms as well as its ontology of the spirit world owe much to the indigenous religious background. Dreams, visions, and ecstatic tongues—gifts of the Holy Spirit—are seen as vehicles of divine power and guidance, recalling aspects both of *orisa* cult-groups and of Ifa divination (Harris 2002), but with prayer substituting for sacrifice as the medium of human address to God. There had been early influences from an American faith-healing group called Faith Tabernacle, but a more significant external input came when, from 1930 onwards, the Aladura became somewhat variably subject to the influence of Pentecostalism, initially through a British group, the Apostolic Church. The outcome was a spectrum of churches, ranging from some of a more home-grown idiom (with African-style music and liturgy, the wearing of white prayer-gowns, elaborate hierarchies of spiritual offices, a rich repertory of ritual symbols, and the use of such items as candles, incense, and holy oil) to those that conformed more to Euro-American Pentecostal norms, with their emphatic scripturalism and aversion to complex ritual symbolism. *Aladura* took for comparison two churches standing toward either end of this spectrum: the Cherubim and Seraphim (C&S) and the Christ Apostolic Church (CAC).

The approach of *Aladura* was "intellectualist" in that, in contrast to studies of new religious movements in the Third World of Marxist and/or functionalist inspiration (Balandier 1970 [1955]; Worsley 1968 [1957]; Lanternari 1963 [1960]), it sought to explain Aladura belief and practice as intellectually cogent responses, given the cultural premises of young Yoruba Christians, to the problems and dilemmas they confronted at a time of midcolonial crisis. From their shared roots, C&S and CAC tended over the years to diverge. C&S, with its more African idiom, tended to revert to what might be called the Yoruba cultural default system, becoming flexible and pragmatic in its search for spiritual power, whereas the more consciously Pentecostal CAC held much more to doctrinally grounded lines of conduct, even against the promptings of Yoruba culture (e.g., its rejection of polygamy or the refusal of medicine in favor of prayer). These differences were related to organizational ones:

> The C&S see themselves ... as a society of people which God had supremely invested with spiritual power, and the prophet or spiritualist ... is their most distinctive religious type. The spiritual clientage is the form of grouping associated with such a man; and this is modified to being the general clientage of a big man, or an association of people after the same spiritual goal. ... Wider organization than these they have found difficult.
>
> CAC members are equally concerned with the fruits of spiritual power, but they are being educated by their leaders to explain it differently. Personal authority of various kinds has always been, and still is important, but the possessors of it have used it to spread the idea that their church is the one which embodies correct doctrines, and so has spiritual power. This has been the work of intellectualist pastors. ... Doctrines are open, public, arguable things, and favor the growth of pastors who expound them; the pastors derive their legitimacy from the church, the embodiment of the doctrines. (Peel 1968: 287–88)

It is evident that this contrast might be rephrased in terms of the DMR theory: the C&S being more imagistic, the CAC more doctrinal—within a fairly narrow band of difference, it is true, but still with the organizational correlates that Whitehouse argued for.

There is a complex ebb and flow at work here. The C&S responded most directly to the dissatisfaction of African converts with an insufficiently inculturated British Evangelicalism: its apparent inability to summon prayer-power for mundane needs and, more diffusely, the converts' hunger for symbolically (that is, imagistically) richer forms of engagement with the divine. The CAC, by contrast, thanks to the influence of their Pentecostal mentors, seemed in some ways to have moved back toward the evangelical baseline—a less imagistic (or at least more doctrinal) form of faith—but yet seemed no less successful for that. I interpreted this in terms of a long-term process of religious rationalization, à la Max Weber, which was linked to the fact that its social bearers were modernizing educated young men. It was this assumption that Fernandez (1978) called into question. He argued, in terms that almost uncannily anticipate those of the DMR theory, that the intellectualist approach to Aladura (further theorized by Horton 1971, 1975) and to African movements more generally projected a kind of "imageless thought" onto them. Instead, because African thought is socially embedded, analysts of religious movements needed to attend to the "argument of images" that they employ. This was applied in his analysis of the Bwiti cult among the Fang of Gabon and the former French Congo (Fernandez 1982), one of the finest studies of an African religious movement ever carried out. The colonial experience was extremely traumatic for the Fang, but what Bwiti offered was less a monovalent solution to its problems than a microcosmic "pleasure dome," created through a complex play of symbols and ritual, syncretizing themes from Christianity, the ancestral cult, and images from the rain-forest environment, from which any adept may take what he or she needs. Bwiti is one of the very few African cults to make use of a psychotropic drug, eboga, in its rituals. Its use of symbols is highly polysemic, and its sermons employ what Fernandez calls "an elliptical riddling style" to produce "edification by puzzlement." If it is a mark of the imagistic mode to generate a "dynamic . . . towards creative elaboration rather than faithful repetition, and the production of local differences rather than regional homogeneity" (Whitehouse 2000: 15), then Bwiti fits the bill perfectly. But at the same time, this implies that the approach advocated by Fernandez, with movements of this type in mind, will be less helpful for those that stand closer to the doctrinal pole, such as the Nigerian CAC.

It is not easy to generalize about the direction of change within Africa Christianity as a whole over the past three decades, but if there is a single dominant trend, it is the rise of neo-Pentecostal or (as it is colloquially known in Nigeria) Born-again Christianity. The Africanizing ethos of the older AICs like the C&S, with their local idioms and resonances, yields to something a great deal more universalist in its sense of itself. Neo-Pentecostalism is a global movement in Christianity, with much circulation of people and media among West Africa, its epicenter in the American South and West, and even such places as Brazil or Korea. There are some similar trends in Islam, as radical reformists with models drawn from the Middle East or the earliest age of Islam attack such long-established West African practices as devotions at the tombs of "saints" (*wali*) or the rituals of *sufi* orders (Brenner 1993). While we may well be drawn to label both sets of phenomena as instances of "globalization," we must not then fall into the teleology of thinking this will explain the phenomena or allow it to blind us to the fact that churches of a strongly local idiom continue to attract many Nigerians.

Surveys of churches in the Yoruba metropolis of Ibadan in the 1990s showed a great burgeoning, not merely of the newest Born-again churches or "ministries" (as they often style themselves) and the older Pentecostals such as Apostolic, Foursquare Gospel, Assemblies of God, etc., but also of the Celestial Church of Christ, a C&S-related body that has the most ritualized practices of prayer, healing, and prophecy of the "white-garment" churches, as the Aladura nowadays are often described. Of the churches once regarded as Aladura, it seems that it is those at either end of the imagistic/doctrinal spectrum—Celestial and CAC— that have grown the most, while churches in the middle—most C&S branches or Church of the Lord (Aladura)— have languished. One great irony is that though Pentecostalism first entered Yoruba Christianity *through* the Aladura movement in 1931, the terms Aladura and Pentecostal are now regarded as mutually exclusive, and fall into different sections of the national umbrella body, the Christian Association of Nigeria. CAC is now emphatic that it is Pentecostal, not Aladura, and has had close relations with some of the newer Born-again groups, especially Deeper Life. A further irony is that the current market-leader among Born-agains, the Redeemed Christian Church of God, actually began as a breakaway from the Eternal Sacred Order of Cherubim and Seraphim, but was radically reconstructed by its well-educated second leader. Like other Born-again churches, it is anxious to make out that a chasm separates it from the Aladura, who are stigmatized as mixing pagan or "demonic" elements into their practices. In testimonies given at Redeemed revival services, former members of the Celestial Church have denounced the Aludura as engaged in "works of Satan," to be renounced by the Born-again.

The fact that people can still be drawn in large numbers to Africanizing churches like the Celestial Church of Christ, even though the main flow of preference is to the more globally oriented Born-agains, should counsel against seeking to explain the success of the latter simply as an adjustment to the spirit of the times. Pentecostalism is a global form of Christianity, but then so is Catholicism, even though since Vatican II "inculturation," or the adaptation of its theology and liturgy to local cultures, has been strongly promoted. But granted that the ethos of global modernity projected by neo-Pentecostalism is part of its appeal, and that this pushes it toward the doctrinal mode, since it has to rely on semantic memory to create understandings that can be shared across an international community of believers, how is Born-again Christianity so successful in combating the "tedium effect" (with consequent loss of motivation) that threatens all forms of Evangelicalism, with its austere symbolic repertory, sustained Bible study, long sermons, and so forth?

Whitehouse's view (2000: 150–55) is that the source of the doctrinal mode presented in missionary Christianity (of all denominations) lay in the Reformation's onslaught on the imagistic practices of late medieval Catholicism. A weakness in his argument at this point is that, in jumping directly from the sixteenth to the nineteenth century, it elides some critical shifts in how the two modes have figured within Evangelical Christianity. We may distinguish three main paradigms in chronological order: Puritanism, Evangelicalism, and Pentecostalism. In the first of these, Puritanism, up to the end of the seventeenth century (or in America the early eighteenth), the doctrinal mode in a fairly pure form could often be applied in religiously uniform communities—Geneva, Scotland, New England—where the tedium effect could, at some cost, be suppressed by social controls. It is hardly a historical accident that it was when these started to break down in the early eighteenth century, making it necessary to find some other means to revive motivation, that a new form of the imagistic mode came into being. Hence Evangelicalism, distinguished sociologically from Puritanism by its focus not on the closed community of the Elect, but on the perception (in Wesley's words) of the world as its parish, and theologically by its voluntaristic conception of God's saving grace freely offered to all who would receive it. Evangelicalism saw itself not as disclosing new doctrinal truth, but rather as reviving the faith of the believer. So in the terms of the DMR theory there was the paradox that, though in one sense it was as doctrinal as any other version of Protestantism—as dependent on preaching and reading the Word—Evangelicalism also made vital use of a new form of the imagistic mode. For it created powerful experiences of divine grace, whose deposit in autobiographical memories—of ecstatic revival meetings, of the moment when one first *knew* the Lord Jesus—would supplement the semantic memories of routine religious instruction. Hence the Methodist societies as they initially related to the established church markedly resembled such splinter groups of the mainline Paliau movement as the Noise or the Second Cult (Whitehouse 2000: 140–46). Compare the name assumed by the movement in colonial America, "the Great Awakening" with the Melanesian cultists' use of the metaphor of "waking up." "Imagistic" is a term that may mislead, if it is felt to point exclusively to visual icons; for the autobiographical memories activated in the Evangelical "religion of the heart" depended not on visual images, but on words and music.

With its institutionalization in churches, however, Evangelical religion tended to slip back to a greater reliance on the doctrinal mode, with little iconic or ceremonial richness to offset the danger of tedium. As John Wesley himself said, in a passage famously quoted by Weber: "I do not see how it is possible, in the nature of things, for any revival of true religion to continue long" (Weber 1930 [1904–05]: 175). So too the Evangelical missionaries of the Anglican Church Missionary Society (CMS) in Yorubaland came to lament the "cold," formal religion (which, reversing Wesley's line of causation, they thought gave rise to "worldliness") of their flock in the second generation (Peel 2000: 250–53). Yet revival—a form of religion in the imagistic mode—was still contained within Evangelical culture as a memory and a hope, at both individual and collective levels, to be periodically reactivated. The 1859–1860 revival in Britain and Ireland (monitored from afar by missionaries in West Africa) led on to the Keswick Convention from the 1870s, which over the next three decades sent out a series of evangelists to conduct revivals at the behest of the Lagos churches. African CMS candidates for ordination in the 1880s–1890s, many of whom were "converted" at these Keswick revivals, were asked to write autobiographical statements of which a key element was their account of this experience.

An issue that needs to be explored in relation to mission is how this Evangelical culture of periodic revival interacted with indigenous historicities in which there were cycles of social renewal, involving such imagistic episodes as antiwitchcraft movements or the accession of new sources of power. Take the case of the Ulster Evangelicals who set up the Qua Iboe Mission among the Anang of southeastern Nigeria. Its pioneer, Samuel Bill, was first moved in the late 1870s by the visit to Belfast of the American evangelists Moody and Sankey in one of the "last waves of the Ulster revival" (Hempton and Hill 1992: 145–58), and started out in Nigeria in 1887. By the 1910s, the Mission was making fair progress under the aegis of colonial rule, opening churches and schools, winning converts, but yet dissatisfied: "The Christians in Ikotobo . . . have not grown in grace as they have grown in numbers. . . . The missionary, joined by a few earnest souls, has been much in prayer for a true revival" (M'Keown 1912: 157). Over a decade later it was still reported: "Our churches and services and all our carefully built organisation are futile for doing God's work without the life-giving Spirit" (Watt 1951: 94). Revival finally came in 1927, triggered by a young teacher but taking the Mission completely by surprise, and produced what was known as the Spirit Movement, marked by witch confessions, mass destruction of idols and charms, contagious enthusiasm, and glossolalia. The missionaries, of course, saw it in terms of the archetypal Day of Pentecost, and of precedents such as the Ulster revival or the Welsh revival of 1904. The Anang precedents are less easy to discern, and certainly some of the immediate conditions, arising from tensions produced by colonial rule, were strictly unprecedented, but later cycles of upheaval suggest that this fluid society with rather unstable chiefly authority—in that, more like Melanesia than the Yoruba were—was prone to cycles of routine and revitalization (Pratten 2000).

Faith missions like the Qua Iboe were already on the cusp between classic Evangelicalism and Pentecostalism, the third main manifestation of the Protestant tradition. The ideal of being born again in the Holy Spirit had been present within West African Evangelicalism from its very origins: it was a prominent theme in the preaching of the Rev. W. A. B. Johnson, the famous German CMS missionary who converted hundreds of liberated Africans during his ministry at Regent in Sierra Leone, as far back as 1817–1823. So what exactly did Pentecostalism bring that was new? Pentecostalism incorporates several of the recurring features of nineteenth-century American Protestantism—perfectionism, premillennialism, fundamentalism, dispensationalism—and also draws down, through its African-American origins, a strong current of African religious sensibility (which would of course reconnect potently with local cultural demand when it got to Africa). Perhaps what most set it apart it from earlier (and largely European) expressions of Evangelical religiosity was the emphasis placed on the physical tokens of divine favor, notably speaking in tongues as the mark par excellence of baptism of the Holy Ghost and miracles of healing. As recent studies of its worldwide diffusion show clearly (Poewe 1994; Cox 1996 [1994]; Corten and Fratani 2001; Martin 2002), Pentecostalism is an extremely protean phenomenon, even within particular countries or churches. Whether its impact is politically conservative or culturally radical, what its natural class affiliation is, what its main practical thrust is—whether holiness teaching, divine healing, gospel of prosperity, deliverance from demons and ancestral spirits, predictive prophecy—are questions all hotly debated (probably because each and all of these alternatives comes up in the appropriate context). Neo-Pentecostalism taps as deeply into the springs of indigenous African spirituality as the older AICs, but manages to do it in an attractively modern and transnational idiom. Its success may be seen, in terms of the present argument, as arising from its unique ability to bring together, sometimes close to the point of fusion, the two modes of religiosity.

The DMR theory is about how the ability of a religion to pass on its revelation is affected by the way it is encoded in memory, not about how the content of that revelation may relate to its context. Still, the connection between religious content and mode of religiosity will always call for attention. A final dichotomy is apparent in the fluctuating religious orientations of both Aladura and Born-agains, which may be called holiness vs. empowerment. Holiness is essentially a concern to conform oneself to the will of God, following the dictates of scripture and prayer, typically by living a life of spiritual self-discipline. Empowerment is where one seeks to enlist the power of God, above all through prayer and revealed means, to achieve a fuller, richer life and to defeat any forces that oppose that end. While holiness looks *inside* the self for the solution to one's existential problems, empowerment looks *outside*. Yet despite this contrast the two orientations have common elements, and holiness can easily "flip over," as when self-discipline comes to be regarded instrumentally, as a means analogous to sacrifice in gaining the favor of a god. In their first encounter with religious modernity, the Yoruba had an early version of the holiness solution presented to them by Evangelical CMS missionaries—change yourselves inwardly, then your institutions will be transformed and "your country will become good"—while they looked to the mission for direct techniques of empowerment (Peel 2000: 127, 152–54). It goes without saying that the missionary version of holiness teaching was firmly in the doctrinal mode.

The trajectories of Aladura (from the 1920s) and the Born-agains (from the 1970s) show striking similarities. Both began as prayer and Bible-study groups largely composed of earnest young people with a marked orientation toward holiness. Faith Tabernacle (CAC's precursor) and the Praying Band of C&S were composed of young literates (Peel 1968: 83–91), and fellowships of "campus Christians" were the germ of the massive Born-again ministries of recent years (Ojo 1988). Chastity and monogamy, abstention from alcohol, regimes of fasting, reliance on prayer alone for healing, not wearing jewelry (in the case of women), and a generally disapproving attitude to the flamboyant display of Yoruba social life were some of its hallmarks. So what are the conditions under which it becomes plausible, even compelling, to so go against the grain of Yoruba culture? Holiness, presenting oneself to God as "a living sacrifice," is an appropriate response to the expectation that the millennium, the end of the present dispensation, is imminent. Premillennialist anticipation was widespread in Nigeria in the years after 1918 into the early 1930s; *End-Time Army* is the title of Matthews Ojo's study of the most holiness-oriented of the larger Born-again churches, Deeper Life (Ojo n.d.). But a complex blend of zeitgeist and Bible-based teaching is needed to hold the holiness orientation in place, and if either condition fades, it may be expected to yield to the perennial Yoruba search for empowerment, where its moral restraints will be resignified as conditions for effective prayer. The concern for empowerment tends to reassert itself when what started as small holiness fellowships grow into large ministries, though differences of emphasis may still remain: Of the larger bodies, Deeper Life still stands toward the holiness end of the spectrum, while the Redeemed Christian Church of God (Ukah 2003) or Winners' Chapel—that name says it all!—stand toward the empowerment end.

In asking how the holiness/empowerment distinction correlates with the DMR contrast, it helps to consider what challenges the two tendencies respectively have to face. Holiness groups need above all to keep their members from slipping over to Born-again churches closer to the general cultural mainstream, that is, those of the empowerment tendency. Their integrity is grounded in the doctrinal mode, in Bible study, sermons, and pamphlet literature, but this is motivationally boosted by the imagistic impact of intense emotions aroused by prayer and the work of the Holy Spirit, particularly in small fellowship groups. The challenge facing the empowerment tendency (which includes most of the largest and high-profile Born-again organizations) is more from rival operators, including Aladura churches like the Celestial Church of Christ, offering similar products in the same crowded religious marketplace. What they most have to do, rather like *orisa* cults in the nineteenth century, is to project a clinching public image of their effectiveness as mediators of divine power. So here the relative importance of the imagistic and the doctrinal tends to be reversed.

Revival is here more of a continuous preoccupation than in the older evangelical churches: Redeemed has a Holy Ghost Night every month, drawing tens of thousands of people to its Redemption Camp off the Lagos-Ibadan expressway.

In cities like Lagos or Ibadan big revivals and crusades take place almost continuously, often with visiting pastors on the Born-again circuit (including prestigious figures from abroad). They are attended by much advance publicity and make the fullest use of all the techniques of religious showbiz as developed in the United States. I earlier noted that the term "imagistic" might seem oddly applied to Evangelicalism, given its poverty of visual icons, as evidenced by the declination from the Catholic crucifix to the plain cross of the Protestants to no cross at all in most neo-Pentecostal auditoria. But visual imagery has been able to stage a triumphant reentry through the Born-agains' confident exploitation of electronic media: TV coverage, videos of preachers and revivals, and video-movies, such as those made by Mike Bamiloye's Mount Zion Faith Ministries. Yet even here all is not imagistic. Complementing these revivals is a network of prayer fellowships and Bible-study sessions, where the doctrinal mode is paramount. Within a fortnight I have seen the leader of the Redeemed Christian Church of God, E. A. Adeboye, conduct a studious afternoon Bible-study meeting at the University of Ibadan's Protestant chapel, and preside at the tumultuous praise-worship and ecstatic spiritual effusions of a Holy Ghost Night. It is in the way that it combines imagistic and doctrinal modes of religiosity that much of the effectiveness of the Born-again movement is to be found.

References

Balandier, Georges. 1970 [1955]. *Sociology of Black Africa: Social Dynamics of Black Africa*. London: Andre Deutsch.

Barber, Karin. 1981. "How Man Makes God in West Africa: Yoruba Attitudes Towards the *Orisa*." *Africa* 51: 497–518.

Barnes, Sandra T., ed. 1997. *Africa's Ogun: Old World and New*, sec. ed. Bloomington: Indiana University Press.

Binsbergen, Wim van. 1996. "Regional and Historical Connections of Four-Tablet Divination in Southern Africa." *Journal of Religion in Africa* 26: 2–29.

Boyer, Pascal. 2001. Religion Explained: *The Human Instincts that Fashion Gods, Spirits and Ancestors*. London: William Heinemann.

Brenner, Louis. 1993. *Muslim Identity and Social Change in Saharan Africa*. London: Hurst.

———. 2000. Histories of Religion in Africa: An Inaugural Lecture. London: School of Oriental and African Studies.

Corten, Andre, and Ruth Fratani. 2001. *Between Babel and Pentecost: Transnational Pentecostalism in Africa and Latin America*. London: Hurst.

Cox, Harvey. 1996 [1994]. *Fire from Heaven: The Rise of Pentecostal Spirituality and the Reshaping of Religion in the Twenty-First Century*. London: Cassell.

De Craemer, Willy, Jan Vansina, and Renee C. Fox. 1976. "Religious Movements in Central Africa: A Theoretical Study." *Comparative Studies in Society and History* 18: 458–75.

Drewal, Margaret Thompson. 1992. *Yoruba Ritual: Performers, Play, Agency*. Bloomington: Indiana University Press.
Durkheim, Emile. 1964 [1892]. *The Division of Labour in Society*. New York: Free Press.
Fernandez, James W. 1964. "African Religious Movements: Types and Dynamics." *Journal of Modern African Studies* 2: 531–49.
———. 1978. "African Religious Movements." *Annual Review of Anthropology* 7: 194–234.
———. 1982. *Bwiti: An Ethnography of the Religious Imagination in Africa*. Princeton, N.J.: Princeton University Press.
Harris, Hermione Mary. 2002. "The Cherubim and Seraphim: The Concept and Practice of Empowerment in an African Church in London." Ph.D. diss., School of Oriental and African Studies, University of London.
Hempton, David, and Myrtle Hill. 1992. *Evangelical Protestantism in Ulster Society 1740–1890*. London: Routledge.
Horton, Robin. 1971. "African Conversion." *Africa* 41: 85–108.
———. 1975. "On the Rationality of Conversion." *Africa* 45: 219–35, 373–99.
Kopytoff, Igor. 1971. "Ancestors as Elders in Africa." *Africa* 41: 129–141.
Lanternari, Vittorio. 1963 [1960]. *The Religions of the Oppressed: A Study of Modern Messianic Cults*. London: MacGibbon and Kee.
Martin, David. 2002. *Pentecostalism: The World Their Parish*. Oxford: Blackwell.
Maupoil, Bernard. 1943. *La Geomancie a l'ancienne Cote des Esclaves*. Paris: Institut d'Ethnologie.
McGaffey, Wyatt. 1983. *Modern Kongo Prophets*. Bloomington: Indiana University Press.
M'Keown, Robert L. 1912. *Twenty-Five Years in Qua Iboe: A Missionary Effort In Nigeria*. London: Morgan and Scott.
Murphy, Joseph M., and Mei-Mei Sanford, ed. 2001. *Osun across the Waters: A Yoruba Goddess in Africa and the Americas*. Bloomington: Indiana University Press.
Ojo, Matthews A. 1988. "The Contextual Significance of Charismatic Movements in Independent Nigeria." *Africa* 58: 172–92.
———. n.d. "End-Time Army: The Charismatic Movements in Modern Nigeria." Unpublished manuscript.
Peel, J. D. Y. 1968. *Aladura: A Religious Movement among the Yoruba*. London: Oxford University Press for the International African Institute.
———. 1990. "The Pastor and the *Babalawo*: The Encounter of Religions in Nineteenth-Century Yorubaland." *Africa* 60: 338–69.
———. 1993. "Between Crowther and Ajayi: The Religious Origins of the Nigerian Intelligentsia." In Toyin Falola (ed.), *African Historiography: Essays in Honour of Jacob Ade Ajayi*. Lagos: Longman, 64–79.
———. 2000. *Religious Encounter and the Making of the Yoruba*. Bloomington: Indiana University Press.
Poewe, Karla, ed. 1994. *Charismatic Christianity and Global Culture*. Columbia: University of South Carolina Press.
Pratten, David. 2000. "From Secret Societies to Vigilantes: Identity, Justice and Development among the Annang of South-eastern Nigeria." Ph.D. diss., School of Oriental and African Studies, University of London.

Rappaport, Roy A. 1999. *Ritual and Religion in the Making of Humanity.* Cambridge: Cambridge University Press.

Sundkler, B. G. M. 1948. *Bantu Prophets in South Africa.* London: Oxford University Press for the International African Institute.

Turner, H. W. 1967. "A Typology for African Religious Movements." *Journal of Religion in Africa* 1: 1–34.

Ukah, Asonzeh F.-K. 2003. "Redeemed Christian Church of God, Nigeria: Local Identities and Global Processes in African Pentecostalism." Ph.D. diss., University of Bayreuth.

Watt, Eva Stuart. 1951. *The Quest of Souls in Qua Iboe.* London: Marshall, Morgan and Scott.

Weber, Max. 1930 [1904–05]. *The Protestant Ethic and the Spirit of Capitalism.* London: Allen and Unwin.

Webster, James Bertin. 1964. *The African Churches among the Yoruba 1888–1922.* Oxford: Clarendon Press.

Whitehouse, Harvey. 2000. *Arguments and Icons: Divergent Modes of Religiosity.* Oxford: Oxford University Press.

Wilson, Bryan R. 1973. *Magic and the Millennium: A Sociological Study of Religious Movements of Protest among Tribal and Third-World Peoples.* London: Heinemann.

Worsley, Peter. 1968 [1957]. *The Trumpet Shall Sound: A Study of "Cargo" Cults in Melanesia.* London: MacGibbon and Kee.

Modes of Religiosity and the Legacy of Ernest Gellner

2

DAVID SHANKLAND

ALBEIT AT A DISTANCE, I have followed for a number of years the emergence of Harvey Whitehouse's "Modes of Religiosity" theories with very great interest and admiration. While it is impossible to be sure, it is my understanding that this body of ideas has not yet been considered in sustained fashion with regard to Islamic society, the area in which I myself have specialized. For this reason, I shall, as well as a specifically ethnographic consideration of the Alevi community in Turkey, offer at least passing reference to the more typical orthodox Sunni movement, and by virtue of this comparison, several rather more general comments.[1]

I should say immediately that I am among the persuaded. It appears to me that Whitehouse's (1995, 2002) characterization of religious movements both fits and illuminates the Islamic world extremely well. It hardly needs to be repeated, perhaps, that in broad the Islamic world has been moving toward what Whitehouse characterizes as a "doctrinal" mode of religious thought. This contrasts with what is demonstrably closer to an "imagistic" mode: one that is celebrated less frequently than the more orthodox "doctrinal," and draws in part at least upon that remembered impact within a less ordered theology he suggests is likely to obtain. The Alevis too certainly illustrate such elements that may be described "imagistic." Nevertheless, I have a number of doubts that, while hardly strong enough to be considered disagreements, suggest certain topics for debate. In part, my concern pertains to that proportion of mind that Whitehouse intends his theories to cover. It would hardly be sensible to claim that memory is the only act of cognition necessary to possess or to pursue a religion. There must be an immense variety of different cognitive tasks occurring simultaneously, each of which may themselves have an impact on a religious style. Whitehouse does not, however, make note of them. Perhaps benefiting by this simplification, "memory" is sometimes used in his work simply as a short-hand for "cognition" itself, enabling him to leave out all those other aspects of mind (such as knowledge acquisition, perception, or consciousness) which may, on investigation, appear to shape religious practice as inexorably as memory itself. It would be interesting then to know more explicitly the "mind-map" that Whitehouse envisages. Without this, is does not seem possible to evaluate his claim as to the prime importance of memory within patterns of religious life.

Gellner on Islam

Leaving this initial worry momentarily to one side, the relationship between social order and religion is surely far closer than Whitehouse permits. In dismissing this, he would appear to have been considerably less than charitable to his predecessors. For instance, the work of Ernest Gellner (e.g., 1969, 1981, 1988) is far more troublesome intellectually to his inquiry than is implied in its rather casual dismissal.[2] After all, Gellner himself suggested that there existed two different types of Muslim "styles" of religious life, styles that are in some ways very close to Whitehouse's "modal" distinction. This is clear not from Gellner's general discussions of Islam, such as may be found in his work on the emergence of modernity, but also from the set of essays, entitled *Muslim Society* (1981), dedicated specifically to his discussion of the Islamic world.

Muslim Society is a complex volume, one that is often criticized.[3] Suspending judgment momentarily, and simply looking at the framework of his argument, Gellner assumes that within the Islamic world, there is often conflict between two different versions of the faith. The first of these is centered upon face-to-face collective ritual led by hereditary or at least sacred leaders, where the community may be largely or entirely illiterate. Worship tends to be expressive and irregular, based more on the ecological rhythm of the pastoral or semipastoral community than any more abstract time-reckoning. Both in life and death, such "saintly" leaders and their tombs may be focal points of religion within the community, which is often closed to outsiders, whether by default or design. Participation, in effect, is only through initiation, birth, or both. Though nominally, or even avowedly, Islamic, doctrine content is often minimal, and the actual practice of religion varies tremendously, not just over a small area but also over time. Often rural, these societies are prepared rigorously to defend their independence in the face of central rule, though at the same time are profoundly prone to fission and internal opposition.

The second version of faith is much more universalistic, proselytizing, and capable of uniting very large groups. Worship is based on a carefully established doctrine, one devoted to removing intermediaries between a worshiper and God, eliminating variation, and asserting the truth of a single text. While devotion takes place frequently throughout the day and adheres to an annual cycle, it is deliberately staggered in such a way that makes it clear that neither the sun nor the seasons are being worshipped. Highly literate and based upon teaching that is thought-out and argued through in minute detail by a scholarly group of specialists, it is at the same time open to all. Not in itself terribly interesting or exciting (though its adherents may be highly skilled in disputation), it nevertheless is capable of spreading quickly and convincing many populations of the truth of its message. Astonishingly stable, it varies greatly only within very large regions, and is capable of crossing the rural/urban divide with ease, so that village worship may often come to resemble that of the larger cities. Far from requiring a separate political organization, it is inclined toward using state power to its own ends, and often merges with it.

For Gellner, life in premodern Islamic societies often oscillated between these two "styles." Influenced by the work of Ibn Khaldoun as well as the more contemporary segmentary lineage theorists, he assumed that tribes outside central control were periodically sufficiently powerful to defeat the urban or sedentary rulers; their rebellion was fueled by religious enthusiasm, by accusations that the urban rulers were committing heresy and becoming lax in religious practice. However, upon taking control of the center, the new victors too would adopt the urban "style" until they decayed in turn, and ultimately were defeated by a fresh rural uprising.

This delicate balance between rural and urban "styles," Gellner assumes, remains at least in part until the transition to the modern world, when the second of these two variants comes to enjoy the greater success. He assumes, broadly speaking, that the internal struggle between the two styles was rendered unequal at the point when the rural style became militarily weaker than the urban. As the preponderance of nation-states became obvious and unavoidable and the state itself supremely powerful, the urban style utterly dominated. Gellner devoted a large part of his analysis to exploring compatibilities between this urban religious style and the modern way of life, asking just why that fusion of religion and nation-state should still be possible in a largely skeptical modern world.

The similarities to Whitehouse's approach are obvious. In part, Whitehouse's argument parallels Gellner's thinking in the assumption of two often-opposed styles of religious life. Indeed, occasionally the correspondence between "mode" and "style" is so close as to make the terms appear to be used almost interchangeably. The two approaches also retain their similarities when a more diachronic perspective is taken into account. This is particularly clear when Gellner's wider historical writings are considered, such as in *Plough, Sword and Book* (1988). His description there of the rise of an "urban, high" style is mirrored very closely by Whitehouse's parallel discussion in chapter 7 of *Arguments and Icons*, where he treats Christianity's assumption of the "doctrinal" mode and its overthrow of the "imagistic" in the Reformation. Nevertheless, while Whitehouse is scrupulously courteous in all his writings, he simply assumes there is no great theoretical import in these similarities. In fact, there is profound relevance.

Causality and the "Trigger"

A possible way to appreciate this is to think once more of the causal processes connecting the two "styles" of religious thought. In as much as a shift may take place from "doctrinal" to "imagistic," the trigger for Whitehouse appears to lie predominantly in the tedium to which repeated rituals doubtless give rise. Gellner does, in fact, consider this question indirectly, in his discussion of Hume in *Muslim Society*, but ultimately suggests that the influence of what, for want of a better term, might be called the sociological (or at least the way that the social order shapes and channels the ideological directions that influence religious thought) is the more significant.

Gellner illustrates why this might be the case through a great deal of highly varied ethnography drawn from North Africa. Stimulated in particular by his earlier fieldwork among the Berbers of the High Atlas (1969), he assumes that in the absence of more formalized law-giving bodies, a highly structured, though unstable, patrilineal kinship system favors the emergence of privileged lineages who, by virtue of that special status, are able to mediate in disputes. Conversely, he suggests that those societies who are more clearly part of the state's social order need immanent divine inspiration far less systematically because the social order may be retained through more formal courts that are authorized by the state authorities. This train of thought, of course, even if now unfashionable, is familiar within social anthropology, at least since *African Political Systems* (Evans-Pritchard and Fortes 1940), and owes too something to Durkheimian sociology.

At present, at least, it appears that Gellner's insistence on the validity of this older stream of thought is entirely justified, and that he in fact has developed a sharper tool than Whitehouse with which to note transitions in the Islamic world. A movement from the "doctrinal" to the "imagistic" mode of religious life has not happened among most of the orthodox Sunni population throughout Islam. In Turkey, for instance, the gradual religious revival that has come to predominate orthodox worship was characterized by dry, almost puritanical interpretations of the faith, in spite of the indisputable and fascinating complexities of the ethnography of Turkish Islam. When men are bored (and they have often complained to me that the mosque ceremony is not of great interest) they appear to turn to that lively, sensuous secular celebration of life that may be found in drink, wine, women, music, or, alternatively (or as well), in that wholehearted embrace of consumerism for which Turkey is famous.

There used to be an "imagistic" escape: in previous centuries the brotherhoods and Sufi mysticism (such as expressed by the Bektashis, the poetry of Hafiz, or in the Rubayyat of Omar Khayyam) celebrated joyous wonderings on the cusp of religion and revelation.[4] However, after the founding of the Republic and the secular state's ban on the brotherhoods, those that nevertheless remain active gradually assumed an oppositional role. Rather than act against the dry strictures of mosque-going worship, they now act as a vehicle to support it; a powerful, coordinated force for the further rise of orthodox practice and doctrine working partly within and partly outside the nominally secular state, the brotherhoods are now emptied of almost all imagistic focus that they may once have possessed.[5]

Thus, for much of the history of the Turkish Republic, boredom relief has been at least largely sought outside the accepted canons of religion. In contrast, the previous vehicles for "imagistic" thinking have become "doctrinal." Would this be possible within Whitehouse's modal schema as it at present is constituted? It seems unlikely. Any response would depend, perhaps, on whether a "mode" is only a way of religion or something rather broader. Here there may be another possible conflation in the way that terms are used. For Whitehouse, it appears that the "doctrinal" or the "imagistic" mode may be both a broad cognitive path *and* a specifically religious characteristic. It is important to clarify this because the answer as to which is intended leads one in different directions. Does Whitehouse use "mode" to refer to a cognitive style associated with certain social or psychological practices in general? Alternatively, of the varieties of human experience, does the term "mode" refer only to religious activity? If the former, why then choose religion for his descriptive focus and not the other connected multiplicities of human life (such as are illustrated in the Turkish population's search for boredom relief in bars, consumerism, and pop music, including the work of the amorphous Tarkan, hated by some religious Islamists as being too overtly sexually stimulating)? On the other hand, if a "mode" is only intended to be a *religious* model, how does Whitehouse account for the seemingly inescapable fact that the ethnographic record illustrates his suggested modes of behavior in nonreligious settings?[6]

The Alevis

We may take a further, more sustained illustration of this conundrum (which to my mind can probably only be addressed by vastly broadening the initial scope of the inquiry, even if it later has to be narrowed simply for practical reasons) by turning briefly to the Alevis. The dominant, seemingly traditional, version of the Alevi faith would appear an ideal candidate for the "imagistic" mode: It is predominantly collective, intermittently celebrated, hierarchical, nondoctrinal, and inspirational. However, ethnographically, the picture is rather complex. The community in the village setting regards itself as being Islamic, but achieves this differentiation in emphasis by maintaining that there are two broad streams of ritual practice, the *Şeriat* and the *Tarikat*. For them, the *Şeriat*, which they regard as being the normal practice of Sunni Islam, is not so much wrong in itself as superficial, and does not reach the depths of human understanding that is characterized by the *Tarikat*. A person may, if they so wish (even if Alevi) follow the *Şeriat* path, but this is not as praiseworthy as their partaking in the more collective *Tarikat*. In turn, they link these two alternative "ways" into the suggestion that there are in fact four ascending paths to God: *Şeriat* is the first and lowest, *Tarikat* the second, where most Alevis find themselves. The third stage, known as *Marifet*, they emphasize little, other than noting its existence, but the ultimate and last stage, *Hakikat*, is to arrive at one with God, to achieve the ability to perform miracles. Ideally, the community's hereditary holy lineages, which they refer to as *dede* (lit. grandfather), *dayı* (lit. mother's brother), or *ocak* (lit. hearths), are on this rank.

Changes over Time

The Alevis' everyday religious practice has changed greatly over time, but so much as I can piece together, it has done so not through any predominance of psychological factors inherent within the ritual practice. Summarizing brutally but I think not inaccurately, conversions to Sunni orthodoxy from the Alevi heterodox movement appear to have been at their height when and where the Ottoman Empire was physically dominant. Indeed, the Alevi villages in the area where I worked maintain that it is possible to follow the conversion from Alevi to Sunni village by village by following the passage of the Ottoman army as it went to war against the Shiite Iranian state, with whom the Alevis were suspected of being allied.

After the formation of the Republic, and when the village was beginning to move from almost purely subsistence agriculture and become more integrated into the modernizing nation-state, opposition to the *dede* lineages frequently emerged from within the villages during debate over who was to control the position of head man, *muhtar*. This opposition was partly structural, in that Alevi villages in the region are typically divided up into distinct and separate village quarters (*mahalle*) that vie for power within the village unit. However, in spite of the Alevis admiration for the secular Republic, in many villages in the region where I worked, such internal opposition took the form of greater emphasis on orthodoxy, and accusing the *dede* of lax religious practice. This opposition was often so successful that the *dedes* lost power completely. Indeed, from the conversations that I have held in villages throughout the subprovince, it would appear that conversion to Sunni Islam in Alevi villages continued throughout the early Republic period, and were certainly not confined to the period of Ottoman rule.

While the history of conversion of any village tends to vary greatly in its specific details, sometimes it appears to have been stimulated by members of the community leaving and attending orthodox religious schools. There, perhaps through poverty not able to pay for their own board and lodging, they would be supported by pious patrons, and expected to continue the good fight after their graduation. Sometimes, these figures would leave their community for good, but on other occasions they would return, full of vigor to convert their fellow villagers. The following account was recorded for me by just such a man, who had left the village in the late 1950s when still a boy to seek his fortune in the local provincial center. There, a former mayor had taken him under his wing, and paid for him to go to the local religious school. Arriving finally back in his home village in the early 1970s, he immediately set about converting his fellow villagers to Sunni Islam, but surprisingly was eventually brought up short by a vivid dream that greatly disturbed him.[7]

> I worked at making my *mahalle* (village quarter) fulfill the "five pillars." During the Ramadan we hired a *mehter* [drum and pipe] team to get them out of bed in the morning before dawn. There were three people who had had a *medrese* [Ottoman religious] education in the village, with their help we formed a group against the *dedes*. We formed a link with the head man of the village at that time. We mended and restored the mosque. We retiled the roof, and put down carpet. For two years, we observed the Ramadan. We offered prayers after the fast's end each evening at the mosque.
>
> Whilst this was going on, one day my life changed through a dream that came to me as I slept. I dreamt that I was on my balcony. I saw a horse coming across the fields in front of me. I saw that the horse was extremely powerful, a war horse, hooves beating the ground. On its back was a strong, bearded man in armour. The horse came on and stopped exactly in front of me. The bearded person on the back, drew his sword, and said,
>
> "I am Hazreti Ali! Mehmet *hoca*, you are going very quickly forward. Stay where you are, or I'll cut off your head!"
>
> He disappeared in a flash. I woke up, drenched in sweat.
>
> I asked myself, who is the most knowledgeable person in *Alevilik* [Aleviness]? Dursun *dayı*, I said. He was the most intelligent, the wisest *dede* of the village. I decided to go to him for advice, because this dream made me very worried. I went to Dursun *dayı* and explained the dream, that I had seen Ali, that he said "Stay where you are, or else I'll cut off your head."
>
> Dursun *dayı* said, "You are attempting a firm partition [of religion] (*şekilcilik*). You should examine the Alevi path: you are not entering its depths. You have devoted yourself purely to the knowledge offered by the *Şeriat*. You should investigate *Alevilik*." I borrowed some books from Dursun, I borrowed some too from one of the other most regarded *dedes* in the area, and also from his *musahip* [religious partner] in the next village.
>
> From the knowledge I gained from them, I learnt that with only fasting and prayers gets nowhere. I learnt that the heart of the matter is humanity (*insanlık*),

the person (*insan*). Slowly I learnt that this was the true meaning of *Alevilik*. . . . From that time on, I ceased to oppose *Alevilik* in the village.

The reconversion of Mehmet *hoca* back into the Alevi fold appears to mark the high point of the rise of orthodoxy in the modern history of the village. That it would remain *Alevi* appears no longer in doubt. However, later in the 1970s, the village began to enter a long further crisis in faith, one that continued over the next two decades. This time, the opposition was not orthodox, but a strong political movement with which the young men in the village allied themselves with the rise of the left wing in Turkey as a whole, becoming often skeptics, or even atheists, in the process. The leadership of the opposition against the *dedes* remained based in the same village quarter that had earlier expressed such piety, but this time was expressed in almost purely antireligious terms.

Here again, something that would not at all appear to be predicted (or even permitted by Whitehouse's theories) occurred. Albeit simplifying a far more complex ethnographic reality, it appears that those who proclaimed this countermovement gave up belief in the religious efficacy of the village's ceremonies. They also often stopped attending them, or did so only under pressure. Nevertheless, they continued to celebrate very significant parts of that same ritual in secular settings, even to express great pleasure in doing so. During drinking ceremonies, festivals, and marriages even the most skeptical Alevis would call for the *sema* ritual dance, play minstrel music extolling Ali continuously, and maintain little touches of ritual, clearly drawn from their religious myth such as touching glasses finger to finger, or passing a little piece of liver to a friend when they had finished taking a sip of strong drink (known as *rakı*). This, they called not religion but their "culture," using the word in direct translation, *kültür*. Thus, for this group at least, belief or literal faith dissipated but their ritual in many important respects continued in a new guise and with a new justification.

In the past few years, perhaps from the early 1990s, there appears to have been yet another development. The movement I have described emerged greatly from within the village, as population rose and the youths became more active in opposition to traditional religious figures. Subsequently, migration from the villages to Istanbul rose greatly. In the new, urban setting, many of the villagers are extremely poor, and have fallen into what might be regarded by many as inappropriate activities from the conventional moral point of view. A very strong movement to bring the village together again has begun, basing its force on an explicitly religious conception of Alevi life, that it is a means of keeping order within the community through sacred ritual. This time, albeit impelled with some force from an exceedingly poor area of Istanbul, and drawing on a wider religious revival in *Alevilik* in Turkey as a whole, religious ritual is being strengthened within the village and its practice of its collective rituals is said by my informants to be on the rise once more.

In sum, a community celebrates its faith primarily through the practices that certainly have aspects in common with the modes of religious life that Whitehouse characterizes as "imagistic." Opposition to the figures who led this style of religious practice was first orthodox, and then subsequently quite the opposite. Instead, its members celebrated their community through collective drinking that incorporated rituals, music, and symbols discernibly associated with Alevi religious tradition. Then again later, in a time of great social upheaval there was a further shift. Religion becomes strengthened again, supported in part by that same generation of once young (but now very worried) men who had earlier felt that faith should be done away with. Their earlier readiness to take part in drinking ceremonies does not decline, but rather is accompanied by a renewed sense that explicitly religious ritual is important to the social cohesion of the community.

At least at present, I have not discerned within Whitehouse's characterization any cause that would permit religious faith to come and go in this way. Indeed (and this is another matter that would need to be clarified), it would appear to be the case that he suggests that when faith dies, so does the ritual. Such a disappearance did not here occur; rather those who lost belief transferred or emphasized their collective activity in a secular setting. Yet, returning to the "trigger," the motivation for change, Gellner's insistence upon the importance of the defining social order *is* sensitive enough to account for this sequence of changes. Some Alevis converted to Sunni orthodoxy when pressured to do so from the outside by substantial force, or when it appeared as if a sense of being "Islamic" (albeit secular) was an important filter with which to integrate with the modern nation-state.[8] Later, in the remaining villages, the youths were able to conceive their religion as "culture" at the point when they felt it was possible to make common accord with the new Republican state through a left-wing radical tradition that they found far more congenial. Then later, when the community was threatened, "Aleviness" began to be interpreted as a religious tradition once more. In other words, the Alevis' conception of religion changes with the social order. The social order is the trigger, not the inner psychology of the believer.

Ritual, Change, and the Social Order

Crucial to my argument is the contention that, however persuasive we may find Whitehouse's depiction of "modes," there is within Islamic society a demonstrable link between traditional social control and religion, just as Gellner proposed, so strong that it can hardly be overlooked. While there is hardly space in a brief chapter to offer an exhaustive ethnographic justification, it may serve as an illustration to look briefly at a ritual series that is extremely important for the Alevi villagers. These rituals are known, in the area where I worked, as the *cem*, the *görgü*, and the "village sacrifice" (*köy kurbanı*) respectively. This description will also provide the opportunity to illustrate just a fraction of the longer sequence of uncertainty and doubt within religious practice that the Alevi communities in Turkey have undergone.

The Cem

Pronounced as the precious stone "gem" is in English, *cem* is the name given by the Alevi to collective rituals that they regard as their principal means of attaining religious fulfillment, very much more important to them than the more habitual Islamic worship in a mosque. A *cem* takes place with both men and women present and, traditionally at least, only at night, and only in the winter months. It has no fixed length, and can often last up to four or five hours. While complex and rich in detail, its principal aim is to worship, to come closer to God through collective, peaceful prayer. It also commemorates the Alevis' allegiance to their patron saint, Haci Bektash, and the twelve imams, including Ali, Hasan, and Hüseyin, through a series of rituals which they refer to as the "twelve duties," *oniki hizmet*.

There is no prescribed number of *cems* that must take place in a year. Rather, they happen when a follower (*talib*) offers a sacrifice to his guide (*dede*). The guide then presides over the collective ritual, and sacrificial meat, usually cooked during the ritual on a hearth in the room, is shared among those who have taken part. Such follower–guide relationships are structured by patrilineage and, in theory at least, unchangeable, having been decided by Haci Bektash himself many centuries ago. This means that a man, when he is born, knows from his earliest childhood of which lineage his *dede* consists, though he will not know which of the individuals in that lineage will eventually emerge to be the most active leader among them. Women are in a slightly more ambivalent position: If they come from a *dede* lineage, they may be known as *ana*, "mothers." Nevertheless, they would normally take their strongest social and political identification from their husband, to whose house they almost always move upon marriage. In all the rituals henceforth, the husband and wife offering the sacrifice may expect to appear together, as a unit, in front of the presiding *dede*.

In order for the ceremony to take place, all who attend must be at peace with one another. This is established, at least in principle, by the presiding *dede* before the ceremony begins. If it does turn out that a party present is in dispute with another, then the *dede* is empowered to attempt to reach a resolution. If he fails, then either the *cem* does not take place at all, or the disputing figures have to leave the room where it is intended to take place. One local, leading figure explained this to me as follows:

Now, if there are small sorts of encroachments on another's boundary, problems of escaping with a girl, we solve them, make them at peace.... The *dedes* ... do not send every subject to the courts. Whether in village or town, except for serious assaults, we make peace among people. We make two hearts one (*iki gönül bir ederiz*). They (the villagers) live in a human way. This is the defining characteristic of the *Alevi-Bektaşi Tarikat*. Those who go to the *Tarikat* of *Hacı Bektaş* never permit a division in their midst.

The Görgü

In the *cem*, the *dede* ensures that the husband and wife who have offered the sacrifice are at peace by questioning them as to the relations that they have had with each other and with the rest of the community, bringing them forward to the center of the room known as "Ali's space," *Ali'nın meydanı*. This questioning is known as the *görgü*. "*Görgü*" is a difficult word to translate, but one possibility is "to be seen," "appear." Alternatively, this questioning may be known as "to die before dying," *ölmeden ölme*. They explain this expression by saying that the interrogation they undergo from the *dede* is parallel to that which they shall receive from Allah after they have died, and on the basis of which they are sent to heaven, or to hell.

Once a year, the questioning of the community is extended, this time to include a couple from every household in the community. When the existence and circumstances of a dispute have become clear, the *dede* suggests a reconciliation based on whether the disputants have shown the correct degree of respect to each other (a young man must respect an older, a wife her husband) or abused one another's rights (*hakkı yemek*). The congregation then must agree with his decision, or else it is not valid. The *dede's* suggestions are supplemented by a "*görgü* committee," *görgü heyeti*, of which he is the head. The other members of the committee are not necessarily *dedes* but must be respected men of the village.

If the problem cannot be resolved, the person disagreeing with the majority must leave, and is said to be fallen, *düşkün*. In this case, at best he or she will be forbidden entrance to religious ceremonies and at worst will not be spoken to or allowed to work with others on daily tasks, or will even be forced to leave the village. If one of a *dede* lineage fails to pass through the center, then the whole of the lineage is forbidden to practice until he or she has done so. The Alevi way of ensuring social order places great emphasis on restoring harmonious relations between people. In any disagreements that I witnessed, the ideal solution to any problem was seen as the public reaffirmation of good relations between the two relevant people by going through an embrace, the *niyaz*. The *niyaz* in turn entails acknowledging the subordinate relationship between younger and older people, so that one of the most important principles of the village social structure is reaffirmed each time a quarrel is resolved.

Social Change

I have offered only the briefest description of Alevi life. However, even this gives certain clear indications: the social order is dependent upon a hierarchy between men that depends on certain lineages being more sacred than others. The celebration of ritual requires the presence of the community and exposes a person's actions to the whole in such a way that can become acutely embarrassing; they are publicly questioned as to their relations with others. As a whole, the elaborate mythological and ritual structure relies upon belief in the literal descent of the twelve imam, as well as the wider cosmology of Islamic thought and its conception of heaven, hell, and the afterlife. The Alevis do possess one religious text, the *Buyruk*, "Command," that they say is written by Imam Cafer.[9] Nevertheless, they do not refer to it very much, rather using the *dede* to explain and to interpret Alevi doctrine during the course of interpretations that they make of the minstrel's songs. Thus, there is a certain, extremely powerful, mutual, and largely unwritten reinforcement: Ritual, social order, ideology, and hierarchy all support each other during the intense, albeit intermittent, experience of the *cem* ceremony.

While ethnographic research among the Alevi has expanded greatly only recently, there are nevertheless sufficient scattered indications in the literature to indicate that this particular, elaborate celebration of belief has undergone great difficulties.[10] There are, indeed, various descriptions from the 1970s and 1980s indicating no *cems* being held at all. In the community where I worked only two took place during the eighteen months over which my fieldwork took place, that is, the winters of 1988 and 1999. The reasons for this are again indisputably extremely complex in detail. Nevertheless, among the reasons for this crisis would certainly be the integration of the rural village communities within the state infrastructure, a growing reluctance to be subordinate to a *dede*, the increasing economic and social heterogeneity of the community through rapid migration to urban centers in Turkey and abroad, and an acceptance by many Alevi men and women that the Kemalist prescription of secularism is in fact an ideal (their term) way to forge citizenship within the new nation.

The Village Sacrifice

Much of this uncertainty was reflected in a village sacrifice, *köy kurbanı* that I witnessed in 1989. A village sacrifice is held annually on the evening after all the households in the village have been through the "die before dying" ceremony discussed above. It is similar to a *cem*, but there are slight differences in emphasis. Instead of one follower offering the sacrifice to their *dede* (thereby bearing the cost of the sacrifice), a small financial contribution is made by every household in the village. Instead of the sacrificial meat being eaten on the spot after the ceremony has finished, each household takes back an equal portion to their home and eats it in their own time.

At the time of occasion described below, at which I was present, the village head man was seriously ill and in the hospital and had decided to offer a personal sacrifice alongside the village sacrifice, the meat of the two animals to be cooked together. The evening began badly. The village head's sacrifice was safely tethered, already blessed by the *dede* during the day, but the village sacrifice was to be brought to the center and a sacrificial song was to be sung over it by a minstrel. After the people had gathered and taken their places, they discovered that the village sacrifice had disappeared. Several people went out to look for it but without success.

Then, a man of the village burst in late, past the restraining hand of the watchman, who was both young and not very bright, and whose prime duty was to prevent incursion. The incoming man was very drunk, so much so that he was unable to stand still as he bowed in front of the *dedes* to receive the greeting before sitting down. The drunken man was taken out, amidst increasing disturbance, and several men saw that he was placed in a stable to cool down. Then the man who had lost the sacrifice was found and brought to the center to be questioned. While he was trying to explain, the sacrifice was located. The congregation began to settle down again, but then the drunken man returned, walking straight to his former place. Again, grumbles began to be heard.

It looked as if the gathering would break up in disarray, and people indeed had begun to stand up to leave. At this point, a young *dede* burst into an impassioned speech and succeeded in holding the assembly together. His long speech is interesting in that it provides an example of the way a *dede* may be able to control an extremely serious threat to the social cohesion of the village.

> There is a saying of *Holy Hüseyin*, "If you would come, come; if you would turn, turn. The goods of those who come, the life of those who turn." This is the forward of the *Kuran*. We are sitting in the *Tarikat* of *Holy Hüseyin*. I beseech you, do not be ignorant of God's divine love. . . . A *görgü* means to bring people together, to listen to their hearts. Here a person of the *Tarikat* comes not to destroy people's hearts but to make them. Let God accept your hearts; let God let no one be inadequate for their path. I am recounting the words of *Holy Hüseyin*. "From those who come, goods, from those who turn, life!" From those who profane here, life departs! Pay attention to this!
>
> People are the *Kuran*. A person must know themselves. . . . Other men worship with five conditions, we are the people of the *niyaz* (embrace). We with the *niyaz* will go to the happy judgment day. What are you becoming? I request, I beseech you. Here in three, five villages remain people of the *Tarikat*. What are you becoming? Your end will be confusion! If we bathe, if we wash it will not go from our backs. Know this for certain! "Agh, I am dying," said my regretted father. He cried and

spoke at the same time. He gave his soul to the longed-for God. He said, "My son, the road is ended." What does this mean? It means that he was a person of faith.[11]

The body is one, the spirit is one, the blood is one, the skin is one. Once you have entered here, siblings are one, wives are one, husbands are one, children are one. There can be a lone voice from no one. From the words of the minstrel, the words of the *dede* a person listens to the words of the scriptures. . .we are the people of the *niyaz*, the people of the *Tarikat*, are we going to be thus people of the *Tarikat*?

Complete silence followed his speech, which succeeded in holding the gathering together. This ceremony took place in the second and final winter that I spent in the village, that is, in 1990. While I have not lived in the community since then, I have kept in close contact. It appears as if the Alevi "revival" referred to above began to take place fairly quickly after my departure. While life in the community is changing rapidly, and in certain respect religion is being reformulated along with those changes, at the time of writing, the Alevi ceremonial life of the community remains in place.

Conclusion

I began this chapter by suggesting that the ethnography of the Islamic world, and particularly that of the community of which I have made a special study, matches the scheme proposed by Whitehouse extremely well. In many ways, the Alevi appear to exemplify the "imagistic." Their ritual ceremonies, each slightly different rather than based on any one text, are intense, sensory-rich experiences that are psychologically markedly different from the far cooler, even scholastic ceremonies within a mosque, where text and prayer is far more clearly prescribed and far less attempt is made to remove the supplicant from everyday reality. This in itself gives a different tone, a difference texture to the proceedings that can hardly be explained or accounted for without introducing into anthropological analysis of religion a psychological or cognitive dimension.

More than this even, the speech that the younger *dede* made to the village sacrifice described above was extremely important. At a time when hardly any *cem* ceremonies were being held, and the village itself was extremely worried about the extent to which outmigration was leading to its effectual cease as an active community, the break-up in disarray of the most important collective ceremony of the year would have been an utter humiliation, and only reinforced their loss of morale. The successful appeal that he makes to the congregation is based on various elements, the importance of their retaining their path and their defining humanity, but it reaches its peak by describing the union with God by his father on the instant of his death. By this, he means not simply the movement of a believer to heaven, but a momentary flash of utter inspiration whereby a supplicant attains the infinite, a moment that is the reward for a lifetime of ceaseless longing for divine love. Both this and the dream recounted by Mehmet *hoca* above appear "imagistic," quite different in persuasive style from the alternative theological, even scholastic debate that Whitehouse calls "doctrinal."

Nevertheless, in spite of my absolute conviction that the "modes" as described by Whitehouse are important, I cannot relieve myself of the doubts that I expressed in the opening passages of this chapter regarding the way that the theories are currently presented. To reiterate: why mode of *religious* life? If the mode in question really has any psychological roots, then surely its cognitive influence goes far beyond religion and affects other social life as well? Why should a "mode" stop being so when it drifts from the religious sphere? It would be extraordinarily artificial (and I am sure that Whitehouse himself would agree) to say that the villagers I describe were in "imagistic" mode when dancing in a *cem*, but that when they mirrored this activity in a drinking session it no longer, in some way, counted as a valid part of their social life. And yet, when someone returns to religion, he or she is then suddenly being "imagistic" once more.

But once this step is taken to permit human behavior more widely as part of our analysis, when then should the cognitive exploration of any particular mode of thought or pattern of life be confined to memory? The fascinating transfer of ritual elements from overtly religious Alevi life into overtly secular life by atheist skeptics is facilitated enormously by music. The minstrel may play for a *cem* ceremony, but he may equally well play and sing at a drinking gathering. Wedding musicians (known as *mehter*) know and play a lively dance taken from the *cem* to the gathered merry crowd. Further, minstrel song is recorded on cassettes and played continuously even by the most hardened of "lefties," to whom it often becomes a form of resistance music. This conscious and sometimes seemingly total immersion into sound is, cognitively speaking, surely a vital factor in the transportation of Alevi culture into different settings, and plays an equally obvious (though perhaps not quantifiable with any precision) role in ensuring the individual and collective cohesion of the secular Alevi movement. Yet, cognitively speaking, the capability to process and understand melody can hardly be reduced to memory, even though they may be closely linked.

Again, I am sure that Whitehouse does not wish to imply that his use of memory stands for a metaphor for all human thought. Nevertheless, it seems to me that if memory is elevated even by default to the *sole* influence on religious formations, then the theory becomes simply too restricting in just this way. Likewise, as I have also outlined, it appears to me inadequate to reduce all influences on religious ideologies to psychological causes. In order to note this, I have considered the application of Gellner's theories to changing Islamic movements in Turkey, and can only reaffirm my conviction of the intellectual soundness of his insistence on the social order as being irreducible to individual psychology. *Order,* the arrangement of life into self-sustaining patterns, after all, is not only a human problem but affects all nature, as Bateson points out: We may not think about it, but we certainly have to obey its strictures in some way, or else there would be no community at all.[12] It appears to me demonstrably the case that this fundamental necessity of existence has a profound impact on religious styles, and indeed that taking this connection into account predicts more accurately than Whitehouse's model the various changes that religious sentiments have undergone within the Alevi movement.

In conclusion, it appears to me a characteristic of millennial movements in academia that they promise a panacea they are unable to supply, and at the same time are vastly too restricted in their original terms of reference. I would urge upon Whitehouse the precise opposite: that the initial focus of the "modes" be widened so as to embrace a far wider sense of variety of human cognition, and not be confined to memory. Then, I suggest that the extent of human behavior that can be explained by the theories be scrupulously understated, with a clear sense of exactly all those areas of human life that the "modal" theory will *not* explain. It is this sense of restraint that surely will enable the "modes of religion" theories to avoid first popular embrace, then equally fickle disillusionment by supporters initially promised so much. It would be, for me at least, a profound disappointment if what is surely the most significant increase in our understanding of religious ideas since Durkheim were to lose its credibility through an insufficient sense of danger at the very moment that the ground is being laid.

Notes

1. See Shankland (1999) and Shankland (2003) for a detailed presentation of the material that I discuss here. The ethnographic quotations are taken from those works. Broadly speaking, the Alevi constitute perhaps 15 to 18 percent of modern Turkey's population, which otherwise is predominantly Sunni. For a description of these and other ethnic and religious communities in Turkey, see Andrews (1989, 2nd edition in press).

2. Whitehouse (2000: 3–4).

3. For a useful collected criticism, see Hall and Jarvie (1996). For a partial reply, see Shankland (2003: chapter 8).

4. On the Bektashis, see Birge (1937); for Hafiz, see Arberry (1947); for the Rubayyat of many versions, see Fitzgerald (1969).

5. This process is discussed in more detail in Shankland (1999: chapter 2).

6. There is one refinement that should perhaps be noted explicitly. The Islamist political movement in 2003 made such substantial gains that it has achieved a majority in the Grand National Assembly and forms the government. A strand of thought within it has attempted to tackle the "tedium" effect, holding lively mass rallies, developing attractive Islamic fashions, and celebrating with "Ottoman Fayres" the evenings during the *Ramazan* after the break of fast.

While not all agree with such celebrations, they have been a noticeable part of the Islamist political success. (See White 2002.) I would certainly rephrase my argument slightly now, and say that while a substantial proportion of the Sunni population turn to nonreligious "tedium" relief, as I have noted, there is in addition a significant desire to reinstill Islamic life in the Republic with everyday excitement while at the same time maintaining literal belief in the truth of its tenets. (See also the work of Mardin 1989 on the philosophy of Said-i Nursi.)

7. A fuller version of this "life" appears in my *Alevis in Modern Turkey*, chapters 1 and 2.

8. The paradox of an orthodox revival within the early secular Republic may be explained in part through the fact that the Republicans simplified as well as secularized the practice of religion in the Republic, thus helping to create a uniform denominator through which citizens could express mutual identification with the national unit. This development is explored beautifully in Meeker's recent work *A Nation of Empire* (2002); see also Shankland (1999: chapter 1).

9. The *Buyruk* has received surprisingly little attention; see however Otter-Beaujean (1997).

10. See, however, the article by Naess (1988), which appears to offer parallel instances to those I note here. For a good place to begin on looking at comparative material on the Alevis, see also Olsson, Özdalga, and Raudvere (1998).

11. That is, as he died he successfully came into contact with God.

12. Bateson (1979).

References

Andrews, P., ed. 1989. *Ethnic Groups in the Republic of Turkey*. Wiesbaden: Dr Ludwig Reichart Verlag.

Arberry, A. 1947. *Fifty Poems of Hafiz*. Cambridge: Cambridge University Press.

Bateson, G. 1979. *Mind and Nature*. New York: Dutton.

Birge, J. 1937. *The Bektashi Order of Dervishes*. London: Luzac & Co.

Fitzgerald, E. 1969. *The Rubayyat of Omar Khayyam*. London: Roger Schlesinger. Gellner, E. 1969.

Saints of the Atlas. London: Weidenfeld and Nicholson.

———. 1981. *Muslim Society*. Cambridge: Cambridge University Press.

———. 1988. *Plough, Sword and Book*. London: Collins Harvill.

Hall, J., and Jarvie I., eds. 1996. *The Social Philosophy of Ernest Gellner*. Amsterdam: Rodolpi.

Mardin, Ş. 1989. *Religion and Social Change in Modern Turkey: The Case of Bediuzzaman Said Nursi*. Albany: State University of New York Press.

Meeker, M. 2002. *A Nation of Empire: The Ottoman Legacy of Turkish Modernity*. Berkeley: University of California Press.

Naess, R. 1988. "Being an Alevi in South-western Anatolia and in Norway: The Impact of Migration on a Heterodox Muslim Community." In T. Gerholm and Y. Lithman (eds.), *The New Islamic Presence in Western Europe*. London: Mansell, pp. 174–95.

Olsson, T., Özdalga, E. and Raudvere, C., eds. 1998. *Alevi Identity*. Istanbul: Swedish Research Institute in Istanbul, *Transactions* Vol. 8.

Otter-Beaujean, A. 1997. "Schriftliche Überlieferung versus mündliche Tradition: Zum Stellenwert der *Buyruk*-Handschriften im Alevitum." In K. Kehl-Bodrogi, B. Kellner-Heinkele, and A. Otter-Beaujean (eds.), *Syncretistic Religious Communities in the Near East*. Leiden: Brill, pp. 213–26.

Shankland, D. 1999. *Islam and Society in Turkey*. Huntington: Eothen Press.

———. 2003. *The Alevis in Modern Turkey: The Emergence of a Secular Islamic Tradition*. London: RoutledgeCurzon.

White, J. 2002. *Islamist Mobilization in Turkey: A Study in Vernacular Politics*. Seattle: University of Washington Press.

Whitehouse, H. 1995. *Inside the Cult: Religious Innovation and Transmission in Papua New Guinea*. Oxford: Oxford University Press.

———. 2000. *Arguments and Icons: Divergent Modes of Religiosity*. Oxford: Oxford University Press.

Is Image to Doctrine as Speech to Writing? Modes of Communication and the Origins of Religion   3

JACK GOODY

IT IS DIFFICULT TO VISUALIZE the origin of religion (practices and beliefs) however defined, unless we are dealing with language-using animals. Primates may be said to have embryonic forms of the main features of human life, having politics (the struggle for dominance), kinship (or domestic relations), and an economy (the search for livelihood) to take the usual anthropological categories, but do they show any evidence of religious practices? The dead, including those of other animals, are sometimes disposed of in formal ways. That hardly indicates religious beliefs. Tylor (1871) saw the basis of religion in such practices, which have drawn the attention of other scholars, and imply some notion of continuity between the dead and the living. But if we follow Tylor further in taking as the minimal definition of religion "the belief in Spiritual Beings," then religious beliefs cannot exist without language.[1] Such an agency, deity, soul, or spiritual force requires symbolization; absence, and distance too, has to be treated in this way. And language is involved not only in such beliefs (perhaps any beliefs) but also in the related actions, such as sacrifice. If one is confined to gesture as a means of communication, one is limited to the here-now, the face-to-face.

The timing of the advent of language is subject to much speculation (see Deacon 1997), but a probable location for the emergence of a full syntactic system is among the Neanderthals, for whom there is some evidence for the use of grave goods at burials.[2] The Advanced Paleolithic saw the appearance of the rich cave art of France. This has been interpreted in many ways, for example, as indicating the presence of complex initiation rituals.[3] Much earlier, the Blombos caves in South Africa have provided evidence of engraved ochre at approximately 70,000 BP, together with bone tools, engraved bone fragments, finely crafted bifacial stone points, and evidence of fishing, all features that archaeologists reject as evidence of "modern" human behavior (Henshilwood et al., in press). Given the complexity of both language and ritual (here religious action), these could not have evolved except over a long space of time. So it is possible, even probable, that the two may have coevolved in the same period, at least at the level of complexity that we find them in any known human culture, though simpler, embryonic forms such as burial practices would have developed earlier.[4] What I am suggesting is that language was a necessary precursor of religion, if not of ritual in the generalized sense of formal behavior ("rituals of eating"). As such, it would have evolved at the same period as images (in the concrete external sense, internal images are of course connected with sight itself).

Developing the notion of "modes of religiosity," Harvey Whitehouse (1995, 2000) has suggested that two major modes can be distinguished, the imagistic and the doctrinal, the latter being associated with more complex polities and specifically with the advent of writing (a protolanguage involving symbolic communication would be much older, possibly going back to the initial enlargement of the brain with Australopithecines), though he has queries about seeing this as having a "determinative" role, suggesting that the doctrinal mode of religiosity may have preceded and eventually triggered the development of writing systems rather than the other way around (see also Mithen 2004). I am not explicitly trying to test Whitehouse's hypotheses, which consist of two "suites of features that are mutually reinforcing." In the first place I do not have access to the kind of psychological data that would enable me to assess the role of semantic memory (frequent repetition of ritual exegesis) as against episodic memory (spontaneous exegetical reflection). What I want to do is to pursue some closely related questions, however, concerning differences in the means of communication.

My major proposition is that if language was central to the origins of religion, then any change or addition to our means of communication should have important implications, and in some respects consequences, for religions as for all fields of social action. Why otherwise would we speak of what Tylor and others called "ethical religions" as "religions of the book"? The book is presumed to make a difference, especially in the formulation of ethical doctrines. In this case "doctrines" instantly become more prominent, more explicit, more "developed" doctrinally, with writing. In this respect, the "religions of the book" have an advantage, if advantage it be, over the religions of oral cultures; they tend to absorb them when they come in contact (Goody 1986: chapter 1). But written religions do not always lack images nor do unwritten ones lack doctrines.

Let me begin first with doctrines. If we associate doctrine with dogma, it was Robertson Smith in his remarkable *Religion of the Semites* (1889) who declared that "antique religions had for the most part no creed: they consisted entirely of institutions and practices." There was no question of orthodoxy as they had no dogma, no doctrines, no "system of beliefs," but only rite and myth (derived from it) (1927: 116ff). About dogma and creed I would agree; possibly I would agree about "system of beliefs" in a systematic sense. But about doctrine I am less certain. Its denial pushes the deintellectualization of early cultures too far. It seems that the elaborate recitation among the LoDagaa of West Africa that constitute what I have called the Myths of the Bagre are "doctrinal" in that they have a didactic function (Goody and Gandah 2002). Where they differ from the "dogma" of written religions, and this touches directly upon the means of communication, is that the doctrines vary considerably over place and time, as Robertson Smith suggests and as Whitehouse sees as a feature of his imagistic mode. I have elsewhere suggested that language-users facing the universe around them have various choices of a doctrinal nature when it comes to formulating a worldview. One version of the myth is highly theocentric (the First Bagre); in it, God, assisted by the beings of the wild, constructs the cultural world in which man lives. Another (the Third Bagre) places much greater emphasis on "man makes himself," on man's own contribution to his well-being. Of course in any society, both Creation and self-improvement are perceived as relevant. God, or the ancestors (culture), has done much to shape our world, but we ourselves, though not omnipotent, have to some extent to be responsible for our own actions. It is the same with notions of the evolution of humanity from an earlier state of (animal) affairs; we are obviously similar to apes in some respects and to living things more generally. On the other hand, the notion of a sudden Creation, a Big Bang (and the associated Creator), brings out our profound differences from the rest of living nature, because we have language and they do not. (Animals are seen as speaking in folktales, but everyone is aware of the fictional nature of such stories.) In each case the opposing possibilities are both available to mankind in their attempt to make sense of the universe. The alternatives exist not because of any factors built into the brain but because of factors built into the brain's use of language. The two kinds of origin stories can be considered as doctrinal, but in oral cultures they never (or rarely) become dogmas because different reciters of myths may switch from one to the other kind of story, in response to the contradictions or complications involved in either. There is no text, no fixed memory, to maintain orthodoxy. For instance, we are both like the primates (and other animals) and radically different from them. To adopt a doctrine of evolution is to emphasize the first and play down the second; the Creation story does just the opposite, even stressing God's unique role in establishing humanity. Was that conceptualization the birth of religion? Was religion dependent upon a recognition not of continuity but of discontinuity, and is that why for so long many churches remained (and some still remain) adamant against the modern doctrine of evolution? The doctrine of evolution undermined their theory of the Big Bang. Much the same contradictory complications are inherent in the emphasis on either mankind or God and other supernatural forces as creators of the cultural environment, on self-improvement or Creation.

These are doctrines, not dogmas. They change into the latter when the utterance becomes a text, that is, with the advent of writing (I am adopting the restricted concept of a text, not the more sloppy one used by many cultural "theorists"). Why? Because a written text, a fixed text in Albert Lord's phrase, embodies one possibility rather than another on a longer term basis. It freezes the acceptance of one alternative. So the doctrine of the Creation is given a quasi-permanent life (though the other alternative may continue to exist at the subdominant level of "popular culture"), which has to be deliberately refuted (as a dogma) rather than adopted more flexibly as an alternative oral version. The written one has to be struggled against in quite a different way, as Huxley had to struggle with Bishop Wilberforce in nineteenth-century Britain. Or biologists with theologians in the South of the United States.

The situation regarding flexibility or closure, doctrine or dogma, resembles one that I have earlier discussed for lists (1997). In oral cultures, a tomato can be included in the category fruit on one occasion and vegetable on another. Or holly in that of bush today and tree tomorrow. When these categories get turned into written lists, such as were and are often taught in early schools, one is forced to make a binary choice. The item has to appear in one column or another, not in both at different times (although as with "doctrines" the alternatives may still be available at the subdominant popular, oral level, where ambiguity can be more easily tolerated, coped with, and incorporated).

For long periods of human history the written version has been preoccupied with theological matters in its texts. That is surely partly because, with few exceptions interpretation of the written word has been in the hands of priests (those figures in Whitehouse's doctrinal mode) whose existence has depended upon the theological story, which has been encapsulated in their texts. The text becomes canonical; a canon is established by including some and excluding others. The exceptions to "ecclesiastical" instruction in the mysteries of writing have been Ancient Greece and China, where supernatural agents have not been totally excluded (especially at the level of ancestor cults or worship, which occupies an intermediary position between the theological and the secular), they have been restricted in the educational sphere of schools, texts, and writing. Significantly, it is these cultures that have had more commitment to secular and nontheological doctrines (such as those of Confucius) than elsewhere.

In oral cultures, doctrines often receive greater elaboration in long recitations such as myths (once again I use the word in its more restricted way as referring to a genre, to a specific recitation) as distinct from mythologies, which are constructed by the observer from a variety of sources. But whereas mythologies, which

I would suggest are nondoctrinal, are universal, being fragmented verbal statements about the relation of humanity to the universe, natural and supernatural, myths as genres of recitation certainly are not. The LoDagaa of northern Ghana have the recitation of the Bagre, which is also the name of a quasi-secret association concerned with the whole gamut of well-being and which has been adopted by some of its neighbors. But most other groups in the area, most notably the well-studied Tallensi, Sisaala, Builsa, Vagalla, and Konkomba, seem to have nothing of the kind, even when they have similar types of association. In other words, among essentially the same general types of acephalous society, some have myths and hence more elaborate doctrines, while others only have fragmented mythologies.[5] In this sense the presence of doctrines, which as I have explained varies over time in the case of versions of the Bagre, also varies markedly over space.[6] Doctrines are not at all universal features of oral cultures.

In northern Ghana, in close conjunction with these acephalous, segmentary societies to which I refer, we find a number of much larger, centralized polities and states in which the religious modalities, like the political ones, are very different. They have a hierarchy of chiefs with courts and political-legal authority, which tend to suppress, exclude, or play down the type of association linked to the long recitations I call myths. They are also affected to various degrees by Islam, which brings with it written texts (above all the Koran and its commentaries), schools, and priests. The latter take over the conduct of many ceremonies of the life as well as the seasonal cycles, and officiate prominently at the installation of chiefs. They also inevitably take over the doctrinal sphere, teaching instead Islamic dogma to the detriment of alternative mythologies, cosmologies, and myths. Once again, some alternative manifestations may persist or change at the popular, oral level, but they are necessarily excluded from the dominant, hegemonic dogma associated with the religion of the book. In northern Ghana, we are dealing with the very periphery of Islam and the spread of Near Eastern religion (until the much more recent impact of Christianity, above all of the Roman Catholic variety). To make the point with regard to such religions, and in order to avoid drawing from the extremely important cluster that emerged from the Near East, notably Judaism, Christianity, and Islam, and that so resemble each other but have often been so hostile precisely because they have dogmas and canons rather than doctrines and "myths," I shall later turn to look at Ancient Egypt.

But first I want to ask if the religions of oral cultures (those without writing) can be described as imagistic rather than doctrinal. Clearly those that lack "myths" (long recitations) and the elaborate doctrines that they embody, must give more attention to the visual, the image external and internal, and to the touch and the smell, rather than to the verbal. The image becomes of greater relative significance, especially in religious activities. But dogmatic (written) religions too are often very committed to the image, even when they are principally dependent on the text, on the (written) Word of God. That is certainly the case with Roman Catholicism and its representation of the crucifixion, as well as with the incorporation of images in painting, in and out of churches, of Gothic sculpture, and of the narratives embodied in stained glass windows. A similar range of images also appears in Hinduism and Buddhism. But while images are often found in conjunction with written religions, some of these are aniconic or have aniconic phases or components. These phases occur in the early history of written religions, when they are trying to establish themselves as a religion of the book (or books). Judaism and Islam both began and continued to be anti-imagistic and aniconic. According to some Jewish scholars, such as Maimonides, even to imagine an anthropomorphic deity was blasphemous. If they went in at all for graphic forms, other than writing, these forms were the closest they could come, favoring abstract rather than concrete designs, which at times resembled the use of calligraphy to present the text, the Scriptures, the Holy Word. While such aniconic tendencies were firmly discarded in later Roman Catholicism, they were present in early Christianity and in early Buddhism, too, despite the later efflorescence of Buddha figures. In these two cases, the objection to images, to figurative representation, even in some cases to internal images, was later set aside. Nevertheless such tendencies remained a possibility within the ensemble of potential religious doctrines, if only because the text offers an encouragement for some to turn the clock back to the earlier phases of the religion. That happened in the Protestant Reformation in Europe where an attempt was made to revive the beliefs and practices of the "primitive" church, including its aniconic stance. Paintings and sculpture were removed from churches (or alternatively defaced), and greater attention was then paid to the text and its explicit doctrines, and to enabling the congregation to get direct access to the Word of God. The word certainly tended to displace the image.

That was also true of some sects of Buddhism such as Zen, which reverted to the aniconic stance of the early Buddhist creed when there were no images of the founder, who was represented only by relatively abstract signs, such as the footprint or the wheel. In China, it was also Confucianism as practiced by the literati that often preferred calligraphy to representational art, both using the same brush, with black and white rather than with color, and adopting a genuinely skeptical stance to supernatural agencies, apart from the ancestors. In Hinduism too it was certain groups of Brahmans, upper custodians of the written corpus of the Vedas, who were skeptical of the iconic character of the Hinduism of the lower castes, and who placed more value on the Sanskrit texts that were their livelihood in every sense. So some religions of complex, written societies were opposed to the image, especially in the upper reaches of the religious hierarchy. But that was certainly not true of all; as the word "icon" itself reminds us, the image could be the very object of worship.

However, despite a certain opposition between image and written word in some religious systems, it is not only in complex, written cultures that we find this rejection of the former. We normally think of oral religions as being dominated, especially in their carvings and masks, in their rituals and ceremonies, by figurative images. But there are some such cultures that not only fail to exploit these concrete forms of representation but even deliberately reject them. And as with the distribution of the myth-genre, this can happen in societies that are found adjacent to one another. The LoDagaa, for example, reject the use of masks whereas their neighbors the Lobi (Lowilisi) in Bourkina Faso do not. Equally they accept representational shrines for ancestors and for beings of the wild but reject them for other deities, especially for the High God himself, whereas their other neighbors have abstract ancestor shrines. The prohibition on representing the High God seems to be very general throughout Africa where, as in Judaism, Islam, or early Christianity, it would be blasphemous to create an image of God: One would in fact be doing his work and threatening his existence by appearing to create the Creator.

The reason for this prohibition on images in some cultures that might have been supposed to be iconic in orientation lies partly buried in theological notions about the role of deity and partly in more widespread secular notions of the kind famously epitomized in Plato's doctrine of forms, where to create an image of an object was to lie, to appear to claim that the image of a chair (or of a god) was the chair (or god) itself when clearly it was not.

The use of images, like the use of doctrines, does not so much characterize modes of religion as the variable orientations within them. On the other hand, without being deterministic on the issue, I would see some broad distinction of a general type that depends upon the mode of storage and communication of beliefs and practices, whether these depend upon oral or written transmission, giving rise in the latter case to texts, to their readers (and sometimes to their writers), to dogmas, and to canons. It is true of course that there are parallel institutions with both modes of communication. Amhate Ba once said of oral cultures that every time an old man dies, a library disappears. To call this a library is neat but misleading, even if there is some parallelism, because the point about a library of texts, of books (*libri*), is precisely that it does not disappear with the death of the author.

Alternative Modes in Ancient Egypt

In order to pursue this question of general difference in religious systems (modes of religion) in oral and literate cultures, that is, as related to the modes of communication, I want to take up my reference to Ancient Egypt, one of the very first written religions, which was also highly iconic because of its development of a type of script, hieroglyphics, that was most closely linked to pictorial representation.

Writing on Egypt, Baines suggests that "it may be best not to think of religion as a unity" (1991: 23). The Egyptians would not have questioned the basis for religious beliefs and processes or asked whether they all belonged together. They had no single term to cover them all.[7] Nor were cultic activities carried out on a national or societal basis, varying as they did from place to place and from time to time; "they never tried," writes Bierbrier (1982: 85) "to work out a systematic relationship for their many gods to be applied over the whole country." The centralized court had a certain effect, particularly after the unification of the country, but that influence did not ensure continuity in the longer term. The preeminence of Ra gave way to that of Amun, and Amun to Aten, the Sun-disc, and back again.

But questions arose on a wider conceptual front, as I have argued happened in other religious traditions. The pharaoh Akhenaten (1377–1359 BCE), who came to the throne as Amenophis IV, has been described as "the heretic king" because he set aside the worship of Amun, which had hitherto prevailed within his dynasty, and directed attention towards Aten, a word that meant "disc," the disc of the sun. Redford suggests that indeed he was perhaps an atheist since he left behind no god at all but only a disc (1984: 170). Others have seen him as devoted to monotheism, as he did away with the Egyptian pantheon of gods.

The motivation behind this move appears in a fragmentary text of a speech the pharaoh gave to the court promulgating his new and unique "deity" (Redford 1984: 172). Two features stood out. Firstly the gods had somehow failed or "ceased" to be operative. Secondly the new god (actually Reharakhty, Re the horizon-Horus, the great sun god of Heliopolis) is described as absolutely unique and located in the heavens. But what also emerges in this religious shift, elements of which were already present in the conceptualization of Re-Amun, is Akhenaten's iconoclasm. In the second or third regnal year we find the abandonment of the earlier falcon-headed man in kilt with scepter and sun disc who confronted the king across a table of offerings. Only the Sun-disc remains. "Where the god's figure once was are now a series of long, straight, sticklike arms which splay down and terminate in human hands (the only concession to anthropomorphism)" (Redford 1984: 173). The sun god is "reduced" to a nonhuman disc representing

> a progressive move to rid concepts of the divine, and even art itself, of all anthropomorphic and theriomorphic forms. Traditional representations or any depictions for that matter!—of the gods are no longer being carved or painted: their emblems, except for those few required for the *sd*-festival [the jubilee], are ignored. . . . Only a few icons connected with the sun-cult continue to be tolerated. . . . Akhenaten was directing a strong counterblast, and doing so consciously we may be sure, against the prevailing involvement of magician and craftsman in the manufacture of the god's earthly "body," his cult image. Pointedly the king alludes to

the Disc as "the one who built himself by himself with his [own] hands—no craftsmen knows him." (Redford 1984: 175)

I have already pointed to the "man-makes-himself" doctrine incorporated in the Third Bagre, but this involved the making of the shrine itself, which often gave rise to doubts. The iconophobia is present in oral as well as many literate cultures, but here an attempt is made to turn it into a dogma.

In the fifth year of his reign, the pharaoh proceeded with the final anathemization of Amun's name at the closing of his huge temple.

> The program of defacement that followed was so thorough that we must postulate either a small army of hatchetmen . . . or parties of inspectors. . . . Everywhere, in temples, tombs, statuary, and casual inscriptions, the hieroglyphs for "Amun" and representations of the god were chiseled out: objects sacred to him were likewise defaced. People who bore names compounded with "Amun" were obliged to change them; and the king led the way. . . . Osiris and his cycle of mortuary gods suffered a like anathemization. Funerary practices might be spared, but only if purged of all polytheistic elements . . . the denizens of the underworld are pointedly ignored in the funerary literature. . . . Even the script and decorative arts are purified of objectionable items such as anthropomorphic or theriomorphic signs; words tend to be written phonetically. (Redford 1984: 176)

He founded "a monotheism that would brook no divine manifestation." In doing so, he committed himself to iconoclasm, to getting rid of icons of a figurative kind, whether human or animal, and favoring abstract forms, even in the script. As in Judaism, Islam, and early and reformed Christianity, iconophobia was associated with monotheism. But it represented more than that; it presumed a failure of the gods as well as a feeling that their images cannot be created by the human hand. These feelings are cognitive in nature and attack the very basis of representation as being man-made rather than "natural." They derive ultimately from man's use of language to represent the world, which under some recurring situations raises doubts about the nature of representation, doubts that are reinforced by the problem of the "god who failed." The god failed when too much belief was placed in his powers. It was an overinvestment of trust that required some cognitive reappraisal. That could take the form of a switch to a different deity (or a different mode of approach) or else to a more radical transformation of the system of beliefs such as we find in that promoted by Akhenaten.

It should be added, however, that Akhenaten's reforms did not result in a permanent or even a long-term shift in the system. With the king's death in 1359 BCE, his coregent Smenkhhare continued to reign for three years. He was succeeded by Tutankhamun who gradually allows other deities to reappear. The new god too had failed, leading to the Time of Troubles. Temples had fallen into ruin, and their remains needed to be restored. Iconophilia was reestablished—"his policy was a strong affirmation that gods did indeed *dwell* in a certain sense in replicas of wood, stone and metal" (Redford 1984: 209), recalling aniconic statements of the Hebrews against shrines of sticks and stones. The Sun-disc does not disappear but is reestablished as the "body" or visible manifestation of a transcendent deity, be it Amun, Re, or Osiris (226). But the first king of the new dynasty following the Thutmosid, Horemheb, finally closed the temples of the Sun-disc at the "heretic's" capital, Akhenaten, taking them down block by block. That at Memphis was also pulled down and its stone reused. The pharaoh's name was eliminated not only from monuments but from the kinglist itself. Orthodoxy had been reestablished.

I have included this movement in the designation puritanical, and indeed "the heretic king" is likened to Luther by his critical biographer, Redford. But the latter also speaks of his concentration of power—he becomes the only son of the heavenly body and receives all the attention by way of offerings; Redford also speaks of his sloth and his court of voluptuaries. However this may be, his "reforms" lie embedded in the core of the previous religion, in doubts about the figuring of gods as men or beasts, in the very process of representing deity.

There is another ambiguous aspect of religion that I want to emphasize. We have seen that what we might call holistic statements about Egyptian religion give rise to a number of problems. Firstly there is some doubt as to the nature of the very concept of religion when applied to Egypt, and even more to oral cultures. Are human activities linked to what we as observers see as supernatural agencies separated from those we conceive of as natural? That is an ancient query, but one that we still have to consider. Secondly, even if there is such a domain, how unified is it in any particular case? Can we describe an Egyptian religion as distinct from local clusters of belief and practice? Thirdly, despite its written sources like the Book of the Dead, which continues to be a recognized part of the "canon" over the millennia, the nature of Egyptian religious activities changed over time. What one can characterize at one point as iconographic and polytheistic becomes at another, under Akhenaten, iconoclastic and monotheistic, perhaps even "atheistic." There are other ways too a religion can change over time or even incorporate alternative possibilities within itself at the same time, giving different emphases to the alternatives in different contexts.

There are contradictions in Egyptian thinking that while not intrinsically part of religious cult are closely related to its premises. Skepticism existed even about the other world. A New Kingdom text claims, "There is no-one who has come back from there" (Baines 1991: 148). Such sentiments, suggests Baines, were likely to have been present earlier on. Skepticism is an intrinsic part of the system of beliefs and could lead to change or modification. In any case notions of this kind, which are inherent in dealing with a future that is both unknown and costly in terms of offerings of goods and services, may lead the actors to take up the contrary path of hedonism, an emphasis on this world rather than the next. The very fact that religion has what have been called counterintuitive elements or premises that are in conflict with the pleasure principle means that its belief system and practices must be unstable over the long term and are subject to reversal of a *va-et-vient* kind. Do we orient ourselves to this world (hedonism in the present) or to the next (provision for a hypothetical future)?

One can see these characteristics as being psychological. I would prefer to say that all human behavior, cognitive in this case, involves both sociological and psychological variables that are very often intertwined. In so far as they are so, psychological variables cannot only be viewed, as cognitive scientists and some biologists tend to do, as part of the "natural," inherited, genetically determined part of the human persona. Such elements exist but do not exhaust the possibilities. Freud's psychology was not always of that kind, much less so Malinowski's. Social psychology in general seeks another course. A concentration on culturally influenced psychology does of course tend to diminish the role of fixed elements, of biology, of universals. That is a mistake on the part of many social scientists, but equally various deterministic schemes, such as Piaget's developmentalism, have been shown to require modification when faced with cross-cultural material. It is therefore an error to limit the psychological to the universal; at the same time the universal may have sociological explanations that relate to the structure of the situation or to the common experience of language-using animals in the face of the world.

Conceptualizing Absence

At the beginning of this chapter I touched on the question of the origin of religion and its relation to modes of communication. If one is looking at the main institutional fields of human behavior, religion is, I suggest, the one that is uniquely human, that is if one separates off the question of morality discussed by Hinde (1999) and concentrates on that of a worldview dominated by supernatural agencies, by gods and deities.[8] There seems to me no problem in accounting for the appearance of worldviews in themselves. These are a consequence of language-using animals facing their environment, of asking questions and inventing answers, of putting an individual's situation into a wider context. Many of these answers will resemble one another and will oscillate between what we would call the natural and the supernatural. Such resemblances could be due to diffusion through learned behavior, and some undoubtedly are (the doctrine of the Trinity for example). Other similarities, such as the notion of ghosts, could be developed from built-in tendencies, as Boyer (2001) assumes following Chomsky's work on language, or could have wider biological roots, as Hinde (1999) proposes. On the other hand, other general similarities could result from necessary convergences in the possibilities offered by the interaction between language and environment.

That seems to me the case not only with worldviews in the abstract but also of religious worldviews that all human societies before the present seem to have possessed, although, in my view, there has always been a skeptical, agnostic element even in the most hegemonic of societies, as we have seen in Ancient Egypt. In the present day the emphasis has shifted and most interaction takes place in a god-free zone. But in long-range comparative terms that development is unusual, an aspect of "modernity" following on the "scientific revolution" and the Enlightenment, part of the overall process of secularization and of trimming, if not discarding, the supernatural.[9]

It is clearly only by using language, by using some form of symbolic representation, that one can "visualize" what is not there, what is not in front of one, what is not the face-to-face and that one can visualize the distant other, either spatially or temporally.[10] The spatial aspect enables one to conceive the world as a whole, the temporal to see it in the past or in the future. It also enables one to symbolize what is absent in the shape of deities, agencies, and forces that might serve to account for, fill in, and make understandable some of the inevitable gaps in man's information about the world, past, present, or future.

The notion of a Creator God fills in the past of the world in which we live, as well as in some cases offering us help in present and future circumstances with which we cannot always cope as readily as we might wish. Other deities fill a similar gap and sometimes act as intermediaries with the High God. It is not surprising that in West Africa and elsewhere (in China for example), the earth as well as major features of the cosmos such as the sun and the rain are seen as having a "supernatural" as well as a "natural" component; indeed the two aspects are scarcely to be distinguished from the actor's point of view. The earth not only provides the fundamental resource for an agricultural livelihood, and indeed the spatial dimension of all life (and hence in West Africa is specially connected with breaches of the peace, the shedding of blood within local communities whose boundaries it determines), but it receives the dead (plants, animals, and men) and regenerates the living crop from the inert seed; the dead indeed assist the living. There seems nothing counterintuitive about attributing these opposing processes and concerns to forces and agencies that include both what we would see as the supernatural as well as the natural. From the standpoint of the vast span and experience of human cultures, it would be strange to do otherwise, especially when language has given us the powers to invent and conceive of absent agencies and forces of all kinds.

Equally the rain and its concomitants, thunder and lightning, are at once essential for the generation of crops and the sustaining of human life and at the same time frightening to humanity. The neonate appears to be programmed to react to loud sounds and sudden flashes, which continue to disturb adults. The lightning itself is later recognized as being particularly terrifying, since it can cause a frightening death or injury. There is the further question of why some people should be struck and others not. There may seem to be no reasonable explanation except that those who have been hit should be singled out to be punished for something they have done, just as a parent singles out a naughty offspring. Intentionality or purposive action is assumed and hence a humanlike agency is deemed responsible; the rain, thunder, and lightning are anthropomorphized.

The problem is not altogether unlike that Evans-Pritchard (1937) has described for Azande witchcraft. If a person passes under a wall and a brick falls on his head, we would describe that as an accident. But the Azande might well attribute intentionality and ask who or what caused that brick to fall on that particular person at that particular time. What agency carried this out and who was behind the act? Obviously it could have been somebody in the community holding a grudge against the victim and attacking him by what we would call mystical means, by witchcraft or sorcery. That is, by agencies that we would not recognize as effective, or alternatively recognize as *supernatural* rather than natural. The identification of the two emerges from the use of language itself, which enables us to symbolize absent forces. The distinction between the kinds of forces, far from being built-in, derives from a long development of thought, eventuating in the Enlightenment but passing through not dissimilar processes in other written cultures, in China for example, with the development of different but parallel methods of proof and argumentation for the evaluation of experience about the world around and inside us. In this way there developed over the longer term that "unnatural" divide between the natural and the supernatural, between the secular and the religious, a dimension that was strongly promoted by the advent of literacy, of boundary-maintaining sets of particular beliefs ("religions of the book") to which you could subscribe or not. From this perspective, it is not so much religious belief that has to be accounted for but its absence.

The opposite holds if we regard the spiritual, the supernatural, and the mystical as counterintuitive. But is it? Does God really counter intuition? Does the flying of witches? To get from here to there silently, as when one assumes a double, flying is the obvious way, the way of the bird. How otherwise would living beings from afar appear close to us as in a dream or a vision? It is true that one would not expect that of one's waking self (distance is distance, a wall is a wall), but there are other situations, in a dream, where that order of things is reversed, when if the world is not turned upside down, then it is at least knocked sideways.

I am well aware that my explanation leans toward that of E. B. Tylor in *Primitive Culture* (1871). But that is not a convergence that worries me. While I can see

language, absence, memory

no evidence for the sequence of religious belief he proposed, it does seem that the ancestor cult or worship depends upon the universal (sociological-psychological) fact that human beings continue their relationships with their kith and kin (others, too) even after they are dead. That also seems true of some animal species, but with humans the notion of continuity is enhanced partly because of the persisting memories of life together, and partly because roles and property are passed down by inheritance so that the dead continue to signify, indeed the more so because of the very nature of their absence, which language both creates and helps to overcome. The continued "existence" of ancestors as ex-humans, epitomized in the careful way humans disposed of their dead in later prehistoric times, necessarily means embodying some of their former characteristics in their now absent and transformed selves. Which characteristics? One is their willingness to continue to aid and punish their descendants; another is their ability to continue to present themselves, possibly as ghosts but also in less material ways. Both these abilities involve assumptions about the way these influences happen and these appearances occur. Mystical and supernatural we would call them, but they form an elaboration of the very notion of the continuity of aspects of the human person after the burial, after the body has been disposed of, indeed of life after death. There is little or nothing that is counterintuitive in all this, simply the elaboration of the ordinary, of conceptualizing absence.

So setting aside Tylor's sequence of religious forms, it seems eminently possible that more complex concepts of deity may well have developed from the commemoration of the dead. One presumably has to begin somewhere in the development of the religious life. The archaeological record can provide little definite evidence of early religious activity, other than, for example, the Neanderthal burial customs, the existence of which seems to imply a notion of the continuity of the living after death. More complex religious forms seem to have developed later, with the Upper Paleolithic and the early Neolithic.

By looking at the impact of language on humanity's perception of the world, and in particular of religious beliefs and practices, we are looking at more proximate, more specific propensities or even "causes" than by positing unlocatable and hypothesized elements of a genetic or biological kind. Of course, both types of explanation are hypothetical, and both also contribute (nothing happens without a genetic or biological base), but the language implications seem more concrete and more directly accessible.

Notes

1. The definition has been contested, especially by those who have opted for the sacred or the holy, but the alternatives seem too vague, and I have chosen to follow Tylor's

commonsense definition. It is sometimes objected that Buddhism is a godless religion. But it offers prayers, gifts, and sermons to absent forces of a mystical kind. It is mystical communication with the absent that language makes possible and that takes a more abstract form in written religion.

2. Immediately before the Advanced Paleolithic, in Mousterian times, the remains of Neanderthal men are widely distributed in Europe and the Near East, that is, with the first *Homo*, though not *sapiens*. At La Chapelle-aux-Saints a Mousterian deposit was found over a grave, cut into the rock floor and containing the crouched skeleton of a Neanderthal man. Similar burials have been found elsewhere in the Dordogne as well as in the Crimea, and on Mount Carmell a whole "cemetery" of ten graves was found, without red ochre or ornaments but an old man clasps the jaw-bones of a large wild boar in his arms (Clark 1969: 35, 53). The Advanced Paleolithic saw a great outburst of human culture, as evidenced by the cave paintings of southwest France. As man's material equipment developed, so too did the material evidence of his beliefs in magicoreligious activities and especially his concern with death and burial. At Grimaldi there was the deliberate placing of the body in an crouched position. One finds the arrangement of skulls and the use of the pigment, red ochre, frequently for funeral purposes and clearly associated with blood. Burials are made in close proximity to the domestic hearth, apparently stressing continuity with the living. Ornaments are found and so too the Venus figures distributed so widely. And grave goods such as mammoth bones are associated with human burials, leading to the great collections of Megalithic times.

3. As far as the advance in culture is concerned, we have more recently to take into account the tools and engravings found in the cave of Blombos 200 km east of Cape Town, which suggest that "symbolic thought" was around in Africa 35,000 years before the Cro-Magnon period in Europe (77,000 BP).

4. The notion of the coevolution of language and the brain has been expanded by Deacon (1997).

5. Fragmented is an inadequate word, since it implies that they derive from a whole, which is not the case. The whole is created by the outside observers.

6. See the introduction to *A Myth Revisited: The Third Bagre* (Goody and Gandah 2002).

7. See Bernardi's comments on Kenyatta's discussion of Kikuyu religion; the nearest equivalents for him were *Igonga* (sacrifice) and *mambra* (sex ritually performed) (1994: 187).

8. I am not trying to reduce religious systems to those beliefs and practices related to supernatural agencies. There are many other aspects. For example they often embody moral and ethical values, but so do other social institutions. They address questions of well-being; again so do others. Cosmology, again. It is gods and similar agencies that are particular to religion.

9. There is a problem in discussing worldviews. One is not talking only or even mainly about the world as a whole but of the world around us, the world in which we live, our social and natural environment.

10. Even meditation, Buddhist or otherwise, depends on language for conceptualizing absence.

References

Baines, J. 1991. "Society, Morality and Religious Practice." In J. Baines et al. (eds.), *Religion in Ancient Egypt: Gods, Myths, and Personal Practice*. Ithaca, N.Y.: Cornell University Press.

Bernardi, B. 1994. "Old Kikuyu Religion *Igongona* and *Mambura* Sacrifice and Sex: Re-Reading Kenyatta's Ethnography." In U. Bianchi (ed.), *The Notion of Religion in Comparative Research: Selected Proceedings of the XVIth Congress of the International Association for the History of Religions*. Rome: "L'Erma" di Bretchneider.

Bierbrier, M. 1982. *The Tomb-Builders of the Pharaohs*. London: British Museum Publications.

Boyer, Pascal. 2001. *Religion Explained: The Evolutionary Origin of Religious Thought*. New York: Basic Books.

Clark, G. 1969. *World Prehistory: A New Outline*. 2nd ed. Cambridge: Cambridge University Press.

Deacon, Terence. 1997. *The Symbolic Species: The Co-evolution of Language and the Human Brain*. London: Norton.

Evans-Pritchard, E. E. 1937. *Witchcraft, Oracles and Magic among the Azande*. Oxford: Clarendon Press.

Goody, J. 1986. *The Logic of Writing and the Organization of Society*. Cambridge: Cambridge University Press.

———. 1997. *Representations and Contradictions*. Oxford: Blackwell.

Goody, J., and S. W. D. K. Gandah. 2002. *A Myth Revisited: The Third Bagre*. Durham, N.C.: Carolina Academic Press.

Henshilwood, C. S., F. d'Enrico, and P. Nilssen. In press. "An Engraved Bone Fragment from ca. 70 ka Year Old Middle Stone Age Levels at Blombos Cave, South Africa: Implications for the Origins of Symbolism and Language" *Antiquity*.

Hinde, R. 1999. *Why Gods Persist: A Scientific Approach to Religion*. London: Routledge.

Mithen, Steven. 2004. "From Ohalo to Çatalhöyük: The Development of Religiosity During the Early Prehistory of Western Asia, 20,000–7,000 B.C." In Harvey Whitehouse and Luther H. Martin (eds.), *Theorizing Religions Past: Archaeology, History, and Cognition*. Walnut Creek, Calif.: AltaMira Press.

Redford, D. B. 1984. *Akhenaten: The Heretic King*. Princeton, N.J.: Princeton University Press.

Smith, W. Robertson. 1889. *Lectures on the Religion of the Semites: The Fundamental Institutions*. 3d ed. London.

Tylor, E. B. 1871. *Primitive Culture*. London: A. and C. Black.

Whitehouse, H. 1995. *Inside the Cult: Religious Innovation and Transmission in Papua New Guinea*. Oxford: Oxford University Press.

———. 2000. *Arguments and Icons: Divergent Modes of Religiosity*. Oxford: Oxford University Press.

Ritual and Deference 4

MAURICE BLOCH

WHITEHOUSE, AND OTHERS WORKING WITH HIM, have put forward a stimulating general theory of types of religious activity, especially ritual. This is a theory firmly anchored within a cognitive framework, something which is too often missing. Whitehouse argues the obvious, but crucial, point that for rituals to continue there must be a mechanism for transmission, and that ultimately, even with literacy or other artificial information-storing devices present, human memory must be a key factor in enabling continuation. He distinguishes two modes of religiosity, "imagistic" and "doctrinal," that rely on different types of memory. One type of religiosity, of which initiation ceremonies are an example he often uses, occur rarely in the lifetime of individuals. For this mode, according to him, transmission is linked to autobiographical memories burned in the mind, so to speak, by the traumatic and emotional nature of the experience. The other type of religiosity is not so emotionally inscribed and relies on the frequency of occurrences of the practices, e.g. the crossing of Catholics. This would lead to a type of internalization that he links with schema theory, but that we can be much more precise about (Bloch 1991).

Although sympathetic with the theoretical ambition of the general enterprise, I have a number of difficulties with the theory, not least of which is my doubt that the distinction can be sufficiently specified so as to lead to the kind of testing envisaged by its inventor. If I take the Merina initiation ceremony (Bloch 1986) as an example, it is unclear whether it should be considered a case of the first or second type of ritual. On the face of it, being a traumatic initiation ritual, it should be classified as "imagistic;" however, there are also at least three compelling reasons to consider it of a "doctrinal" type: (1) the organizers cannot draw on their experience of their own circumcisions in any significant distinctive way since they were usually younger than two when they were themselves circumcised; (2) the organizers draw on their observation and participation of the many circumcision rituals they attend, usually every year; (3) the basic elements of the ritual are simply an elaboration on the Merina blessing done by elders for the benefit of juniors, a ritual practice that, in some form or other, occurs probably as frequently as a devout Catholic crosses him- or herself. Nevertheless, such blessings can serve as a mnemonic framework for the rarer circumcision ritual.

The problem of distinguishing between the two modes also occurs in a number of less straightforward ways. Whitehouse argues that the two modes of religiosity lead to very different types of exegetical activity; however, I argue below that this is not so.

Thus, according to Whitehouse, often-repeated rituals are not likely to involve spontaneous, individual, exploratory exegesis that genuinely connects with specific practices, since these are done quasi-automatically and the rationality underlying the actions is never spelled out. Whatever exegesis exists is external, fixed by masters of orthodoxy, and does not concern the ordinary practitioner. On the other hand, traumatic, rare, and emotionally arousing rituals are not likely to be accompanied by fixed exegesis either but nevertheless enable "rich and revelatory religious experience," a kind of individual transformation of the implicit message of the symbolism into private yet explicit and fluid exegeses (Whitehouse 2002).

Whitehouse's concern with exegesis is part of a long line of anthropological struggles with the "meaning" of rituals. Since people in many parts of the world devote large amounts of energy on practices that have been called rituals, anthropologists feel that it is their job to explain why people do such things and that such an explanation requires decoding what these practices *mean*, presumably for the practitioners. The obvious way would be to ask them, but informants turn out to be singularly unhelpful. They claim that they don't know why they do what they do, they say that they do these things the way they do because that is the way their ancestors did them, and they often assert that they can't even understand the words they use. Worse, when one can extract explanations from some people, these individuals often turn out to be either concocting private and fleeting musings, probably set in train for the first time by the anthropologist's questions, or, in the case of religions with expert literate practitioners, merely mouthing standard responses that clearly remain totally external to the feelings and understandings of ordinary people.

As a result, anthropological writers have been concerned with the puzzle caused by the observation that, while it is clear that rituals seem to be, in part at least, communicative acts—in that some kind of nontrivial information is conveyed and is involved for both participants and observers alike—it seems very difficult to be satisfactorily precise about what this content might be. It has even been suggested by many, including myself, that a precise decoding of the message of rituals is necessarily misleading (Bloch 1974; Sperber 1974; Lewis 1980; Humphrey and Laidlaw 1994). Some have gone so far as to argue that rituals are simply meaningless (Staal 1979), though exactly what such a claim would amount to is very unclear. However, one reason for arguing in this way is simply that, in the field, we are frustratingly and continually faced with informants who say that they don't know what rituals mean or why they are done in this or that way. Nonetheless, what stops anthropologists adhering easily to the thesis that rituals are meaningless is that these very same informants who a minute before admitted they did not know what elements of the ritual were about, add, at the same time, puzzlingly and portentously, that these elements mean something very deep and they insist that it is very important to perform them in precisely the right way.

In fact, anthropological discussions often suffer from the fact that they conflate the problem of writing the ethnography of ritual (symbolic analysis) and the problem of understanding the meaning of what is going on for the participants. But leaving this point aside, anthropologists nevertheless often leave us with the rather lame point that rituals convey something or other that is vague but somehow powerful. Notably, this is so for the two types of rituals identified by Whitehouse's theory. Here I want to follow a tradition in ritual analysis that, instead of being embarrassed about vagueness, makes it its central concern. This is what I want to be precise about. Furthermore, I want to go much beyond my predecessors, myself included, in arguing that the vagueness of ritual offers us a clue to the nature of much human social knowledge and of many learning processes.

Repetition

One feature which has often been noted in discussions concerning ritual is the presence of repetition (Leach 1966; Bloch 1974; Rappaport 1975; Lewis 1980). In fact, the term "repetition" in these discussions is used to refer to quite a variety of phenomena, all of which are commonly present in rituals.

First of all, the same elements or phrases are often repeated in the same performance, sometimes to a bewildering extent. For example, in the type of Malagasy circumcision ritual referred to above, the same phrase can recur several hundred times, perhaps even more; similarly, in Christian rituals, the word "Amen" is also said many times. Secondly, there is the fact that whole rituals are often repetitions one of another. One weekly Mass is in many parts much the same as that of the week before. Finally, actors in rituals guide much of their behavior in terms of what they believe others, or themselves, to have done, or said, on previous occasions. In this sense they are repeating either themselves, or others. Indeed, any act, whether a speech act or otherwise, that appears to originate fully with the actor cannot properly be called a ritual in English.

It is repetition of this latter type that I want to concentrate on. At least some, if not most, of the actions involved in the kind of phenomena mentioned above are understood, by actors and observers alike, as repetitions; that is, they are acts, whether speech acts or acts of another kind, that do not completely originate in the intentionality of the producer at the time of his or her performance. This point is most important and, with the notable exceptions of Humphrey and Laidlaw (1994) and Keane (1997), whose arguments are somewhat similar to mine, has not been stressed enough in the literature. It means that what is involved in ritual is conscious "repetition," either of oneself, but much more often and much more importantly, of others whom one has seen or heard perform the ritual before. All rituals thus involve what can be called "quotation," if we use the term to refer not just to language, but to all repetitions of originators. These originators must have some sort of authority, and this authority justifies quoting them, as in the Lord's prayer or the Christian communion service.

Familiar statements given to anthropologists by participants in rituals, such as "We do this because it is the custom of the ancestors," "We do this because it is what one does at these events," or "We do this because we have been ordered to act in this way," imply conscious quotation.

Therefore, the inevitable implication of such statements is that, both for participants and onlookers, it is not just the specific present context of time and place that frames the intentionality of the acts of the ritual actor and that is relevant to fully understanding them, but also the past time and space context of specified, or unspecified, previous occurrences of the repeated/quoted acts. As Humphrey and Laidlaw put it, in a way that echoes a point I made in an earlier article (Bloch 1974), "ritualisation transforms the relation between intention and the meaning of action" (Humphrey and Laidlaw 1994: 90).

When a Malagasy, during a circumcision ceremony, sprays water by way of blessing on those present, everyone knows that he or she is doing this kind of action in this way because this is "what one does," that is, the tradition. This means that whatever the elder feels like at the time, and the way he perceives the situation, will be insufficient to explain, and is well known to be insufficient to explain, why he is using water at that moment. Compare this with a situation wherein he was merely reaching for water from a stream; in this case most observers would find it sufficient, not necessarily rightly, that, given his background knowledge, the twin facts that the person was thirsty and that he saw the water in front of him—that is, his beliefs and desires, in the psychological/philosophical sense of the terms—was all there was to it.

The fact that rituals involve, and are known by everyone concerned to involve, quotation, in the broad sense in which I have been using the word, is not all there is to a phenomenon such as a Malagasy blessing, but it is surely a highly significant part of it. In what follows I turn to an examination of what this fact might imply, given the centrality that has been accorded to the reading of the intentionality of speakers for semantics in general and for linguistic utterances in particular.

Deference, Understanding, and Truth

Rituals therefore are acts of repetition or quotation. Such a remark places ritual within what externalist philosophers have identified as a central aspect of human thought and communication (Putman 1975) and which has been called by some "deference" (Burge 1986), that is, reliance on the authority of others to guarantee the value of what is said or done. What makes such an observation particularly interesting for anthropologists is that deference fundamentally alters the relation between understanding and holding something to be true. It seems common sense that to hold something to be true one must also understand it. This, however, is not the case when deference is involved, especially when deference is linked to quotation.

Roughly, we can say that, in pragmatic theories of the Gricean family type (Grice 1971; Sperber and Wilson 1986), understanding meaning is seen to necessarily require not only knowledge of the lexicon and of the syntax employed, but also the unconscious reading of the mind of the speaker and of what she intends as she utters the sounds. Without such "mind reading" the words are, at the very least, so open to a wide range of ambiguities that it is impossible for the hearer to process them successfully. Such a theory is all the more interesting in that it makes the understanding of language depend directly on what many would now argue is *the* key distinguishing feature of *Homo sapiens sapiens*, the so-called theory of mind, which enables a person to "read" the mind of others and which separates mankind fairly sharply from all other animal species (Premack 1991).

Quotation implies an obvious modification of the simple Gricean principles considered above. It throws the hearer back to trying to read not only the mind of the speaker, but also the mind of the speaker who is being quoted. Given the metarepresentational ability of human beings, this is easily done, even if we are dealing with further degrees of metarepresentation (Sperber 2000). In this case, once the quoted sentence is understood, its truth or otherwise can be considered.

Quotation, however, offers another possibility. This is a kind of abandonment of the examination of the truth of the quoted statement, because one is only concerned with the fact that the statement has been made and that the speaker has been identified. If this speaker is worthy of trust, one can assume that what has been said is true without making the effort of understanding. In such a case deference is combined with quotation, and it accounts for the rather odd possibility that one may hold something to be true without fully understanding it. If one trusts the source sufficiently, understanding is not necessary for the truth to be accepted, as is illustrated by the following example given by Origgi (2000). She tells us of a follower who is convinced of the truth of a statement made by a leader who asserted that there are too many neo-Trotskyites in their party, even though she knows that she has no idea what a neo-Trotskyite might be. She will then be happy to transmit the information to another without understanding it. This might seem an unusual scenario, but a moment's reflection will confirm that we are all, to varying degrees, in much this same sort of situation, most of the time.

Deference and Social Life

What is particularly interesting for anthropologists in an example such as the one just given is that not only do such occurrences crop up continually but that their occurrence is not random in the course of social life. Situations when the truth of certain propositions is to be accepted through deference, and therefore not necessarily understood, are socially and culturally organized and regulated. Living in a partially institutionalized form of life, which is what is meant by living in society, means that there are moments, concepts, and contexts the why and wherefores of which one may examine and moments, concepts, and contexts where this is inappropriate. For the reason we have seen above, this means that the latter need not be understood.

Thus, social life "manages," so to speak, the occurrence and the nature of deference through different types of institutional devices and therefore, at the same time, it establishes an economy of the necessity of understanding. It is clear that living in a socially organized system, even the apparently most ad hoc, nonetheless involves moments of compulsory deference, in the sense used above. There are moments when there are, not only limits to understanding, but limits to the appropriateness of attempting to understand. The ordinary continual deference of practical life does not simply involve delaying our search for intentionality, but often apparently largely *abandoning* it. This means that all normal human communication involves a mixture of searching for meaning, our own and that of others, and *also* not searching, moments of understanding and not understanding. When young children exhaust their parents by endlessly asking "why" questions, they may well be training their judgment of when to search and when not to search. Consider the example of someone who tells us that the cat is on the mat; in such a circumstance we may well search for the reason why they want to inform us of this fact, but we would be very unwise to waste our time searching for the reason why they chose that particular sound to convey the concept "cat."

We have seen why deference makes holding something true without understanding it possible, but there is also a reason why social life makes this abandonment of the search for meaning common. The reason is that the experience of living in a historically constructed system means that deference continually occurs without the individual who is being deferred to being easily identifiable. As a result, intentionality cannot be "locked" onto an intending mind and therefore understanding cannot be "clinched." People around us and ourselves are clearly deferring to others. But if we were so unwise as to want to examine these others more closely, they would turn out to be deferring to yet others, and so on, without the process having any clear boundary. This is because humans live and act within a set of conventions, which are no doubt the product of a long historical process of communication and quotation, and which are experienced as "given," that is, without specific minds intending them. These are the conventions that have been so internalized as to be completely unconscious. Anthropologists sometimes call them culture or habitus and sometimes give them other names such as structure. In other words we are continually deferring to others, but we do not catch sight of the minds we are deferring to. For we are not simply reading human minds, we are reading historically constructed human minds. We do not simply understand others and ourselves; we always, to varying degrees, but semiconsciously, understand that people around us are deferring to invisible and indeterminable others and that therefore we should limit our attempt to understand them. What this means is that complete understanding is impossible because, as noted above, full understanding requires that, either immediately or at one or more remove, as in quotation, it is in the end possible to imagine the intentionality of some mind or other. But, if it is not possible to identify clearly an original intentional being, meaning can never be grasped.

Of course, such indeterminate deference is much of the time unconscious, but this is certainly not always the case. The case of the follower accepting the belief about the neo-Trotskyites is a case where it is quite possible that the act of deference becomes conscious, although, there, the person deferred to is clearly identified. What difference this consciousness of deference makes has not been, as far as I know, much explored in pragmatics, or in philosophy, but since it is so prominent in ritual and religion and so closely linked with the question of exegesis, we will have to consider the question.

There are therefore three elements in human communication that can be combined: (1) quotation and deference, (2) consciousness of deference, (3) lack of clarity as to who is being deferred to. When all three are present, we have the phenomena that in anthropological English are commonly referred to as ritual. Because the combination of these three elements is likely to lead to limited understanding, it is not surprising that this state of affairs is frequent in ritual.

Deference and Religion

Now we have the tools to examine what all this might mean for ritual and religion. At first, I examine two apparently simple deference scenarios, both of which correspond quite closely to the Origgi story about the neo-Trotskyites. The first concerns learning the Koran in Muslim schools, and the second concerns spirit possession.

Reading or reciting the Koran, which is the central purpose of Muslim education, apparently involves a simple type of quotation on the part of the student since the speaker is merely quoting a single other intentional mind: that of God, to whom he defers totally (Eickelman 1978). The student should, ideally, learn the Koran perfectly by heart and so become a totally transparent medium just like Mohamed himself. He should become a sort of tape recorder, so that his intentionality, and thus his understanding, disappear or become irrelevant to the text. As a result, the speaker or the hearer can focus entirely on the presence of God in the words. The student should efface himself as much as possible.

Another example of such ideally "transparent" quotation is spirit possession. Theoretically, the utterer of sound has totally surrendered her body, and especially her vocal organs, to the being who temporally possesses her. In this case too, the locus of emission of the sound should ideally disappear. Asking the student of the Koran, or the medium, to explain her choice of words or content—that is, to provide an exegesis, would clearly be to deny her complete deference.

These two examples may seem simple, but in fact they involve two quite different elements. The pupil learning the Koran, and others around him, believe that what is proposed there is true and they must assert it whether they understand it or not. The medium has so effaced herself that the assertions that come from her mouth must be true, because the spiritual source speaks irrespective of her understanding. This is straightforward. However, one might expect that such practices might simply place at one remove the effort to understand. Having got the pupil or the medium out of the way, it should be possible to concentrate on understanding God or the spirit. This, however, does not seem to be the case. In such practices the act of deference takes center stage and everybody joins with the pupil or the medium in abandoning their intentionality and in making themselves transparent to whoever's words they are quoting, which strangely fade out of focus.

The medium or the student is implicitly claiming truth for his utterance at the very time that he is denying the relevance of understanding what he is saying. The devout Muslim aligns him- or herself with the position of the student and therefore accepts the deference. It seems probable that the spectator at a séance never imagines a direct relation with the spirit but always a relation via the medium, in which case the deference comes into play also, probably because of the drama of his self attack. The effort in being transparent, that is, in deferring totally, is the real focus of the action.

In such cases we have two of the elements isolated above: deference and the consciousness of deference, even though this may ultimately disappear. What is not present, however, is the third element discussed above: the indetermination of the originating mind. It is clear that it is God who is the source of the Koran or it is Great-Grandmother who is the spirit. But what happens when such definition disappears? It is to this that I now turn.

Ritual

It is the presence of the third element that characterizes much ritual and, more especially, those ritual elements that are most strongly resistant to exegesis. In such instances quotation, and therefore deference, is obviously taking place, but it is not clear who is being quoted or deferred to.

As noted above, a very common experience among anthropologists who ask why someone is doing something in a particular way in a ritual is to be answered by such phrases as "It's the tradition," "It is the custom of the ancestors," "It goes back to early history," and so on. Now, these apparently frustrating answers are nonetheless interesting in many ways for they combine explicitness concerning deference and awareness of imprecision about who exactly is the originating mind behind the practice.

The reference to tradition, or the ways in which things have always been done, or to the ancestors, clearly does throw the attention of the participants *away* from the intentionality of the actor but *to where in particular* is not so clear. Sperber, in a famous earlier paper, gave an example of this sort of thing when talking of a man who had asked him to shoot a dragon. He, quite rightly, stressed that we should bear in mind the quotational character of such a request. The man was not fully committed to the existence of dragons but was quoting others whose minds were questionable (Sperber 1982). This situation seems to me different from rituals. Rituals are even vaguer as to who the individual mind originating the message might be. Scrutiny of the source of the authority inevitably leads the inquirer into an endless regress. Thus, although we normally think of tradition as something being handed forward from the past to the present, the appeal to the *authority* of tradition, something that is socially much more central, involves being handed back from the present toward an indeterminable past destination.

If we imagine the participants, or the observers, in such rituals as the Mass, or the Malagasy initiation ritual, or making the sign of the cross, trying to work out who intended what they are doing to be done so, in other words trying for exegesis, they are going to be in a difficult situation.

Exegesis, that is, the search for original intentionality, is in itself perfectly reasonable, and although frustrating, almost inevitable. After all, we are dealing with people with human minds, that is, with animals whose minds are characterized by an intentionality-seeking device that is normally exercised ceaselessly, one might almost say obsessively, sometimes consciously but often unconsciously, and that enables them to read the minds of others and thus coordinate their behavior with them. But in a ritual, these poor little animals, amongst them poor little anthropologists, appear to be faced with an impossible situation because the search for intentionality leads them ever further back, to ever more remote authorities, but without ever settling anywhere with any finality. This is the predicament of participants who might unwisely ask themselves why on earth they are doing this or that, as well as that of mere onlookers asking the same question.

This Kafkaesque nightmare of being endlessly referred back to other authorities can only be rendered bearable in one of three ways:

1. The first is the most straightforward. One can attempt to simply switch off the intentionality-seeking device, an attitude which could be described as retreat or "putting on hold" or "letting things be." This switching-off requires some effort as, given the way our minds work, it is unnatural, but it can be done nonetheless. Saying that what you do, or what you say, is because of "tradition" may in some cases be nothing more than an expression of this attitude. The refusal to look for intentionality, however, presents the participants with a disappointing propositional thinness. It is doubtful whether it is at all possible to entertain any relevant propositional content without placing it within the framework of propositional attitudes. And it is obvious that one cannot detect propositional attitudes without imagining a mind to which these attitudes belong. It is as if, when we are very tired and kept awake by a hubbub of voices, we apparently make out somebody or other saying, "Raindrops are Jesus macaroons." In such a situation, we might make no effort to discover the intentionality of the speaker and hope to go back to sleep as quickly as possible. My early memory of Catholic rituals is of this sort. It is probably accurate to say that such a proposition, totally devoid of attributable intentionality, has no meaning, or at least no speaker meaning, to use a Gricean distinction. The only thing we have got from it is the realization that it involves the use of proper language, therefore that it probably has potential for speaker meaning. Clearly there is here no understanding, and it is far from clear whether anybody in such a situation even holds the propositions to be true.
2. The second possibility is much more common but will also appear in a number of somewhat exceptional situations, being faced by an overly inquisitive anthropologist being one, but not the only one. Then, for some reason, it will seem necessary to make an effort to understand what is going on. At first, one is tempted to search in the dark recesses behind

the producer of the ritual acts, who after all we know is only quoting someone, somewhere, who might have meant to mean something. (Doing this without paying attention to informants is called functionalism in anthropology.) But it's dark behind there, for, as soon as someone seems to come into focus, they become transparent as they reveal another person behind them. They are only deferring to someone else, further back, who, when focused upon, becomes similarly transparent, and so on. Finally, we give up searching for meaning, though not in the same total way as the giving up I discussed in case 1 and for the following reason.

All this frustration only occurs over the problem of searching for the intentionality of the initiator of the message. By contrast, the intentionality of the speaker, the singer, or the actor in the ritual is not more problematic than those of the spirit medium or of the pupil learning the Koran who were discussed earlier. The intentionality of all these people can simply be read as deferential, and this act is greatly valued. The search for intentionality is therefore switched to the unproblematic examination of the intentionality of the transmitter, the situation that Humphrey and Laidlaw describe for the Jain *Puja* (Humphrey and Laidlaw 1994). And when people tell us that they don't know what such a phrase means, or why such an act is performed, but that it is being said or performed in this way because one is following the customs of the ancestors, they are surely telling us that what they are doing, saying, singing, is above all *deferring*. In such a case there is no exegesis to be expected from the participants, and it is indeed offensive to ask for it, as this denies what they are doing. The reason they do not understand the content of what they are doing is that its originators cannot be localized as intentional minds, and no speaker meaning can thus be attributed to them. However, this indeterminacy does not eliminate the authority behind the content, an authority that claims truth for it. It is this situation that so puzzles the decoding anthropologists, but that is exactly what is analyzed by Burge: that is, claiming truth for what one does not understand. This situation is simply muddled by traditional worries about the presence or absence of exegesis, though it is possible that, in such a case, the people involved will accept that exegesis from somebody else is possible and that experts, somewhere or other, know the "meaning" of what is going on.

3. It is possible, however, that even this solution to the problem is unsatisfactory. In rare but important moments, people are going to ask themselves, or others, why things are done or said in this or that way, and they will not give up in spite of the apparent difficulties encountered in

their search. Their mind-reading instinct will just not leave them alone. This kind of determination is what in Whitehouse's theory is deemed to cause "rich and revelatory religious experience." Thus, one wants to attribute speaker meaning to what is going on but in order to do that one must inevitably create some sort of speaker. Normal speakers are not available since these will become transparent as soon as they are considered and will therefore perform the disappearing act discussed above. Again, this situation is identical whether we are dealing with frequently or rarely occurring rituals, since participants may wonder about the meaning of an action such as crossing oneself, or seeing others cross themselves, as rarely, or as frequently, as they might about the meaning of a plant in a New Guinea initiation ritual.

The solution to the problem of wanting to locate meaning without having normal originators to that meaning is to merge all the shadowy transparent figures into a phantasmagorical quasi person who may be called something like "tradition," "the ancestors as a group," "our way of doing things," "our spirit," "our religion," even perhaps "God." These are entities to which "minds" may just about be attributed with some degree of plausibility, thus apparently restoring intentional meaning to the goings-on of ritual. The apparent specificity of such entities thus appears, at first, to solve the problem of the indeterminacy of the intentional source. After all, we are familiar with the attribution of humanlike intentional minds to things like mountains, or dead people (Boyer 1996), so why not to an essentialized tradition? There we are in a situation that is somewhat similar and somewhat dissimilar to that of 2. It is similar in that the message is held to be true whether it is understood or not. Again, the act of deference is consciously present and valued in and of itself. However, the act of deference does not hold center stage as much as in 2, because speaker meaning becomes an alternative point of interest. Nonetheless, this is no ordinary speaker meaning to the extent that the "speaker" is no ordinary mind, the kind of mind we instinctively know how to interpret with great subtlety because of our probably innate "theory of mind." In fact, I would propose that the precision of our understanding varies with the degree that the phantasmagoric initiators are close or distant to ordinary minds. Thus, the mind of an entity called "the tradition" would be more difficult to interpret than that of an entity called "the ancestors," but that is, in turn, probably more difficult to interpret than a singular spirit, simply because the concept of plural minds is not what we are equipped to understand. The difficulties of exegesis in such cases should thus correlate with the degree of the normal, humanlike characteristics of the entities who halt the endless regress caused by deference.

The three variants discussed above are of course not distinct in time or place. Individuals may slide from one to another during a particular ritual. However, the form of the ritual and the entities invoked will ensure the general organization in most people's minds of relative degrees of understanding. This is because the problems of attributing clear meanings to what is done all result from the central fact that ritual involves high degrees of deference. This emphasis actually fits well with quite the different type of discussion of ritual I developed in *Prey into Hunter* (Bloch 1992), where I argue that the first element of ritual is a kind of dramatized self attack by participants, an attack against their own intentionality, so that it may be replaced. What I identified as the preliminary violence in ritual (for example: the weakening of the sacrificial animal, which stands for the humans involved) can be seen as the theater of deference. Rituals are moments when the actors make themselves transparent so that other intentional minds can be read through them. Once again what characterizes ritual is conscious deference.

However, as we have seen, deference is a common aspect of human life. It occurs whenever we do something, or believe something to be true, relying on the authority of others, something that we do constantly. If people are always partly, but very significantly, living in a sea of deference, this is largely an unconscious fact. But nevertheless, it is a fact that hovers not very far from the level of consciousness, and that can, and often does, cross into the level of consciousness. As Putnam (1975) stressed, people are almost conscious of the fact that they are constantly relying on the understanding of others and that they normally act in terms of beliefs they do not fully understand, but which they hold valid because of their trust in the understanding of others. This is also the situation described by Hutchins, which he defines as "distributed cognition" (1995). People therefore allow themselves to depend on others. By and large, this a good feeling, while at other times it is oppressive. But, when one is in trouble, and one does not know what to do, one allows oneself to be taken over by the knowledge and the authority of others; it is only sensible, and there is nothing much else that one can do.

Now I am arguing that ritual is just that—in a rather extreme form, rituals are orgies of conscious deference. But if this is so, the search for exegesis is always misleading. This is not because it is impossible. Clearly exegeses exist, whether private or shared, whether the secret of experts or available to all, whether conscious, semiconscious, or unconscious. But they are beside the point of the central character of ritual: deference. In that crucial fact, Whitehouse's two types of religiosity are reunited.

References

Bloch, Maurice. 1974. "Symbols, Song, Dance and Features of Articulation or Is Religion an Extreme Form of Traditional Authority?" *Archives Europeenes de Sociologie* 15: 55–81.

———. 1986. *From Blessing to Violence: History and Ideology in the Circumcision Ritual of the Merina of Madagascar*. Cambridge: Cambridge University Press.

———. 1991. "Language, Anthropology and Cognitive Science." *Man* 26: 183–98.

———. 1992. *Prey into Hunter: The Politics of Religious Experience*. Cambridge: Cambridge University Press.

Boyer, Pascal. 1996. "What Makes Anthropomorphism Natural: Intuitive Ontology and Cultural Representations." *Journal of the Royal Anthropological Institute* 2: 83–98.

Burge, T. 1986. "Individualism and Psychology." *Philosophical Review* 95: 133–201.

Eickelman, Dale. 1978. "The Art of Memory: Islamic Education and Social Reproduction." *Comparative Studies in Society and History* 20: 485–516.

Grice, H. P. 1971. "Utterer's Meaning, Sentence Meaning and Word Meaning." In J. Searle (ed.), *The Philosophy of Language*. Oxford: Oxford University Press.

Hutchins, Edwin. 1995. *Cognition in the Wild*. Cambridge, Mass.: M.I.T. Press.

Humphrey, Caroline, and James Laidlaw. 1994. *The Archetypal Actions of Ritual*. Oxford: Oxford University Press.

Keane, Webb. 1997. *Signs of Recognition*. Berkeley: University of California Press.

Leach, Edmund. 1966. "Ritualisation in Man in Relation to Conceptual and Social Development." *Philosophical Transactions of the Royal Society* 251: 403–408.

Lewis, Gilbert. 1980. *Day of Shining Red*. Cambridge: Cambridge University Press.

Premack, David. 1991. "Does the Chimpanzee Have a Theory of Mind? Revisited." In R. Byrne and A. Whitten (eds.), *Machiavellian Intelligence*. Oxford: Oxford University Press.

Origgi, Gloria. 2000. "Croire sans Comprendre." *Cahiers de Philosophie de L'Universite de Caen* 34: 191–202.

Putman, Hilary. 1975. "The Meaning of 'Meaning.'" In K. Gunderson (ed.), *Language, Mind and Knowledge*. Minneapolis: University of Minnesota Press.

Rappaport, Roy. 1975. "The Obvious Aspects of Ritual." *Cambridge Anthropology* 2: 3–61.

Sperber, Dan. 1974. *Le Symbolisme en General*. Paris: Hermann.

———. 1982. *Le Savoir des Anthropologues*. Paris: Hermann.

———, ed. 2000. *Metarepresentations: A Multidisciplinary Perspective*. Oxford: Oxford University Press.

Sperber, Dan, and Deirdre Wilson. 1986. *Relevance: Communication and Cognition*. Oxford: Blackwell.

Staal, Franz. 1979. "The Meaninglessness of Ritual." *Numen* 26: 2–22.

Whitehouse, Harvey. 2002. "Religious Reflexivity and Transmissive Frequency." *Social Anthropology* 10: 91–103.

The Doctrinal Mode and Evangelical Christianity in the United States

5

BRIAN MALLEY

I<small>N</small> *A<small>RGUMENTS AND</small> I<small>CONS</small>*, Harvey Whitehouse describes Protestant Christianity in its immediate post-Reformation and early-twentieth-century missionary forms as an example of a religion dominated by the doctrinal mode: ritually repetitive; focused on beliefs rather than images; envisioning a large, faceless, hierarchically organized community. Many of the characteristics that led Whitehouse to identify these forms of Christianity as doctrinal in orientation also characterize the diffuse and amorphous form of Christianity in the United States called evangelical Christianity. In this chapter I argue that although American evangelicalism is overall a good fit with Whitehouse's doctrinal mode, it raises serious questions about the motivation for frequent repetition and suggests that the doctrinal mode is more self-sufficient than Whitehouse allows.

"Evangelical" is, at present, a multiply defined term both within U.S. Christianity and within scholarship on U.S. Christianity (cf. Noll 2001: chapter 2; Harding 2000: xv–xvi; Smith and Emerson 1998: appendix B). The American religious scene is complex, and there is no fully satisfactory way of identifying the population at the focus of this chapter. Doctrinally, they believe in the inspiration and authority of the Bible and the saving death and resurrection of Jesus Christ. They also regard the Protestant Bible as the authoritative word of God. Although they use the term "evangelical" to describe themselves, this term is often used also to include Pentecostal/Charismatic and African American groups, who are not treated here. This discussion is based on ethnographic fieldwork at Creekside Baptist Church[1] in Ann Arbor, Michigan. Creekside Baptist is a highly educated, predominantly white church with 350–400 attendees on a typical Sunday morning. In addition to participant observation from 1998–2001, I conducted interviews and a survey. I also interviewed other pastors of similar churches in Ann Arbor and neighboring Ypsilanti, and read widely in evangelical literature.

Creekside Baptist generally fits Whitehouse's description of a religious system in the doctrinal mode: The style of codification is predominantly verbal; the frequency of transmission, relatively high; the level of arousal, generally low; memories, schematic; and transmission, narrative. On the sociopolitical side, cohesion is diffuse; spread is rapid; uniformity is high; and the scale is large. Because these are well-known characteristics of evangelicalism generally (a point to which I will return momentarily), I will not evidence them here.

With respect to two features, however, Creekside Baptist does not fit Whitehouse's characterization of the doctrinal mode. Whitehouse characterizes doctrinal mode systems as large-scale, with a vertical, hierarchical social structure. Yet Creekside Baptist is an autonomous church, with a relatively weak hierarchy. Like many other churches, Creekside Baptist is part of a larger conference, but all of its decisions are made internally. Its participation in the conference has little impact on the church's operations.

Internally, decisions at Creekside Baptist are made by the congregation, the pastors, and a board. Many day-to-day decisions are made by the pastors. More important decisions are made by the board. Critical issues are brought before the whole congregation.

While authority is not evenly distributed within the church, what hierarchy there is must be regarded as highly tenuous. In general, those who wish to be involved in the church can be, and practical authority basically accrues to people in proportion to the degree to which they are willing to take responsibility for church affairs. It is a volunteer organization, and ultimately, it is those who do who decide what's done. The pastors have a kind of general, spiritual authority, but it is not regarded as binding, and the pastors are in fact very much at the mercy of the congregation: Not only can they be directly fired, but a series of unpopular decisions can lower church attendance (and donations) to levels that threaten the entire institution. In short, Whitehouse's prediction that doctrinal institutions will be large-scale and centralized is not borne out by the case of Creekside Baptist.

In some of these characteristics, American evangelicalism, as evidenced by Creekside Baptist, fits a widespread stereotype of Protestant Christianity. In a very general sense, the data presented here must have been known or suspected by Whitehouse prior to his theoretical proposal, and hence cannot be regarded as a fully independent test of his theory. But it cannot be dismissed either: If the data had been really fully known, Whitehouse's predictions would presumably have accounted for them. Moreover, the stereotype of Protestant Christianity is empirically inaccurate on many points, and there would be no reason a priori to expect the stereotype to help, rather than hinder, his theory's accuracy. So while American evangelicalism is not a fully independent test case, neither are Whitehouse's predictions foregone conclusions.

Although the overall shape of American evangelicalism fits quite closely with Whitehouse's description of a religion in the doctrinal mode, their practices do suggest alternative explanations of doctrinal repetition and the durability of the doctrinal mode. I suggest these as amendments or additions to Whitehouse's theory.

Repetition

Whitehouse suggests that the repetition of doctrines is a precaution against "unintended deviation" (Whitehouse 2000: 171). Since deviation from Christian orthodoxy is usually considered heresy, I will set the stage for an evaluation of Whitehouse's specific claims by briefly examining heresy among evangelical Christians.

The term "heresy" does not seem to be much in use among evangelicals today. By heresy, I mean doctrinal error regarded as sufficient to motivate the refusal of fellowship. The people of Creekside Baptist are not much concerned with heresy. Some beliefs are regarded as so foundational that departure from them is heretical, but they are very few. Apart from the basic gospel message and the doctrine of biblical inspiration, there are few compulsory elements of orthodoxy. Much is left up to individual judgment. In principle, heresy could be a problem, but it is largely avoided through the process by which leadership is selected. Individuals may have heretical beliefs, but these ideas are little disseminated because these individuals are not in leadership roles. To the best of my knowledge, no instances of (potential) heresy arose at Creekside Baptist during the period of my fieldwork. The following observations, therefore, are drawn from my wider reading in evangelical literature rather than from firsthand observation.

The debate I will examine is the inerrancy controversy. Since the end of World War II, evangelicals[2] have begun arguing over whether the doctrine of biblical inspiration—the belief, on which all parties agree, that the Bible is the inspired word of God—entails the *inerrancy* of the Bible.

Many evangelicals maintain that the Bible, properly interpreted, is inerrant not only in matters of faith but also in incidentals of science and history. It is worth spelling out some of their more common claims as they understand them.

- The Bible is held to be thoroughly true on every matter it touches. It is not held to be a science or history textbook, but is thought to be true on whatever matters of science and history it happens to record.
- The Bible's acknowledged use of figurative, phenomenological, or otherwise special language, while feeding some hermeneutical disagreements, does not bear on issues of its veracity. The Bible's use of figurative language does not constitute error.

- The Bible, at least in the original autographs, is the very word of God. To impute error to the Bible would be to impute either deception or ignorance to God. Because God is omniscient and truthful, error in the Bible is theologically impossible.
- Nonetheless, the Bible is "accommodated" to its cultural context. When Jesus said that the mustard seed is the smallest of all seeds, he said something that is not absolutely true. Yet it would have been impractical and distracting for him to say that a then-unknown North American seed is the smallest of all seeds.

They also point out that the Bible has been vindicated by archaeology and history in many passages where nineteenth-century scholars had claimed it was in error. Their open challenge is for someone to show a clear and definite error in anything the Bible says.

Other evangelicals, perhaps as a result of evangelicalisms' reengagement with secular scholarly and scientific discourses, have adopted a less demanding interpretation of inspiration.

- The Bible is held to be thoroughly true in spiritual matters, but may contain error in matters of science and history. The Bible touches on scientific and historical matters only incidentally, and nothing important hinges on its exact truth in these details.
- Just as God accommodated himself to humankind in sending the eternal Son of God to appear as a mere man, so God has accommodated himself to humankind by sending the great message of salvation to prophets and apostles who were in every way men of their own times. We do not need to be committed to their understanding of the physical world any more than we are to their acceptance of slavery or other aspects of their cultures.
- Error in the incidentals of the Bible does not reflect on God, save as evidence of his mercy in communicating with frail-minded humans.

In practice, this "limited inerrancy" view is often the consequence of specific difficulties with the biblical text—people hold to this view because they have encountered some portion of the Bible that cannot easily be made to square with accepted scientific or historical fact.

This issue continues to provoke serious debate in centers of education, denominations, and local churches. (Creekside Baptist Church is committed to inerrancy, though a survey I carried out indicates that a substantial minority does not affirm the inerrancy of the Bible.) Most parties in the debate have been very reluctant to sling the term "heresy" at their opponents. Nonetheless, each side regards the other as teaching a false version of an important doctrine, and each has claimed that Christian tradition is on its side (Lindsell 1976; Rogers and McKim 1979; Woodbridge 1982; Geisler 1980; Bush and Nettles 1999). The inerrancy controversy would seem then to be a fair example of an orthodoxy-versus-heresy debate.

Is either position the result of faulty recollection? No. Both sides are well-motivated, reflective, researched positions. More importantly, neither side is a departure from a well-established tradition: Both sides can find statements from classic Christian thinkers that seem to support their understanding of inspiration, and it seems that both the tradition as a whole and some important thinkers individually have been ambiguous on this point. It is therefore not even possible to construe either position as a departure from a preexisting orthodoxy. Until recently, there simply *was* no consistent message that *could* have been misremembered. The classic heresies—Gnosticism, Docetism, Arianism, etc.—seem to have had similar histories.

Whitehouse does not claim that all heresies are the result of faulty recollection. He does not even claim that the repetition of doctrines is a precaution against heresy. His claim is that the repetition of doctrines is a precaution against *unintended deviation*. The (potential) heresy discussed above is clearly intentional. Those professionally involved in evangelicalism may worry about heresy, but they are *not* worried about the sort of unintentional variation that results from lapses of memory. Failures of memory are not considered heresies, and have never, to my knowledge, motivated the withdrawal of fellowship.

The fact of repetition is not in doubt. There is, in practice, a great deal of repetition in evangelical sermonizing. It would be uncommon for sermons to cover *exactly* the same ground, but they do overlap considerably. (It might be that people aren't very attentive in church: The children's ministry coordinator once told my wife that, on average, an announcement has to be repeated *six* weeks in a row before *half* the people in church will know it.) Some major themes, like those of God's love and forgiveness, are repeated almost every week.

I would like to suggest that this repetition does have, as Whitehouse suggests, a *reminding* function, but that the purpose of the reminding is not so much to avoid doctrinal variation as it is to increase the relevance of the doctrines by regularly repriming them in memory. Evangelical Christians have the general goal of bringing their entire lives—all their attitudes and behaviors—into submission to God. They want to conform their lives to God's will. In a few cases they believe that God has given specific guidance: don't steal; don't get drunk; don't cheat on your spouse. But most situations involve some effort at discerning what God's will is in that specific situation. This is usually done by appealing to the Bible's general principles and deducing from them the appropriate course of action in one's situation. Ethics are controlled not by a specific list of do's and don'ts, but by a general interpretive framework connecting real-life situations to the word of God.

The goal of conforming one's life to the will of God, however, extends far beyond ethics. It includes also one's attitudes, thoughts, and feelings. Evangelical Christianity is supposed to be a matter of one's whole lifestyle, of being transformed by one's "relationship with God." Evangelical Christians speak of being "renewed in their minds" (alluding to Romans 12:2) and developing a "Christlike character" (alluding to Ephesians 4 and other passages). This transformation of perspective is accomplished by regular prayer, the (preferably daily) reading of the Bible, and participation in worship services. The sermon is conceived as a time for instruction in which the pastor shares new insights about how the Bible speaks to their daily lives.

The reminding function of the sermon is best understood in light of this overall program. The goal of the pastor in reminding the congregation of basic doctrines is less to prevent their distortion than to refresh an evangelical perspective that tends to be lost amid the business of weekday life. I have even heard pastors preaching on I Peter 1:12–13—"So I will always remind you of these things..."—say explicitly that the function of preaching is not only to teach but also to remind. The repetitious and the novel portions of a sermon have the same goal: to help people connect biblical teaching to their everyday lives. The repetitive portion does this by repriming fundamental doctrines in memory: The woman who comes in discouraged is uplifted as she is reminded of God's concern for her; the man contemplating a child-care decision is reminded of his ultimate values. The novel portion of the sermon suggests new ways in which the Bible might be seen as speaking to daily life: Jesus's dining with tax-gatherers illustrates how evangelicals are to reach out to the needy; Abraham's willingness to obey God even at the cost of sacrificing his own son shows how important faithfulness is. In both its repetitive and its novel parts, the sermon is designed to help people live in the light of the word of God.

There is no reason that sermonic reminders cannot have multiple purposes. I cannot say that worry about unintentional deviation from orthodoxy *never* motivates doctrinal repetition. But I do think that it is an extremely minor concern when compared to intentional variation and the tendency to secular distraction.

Interaction

Whitehouse suggests that the doctrinal mode is dependent upon the imagistic mode for its survival. As a religion almost entirely doctrinal, it is hard to see how evangelical Christianity in the United States has survived the tedium effect. On Whitehouse's model it should become, literally, "bored to death." Yet it has not.

There is not, in my view, any great mystery as to how modern evangelical Christianity survives. It has shown itself to be an adaptable tradition, and its doctrines, if sometimes dryly expressed in print, resonate with evangelicals' lived experience in important ways, constantly reshaping their life-space. Sermons, books, magazines, newsletters, and radio programs constantly provide new food for thought. Evangelicalism is alive intellectually and socially, sufficiently so to offset the tedium effect. Yet this may not be the whole story. While modern noncharismatic evangelical Christianity is almost exclusively doctrinal, it is possible that the *motivation* for continued participation may occur individually, and so may not be manifest as a social movement. The profile that Whitehouse describes in his description of interacting modes (2000: chapter 6) emerged because (among other things) the intense emotional experiences happened also to be social, such that small groups of people went through these periods of reinforcement together. If they had gone through them separately, individually, then there may have been no social pattern of oscillation. It is possible that, in evangelical Christianity, individuals are going through intense religious experiences on their own, and so small, emotionally intense splinter groups do not emerge, but the movement as a whole gets renewed energy. Many evangelicals do indeed report special experiences, and there is a recognized genre—the personal testimony—in which a person recounts a personal crisis that led to either conversion or a renewed commitment to the faith. At Creekside Baptist, testimonies are shared several times a year as part of the service, and much more often in less formal settings. The crises can be of many sorts: drug addiction, chronic depression, cancer, infertility, serious doubt, etc. Testimonies recount the crisis and narrate how God helped the individual through the problem. Formal testimonies usually end with the problem solved and the individual stronger in the faith than before. The worse the crisis or the more miraculous the resolution, the better the story and the more likely the testimony to be repeated or publicly performed.

But, in my experience, all adult evangelicals have some such story to tell. Not all stories are dramatic, and some are too embarrassing to be widely shared, but virtually everyone has encountered some form of personal difficulty that has challenged him or her to trust God more profoundly, or to obey God's commands more thoroughly, or to develop new levels of patient resolve. And the crises need not always be ideally resolved: Sometimes the most a person can say is that he or she made it through and learned something about him- or herself along the way. But whatever the material outcome of the crisis, testimonies always bear witness to deeper faith and renewed commitment.[3]

Moreover, renewed commitment need not wait for a crisis. My survey showed that most people at Creekside Baptist engage in private devotional Bible reading and prayer. Devotional activities are intensely private, but I was able to talk with people—in general terms—about their devotional practices and experiences. Devotional activity is usually conducted with the hope that God will "speak" to the devotee. The metaphor of speech is used, though few people report ever hearing words. God is usually thought to speak to people through impressions, novel insights, sudden conviction, inexplicable comfort, and other subtle means. The belief is that in the devotional time the individual is taking time to be alone with God, to communicate with God by hearing what God has to say and by expressing him- or herself to God in prayer. Most of the participants whom I interviewed told me that they did their devotional reading in the hope that God would somehow speak to them individually in their particular circumstances. That is, they hoped for individual illumination and conviction. They did not always get it, but everyone seemed to have experienced it on a semiregular basis. They described this experience as "refreshing," "renewing," and "encouraging"—all of which suggest renewed motivation.

There is, therefore, some reason to believe that individuals are having emotional experiences, of varying degrees of intensity, on their own, and that they are then bringing this energy back into the church as a whole. The overall institution benefits from these private experiences and the renewed motivation of individuals, but the individual nature of these experiences means that they do not generate tightly knit groups. The reinforcement is individual, but the institution benefits. Whitehouse's picture of interaction between the religious modes, while provocative as a model of wider tendencies beyond New Guinea, seems not to be the only means by which doctrinally heavy religions can survive.

Although American evangelicalism raises questions about the motivation for repetition and the necessity of interaction between the doctrinal and imagistic modes, the overall picture generally supports Whitehouse's theory.

Notes

1. A pseudonym.
2. In this discussion the criterion for identifying someone as an evangelical is self-identification as such. Use of belief in the traditional doctrine of inspiration (which includes but is not necessarily limited to the orthodox doctrine of inspiration) as a criterion for identifying evangelicals would beg the question.
3. Presumably those whose faith does not survive are not present to tell their story!

References

Bush, L. R., and T. J. Nettles. 1999. *Baptists and the Bible*. Nashville, Tenn.: Broadman & Holman.

Geisler, N. L., ed. 1980. *Inerrancy*. Grand Rapids, Mich.: Zondervan.

Harding, S. F. 2000. *The Book of Jerry Falwell: Fundamentalist Language and Politics*. Princeton, N.J.: Princeton University Press.

Lindsell, H. 1976. *The Battle for the Bible*. Grand Rapids, Mich.: Zondervan Pub. House.

Noll, M. A. 2001. *American Evangelical Christianity: An Introduction*. London: Blackwell.

Rogers, J. B., and D. K. McKim. 1979. *The Authority and Interpretation of the Bible: An Historical Approach*. San Francisco: Harper & Row.

Smith, C., and M. Emerson. 1998. *American Evangelicalism: Embattled and Thriving*. Chicago: University of Chicago Press.

Whitehouse, H. 2000. *Arguments and Icons: Divergent Modes of Religiosity*. Oxford: Oxford University Press.

Woodbridge, J. D. 1982. *Biblical Authority : A Critique of the Rogers/McKim Proposal*. Grand Rapids, Mich.: Zondervan Pub. House.

Embedded Modes of Religiosity in Indic Renouncer Religions

JAMES LAIDLAW

As Harvey Whitehouse has himself noted (1995: chapter 8; 2002a), his distinction between two "modes of religiosity" is in one respect not original. A good many writers on religion have put forward similar dichotomous distinctions: similar not only in the fact of being dichotomous, but similar also in content. Whitehouse cites among others Weber, Benedict, Gellner, Goody, and Barth, and examples could be multiplied, including one of the originators of modern social analysis of religion, David Hume (1976 [1757]). These authors have all drawn attention to a difference between, on the one hand, religions of regular, ordered ritual, characterized by doctrinal orthodoxy, and associated with large impersonal organizations, and, on the other hand, religions of ecstatic ritual, doctrinal and ideological ferment, and more personal and cohesive communities. The patterns of well-attested historical and ethnographic facts that give Whitehouse's distinction its intuitive plausibility have been noticed before, and have led a range of authors with quite various concerns and intellectual styles to formulate at least superficially similar distinctions.

Part of the claim to originality for Whitehouse's formulation of this dichotomy lies in the fact that it is not just a pair of ideal types, with lists of contrasting features. It has been the drearily predictable fate of many apparently audacious analyses in the human sciences, including anthropology, to begin as a clear analytical distinction and then be expressed instead, in response to skeptical challenge, in softened or blurred form, for instance as a continuum. Such modifications are generally reassuring for the particularistic and even the relativist inclinations of many anthropologists, and handy enough for descriptive commentary on individual ethnographic cases, but they retain no real explanatory ambition or power. There is some hope that Whitehouse's distinction is so formulated that it need not, indeed cannot succumb to this kind of reformulation.

The grounds for this hope lie in the idea that the two modes are dynamically divergent. Whitehouse does not quite go so far as to say that it is impossible for them to coexist, but it is central to his thesis that each mode is an internally coherent complex of sociopolitical features, grounded in distinct cognitive mechanisms. Their coexistence is problematic. They may both be found in the same broad social context, but they will always be separate and different, and they will always be locally recognized as such, which is to say they will constitute what Whitehouse calls, "clearly demarcated domains" or "discrete fields of operation" (2000: 1, 5, 126, 130, 147–49; 2002a: 309). Moreover, they will be in dynamical tension. Imagistic splinter groups will tend to challenge routinized doctrinal traditions, and doctrinal traditions will tend to seek out and suppress expressions of imagistic religiosity. Muddle in the middle, the theory predicts, should not be able to continue for long. Hence the modes are described as "basins of attraction" (2002b). Religious movements or organizations will roll toward the dip in the landscape of logical possibilities represented by one or the other of the two models. There is no stable point for them to come to a standstill in between.

How should we assess this aspect of Whitehouse's theory? How strong should we expect the effect of the "divergence" between the two modes to be? How steep and deep are the basins of attraction?

In this chapter I discuss the application of the "modes of religiosity" model to the Indic religions of renunciation, specifically Jainism and Buddhism, although what I say has relevance too for Hinduism, insofar as renunciation is an important value and practice in Hindu traditions. I shall suggest that the distinction between the two modes, and also the associated notion of interacting modes, throw light on some core features of these religions. However, I shall also suggest that insofar as the model of the two modes is applicable to these religions—and I shall register some important qualifications on this question—the religions in question appear to contain and indeed to be organized around enduring syntheses of, roughly speaking, "doctrinal" and "imagistic" modes. This is something that Whitehouse predicts should not be possible. This unanticipated configuration does not in itself disprove his claim that the two modes are divergent, though it does show limits to the force of this divergence.

Buddhism began in the Ganges basin, around the fourth century BC, as one of a number of competing religious movements organized around groups of traveling renouncers. A formerly largely pastoral society was developing new towns and cities, centers both of expanding trade and of newly centralized kingdoms. The renouncer movements drew their followers from these urban centers. All rejected the then-dominant communal religion of priestly Brahmanism, focused on rites of sacrifice, but otherwise they were intellectually rather diverse. Each taught a different conception of the human condition, and of the nature of fulfillment or perfection, and they experimented with meditational and other religious practices. The surviving literature indicates that they debated actively with each other on matters of membership and structure as well as metaphysics and ethics. But they were alike in being composed of relatively small groups of men and women who actually left their homes and committed themselves full-time to a wandering religious life, together with much larger and looser followings of devotees and patrons. These followers all accepted, even if they did not act upon, the premise that human perfection demanded the renunciation of ordinary domestic and social life for a life instead of directed religious exertion. Thus these movements were known generically at the time as "those who strive," or *sramanas*.[1]

Most of these *sramana* traditions had died out in India by the eleventh century. The only one to have survived there is Jainism, a religion that has older roots but the last of whose legendary twenty-four founding renouncers (the Jinas) was an elder contemporary of the Buddha, known to the Jains as Lord Mahavira.[2] Like the Buddha, Mahavira taught his disciples that life in this world is inherently unhappy, and that the only way to escape it is through cultivating equanimity and rigorous detachment from worldly interests. He differed from the Buddha in that he believed severe austerity was necessary to accomplish this. When the Buddha described his path as "the middle way," the contrast he was drawing was, among other things, a contrast to the extremes of Jain asceticism.

The subsequent social histories of these traditions have been very different. By the time Islam became widely established in peninsular India, Buddhism had largely disappeared there, although it had meanwhile spread through much of eastern Asia. Theravada Buddhism, the form that remains closest to its *sramana* origins and closest also to Jainism, became the state religion in the kingdoms of southeast Asia, and therefore the communal religion of vast peasant populations. It has remained so through the colonial and postcolonial eras. Jainism, by contrast, has continued as an unbroken tradition in India, but it has never been the religion of any other than a small minority, mostly urban and mostly shopkeepers, traders, merchants, and financiers. Its relatively small following has been disproportionately influential, and not only because it is on the whole quite rich. The very severity of Jain renouncers' lives seems to give them a certain authority, and Jainism is at least in part responsible for the prevalence of vegetarianism in the upper strata of Indian society. But the cultural influence of the *sramana* movements in general is much wider and more pervasive than this. The traditions that have gone on to form modern Hinduism have been profoundly influenced both by the teachings and by the form of the *sramana* movements. Successive movements of Hindu *sadhus* that are recognizably descended, both in their ideas and in the forms of organization they employ, from the *sramana* movements, have continued to be among the most dynamic features of that religion. Louis Dumont may have gone too far when he described the relationship between these renouncers and their lay followers as "the secret" of all the Indic religions—Buddhism, Jainism, and Hinduism (1960). But many other authors besides him have perceived that there is something distinctive and important in the structure of the *sramana* movements that has profoundly shaped all these religions, and that is as yet not fully understood.[3]

The anthropology of Buddhism[4] has been dominated by the question of the relationship between Buddhist doctrine on the one hand and popular Buddhist religion on the other. The latter has seemed to most commentators—including many educated Buddhists in the region—to differ intellectually and morally from the inherited tradition of the Buddha's teaching.[5]

A complex body of doctrine, codified in the Pali canon and in the textual traditions that followed, was spread and then transmitted more or less faithfully for centuries throughout agrarian society in the kingdoms of southeast Asia. The agents of this transmission were the monastic orders, hierarchical organizations under royal patronage with great monastic centers but also small temple-monasteries in nearly every village. The custom of temporary initiation meant that literacy and the pedagogic disciplines for transmission of the canon and commentaries, which depended heavily on memorization and recitation from memory, spread knowledge of Buddhist teachings widely throughout these societies. The local cults are different. They have differed from place to place, as have the deities and spirits on which they focused, but in general they are in marked contrast to doctrinal Buddhist values and beliefs. Warrior gods and violent goddesses, spirits of the unsettled dead, animal deities, and heroic ancestors have been worshipped in rituals that depend much more on vivid visual imagery and other sensory stimulation, and on forms of expression of intense personal devotion, than they do on accurate or comprehensive rehearsal of doctrine. Perceptions of logical, aesthetic, and ethical incompatibility between these manifestations of popular religiosity and doctrinal Buddhism have led many commentators to raise the question—even if in the end they have generally answered in the affirmative—of whether the religion practiced by most village Buddhists in southeast Asia is really Buddhism at all.

Similar questions have suggested themselves in the case of Jainism, in some ways even more forcefully. The life prescribed for Jain renouncers is more ascetic, with particular stress on the need to abjure all material possessions. Indeed, in some Jain traditions, the monks go naked because they may not possess even clothes. Yet the Jain laity is a generally wealthy commercial elite. Their temples are often gloriously lavish and richly decorated. They contain statues of great renouncers of the past, from the quasi-mythological Jinas and Lord Mahavira himself to more recent renouncer saints, but they also contain images of local deities, like those found in the equivalent Buddhist temples. These include mustachioed warrior deities, formless blobs representing the spirits of the land, many-armed goddesses, animal-headed deities, and *nagas*, or cobra-spirits, who are prominent in the popular mythologies of the region.

The terms in which both Western scholars and local religious reformers have discussed these matters over the last century and more, both in Buddhism and in Jainism, echo to some extent those of Whitehouse's analysis. On the one hand, we have a doctrinal tradition, a logically consistent set of teachings transmitted by a large-scale, dispersed, and formal religious organization, and on the other, various similar and connected but essentially small-scale and local cults, focused on ecstatic and devotional ritual practices. The latter certainly overlaps with what Whitehouse terms the "imagistic." Inquiry by Western commentators, and indeed internal religious debate, has focused on questions of how the two are related.

The indigenous historiography of both traditions tells of oscillations between periods of "reform," in which charismatic leaders in the doctrinal tradition, usually monks but sometimes also kings, pioneered separation between the doctrinal and the local religions, and often also led attempts to suppress ecstatic and devotional practices. These are punctuation marks in longer periods of gradual accommodation and assimilation, in which Buddhist or Jain monks would adopt and adapt practices from local traditions, and the two would become increasingly entangled. This aspect of indigenous tradition, the idea of periodic accommodation and reform, which is of course the story of an interaction told very distinctly from one side only, on the face of it looks compatible with Whitehouse's account of interacting modes (2000: chapter 6). Such narratives might even be said to be not so much examples of what the theory describes as yet other formulations, in a religious rather than a social-scientific idiom, of the same much-observed dichotomy. If that is so, is the theory that seeks to explain this pattern, in terms of intrinsically divergent modes of religiosity, similarly confirmed?

At first sight it might seem so, but there are problems. The Jains today are divided into several competing sects and schools, and each of these without exception traces its inception to a process of reform in which nondoctrinal practices were purged and replaced by others more in line with transmitted doctrine. And each tradition continually engages still in internal debates about the line between acceptable and unacceptable practices. The latter invariably include those identified by Whitehouse as imagistic practices—ecstatic and possession practices, and use of powerful visual imagery and other sensory stimuli to create heightened emotional states. At first sight, the terms of Whitehouse's theory appear to correspond with some important dynamics of Jain religious history. The apparent fit here is, however, deceptive. Although there is perennial concern and debate about popular lay religious practice, this has never given rise to the most profound dissension and it has never been this that has led to schism, which has instead always been about the correct form of renouncers' ascetic practice. And that, as we shall see, is not a matter of suppressing manifestations of the imagistic mode; in fact it is quite the contrary.

Oscillations of reform and accommodation between the doctrinal tradition and popular devotional and ecstatic practices have occurred so frequently (indeed they never really cease) precisely because the separations they effect have never been particularly dramatic or decisive. As Gombrich and Obeyesekere (1988) put the matter, in the case of Buddhism, the doctrinal soteriology has existed in a remarkably stable "traditional synthesis" with local spirit religion. Indeed, as Gombrich (1971) brilliantly demonstrates, practicing Buddhists were aware that the doctrinal tradition was itself incomplete, as it left unanswered many questions that were important to them (Are there gods? What are dreams?, etc). This integration was successful in incorporating mass peasant societies into Buddhist civilization and in securing faithful transmission and preservation of Buddhist teaching over very long periods of precolonial and colonial history.

Virtually all the ethnographical description we have of Theravada Buddhism has emphasized how intimately interconnected the doctrinal tradition was and remains, in practice, with local cults.[6] David Gellner (2001) has usefully summarized recent anthropological work along these lines. Some authors, such as Tambiah, have insisted that the distinction between the two is wholly artificial—that they can only be understood as part of a single complex whole (1970, 1984), and that this has been the case from the foundation of Buddhism as a sociohistorical phenomenon (1976). But even those who maintain the historical and logical integrity of the doctrinal tradition stemming from the teachings of the historical Buddha have emphasized how thoroughly integrated it came to be with local non-Buddhist forms (e.g., Gombrich 1971, 1988).

The predominant theme of the anthropology of Jainism, similarly, is that although there is a pronounced contrast between doctrinal Jainism and much of the popular nondoctrinal religion of practicing Jains, and although this contrast is registered and asserted by Jains themselves, there is also a profound integration between the two, and this too is indigenously recognized. The strictly ascetic daily regime of study and meditation followed by Jain renouncers, and the extended fasts they are required to take, are the model for asceticism that is widely practiced by the laity. Even though the laity do remain laity—they do not abandon their homes and families or the attachment to values of normal human flourishing and well-being—they do nonetheless remain committed to the doctrinal ideology, practice it to some degree, and play a part in transmitting it. Thus Cort (2001) has argued that what he calls the "*moksh-marg* ideology" is only a part of the Jain tradition, which embraces also the "realm of value of well-being." Babb (1996) has likewise shown that apparently contradictory aspects are part of an integrated "ritual culture." One can argue indeed that popular religion, although it does not in itself conform to the doctrine, has been an essential vehicle for its transmission and reproduction. This is so not just in the obvious sense that if rigorously followed, the doctrinal tradition would die out in a generation. The sense ordinary Jains have that the impossibly demanding and literally life-denying asceticism of Jain doctrine is in a strong sense *their* religion is possible only because it is for them, in practice, elaborately integrated with practices that also express quite contrasting life-affirming values (Laidlaw 1995).

Furthermore, both Jain and Buddhist traditions themselves also contain powerful representations of this conception of how things are—representations that are much more widespread at a popular level for most of their histories than the high-culture traditions mentioned above that tell of dynamics of degeneration and reform. These representations express the idea of the permanent subordination and inclusion of local deities, and devotional ritual practices relating to them, into the Jain and Buddhist pantheons and the religious and ritual life presided over by the monks of the doctrinal traditions. Most common are stories of fierce, territorial deities and spirits who become convinced of the rightness of the *sramana* doctrine, and therefore become devotees and servants of the Jinas or the Buddha, their power thereafter being used in the service of one of the latter's teachings and for the protection of his followers. Ritual practices of devotion, magic, and ecstatic trance and possession that have not been permitted in relation to the Buddha or Jinas themselves, or in the central spaces of their temples, have flourished instead in cults of protector deities.[7]

Gombrich (1971) has argued persuasively that this kind of accommodation does not constitute corruption of Buddhism. The core of Buddha's teachings—the soteriology—was transmitted remarkably faithfully in part precisely because it existed in "traditional synthesis" with spirit religion (Gombrich 1988; Gombrich and Obeyesekere 1988).

Both popular Jainism and popular Buddhism include and are indeed largely composed of what Whitehouse refers to as "imagistic practices," but this is a potentially misleading expression. Although Whitehouse occasionally writes as if they were, not every religious practice that involves the deployment of visual imagery is on that account "imagistic."[8] It is not even clear that his own paradigmatic examples of imagistic religiosity—initiation cults and messianic movements in Papua New Guinea—are really very notable, comparatively speaking, for their deployment of visual imagery. In these cases it is not typically arresting images that trigger the crucial episodic memories, but mortal terror and physical pain. When considering popular religion that might indeed not be "doctrinal," in the sense that it does not conform to orthodox dogma, it is important not to be misled by the terminology, or by the mere presence of visual imagery, into thinking that we have a case of what Whitehouse refers to as imagistic religiosity.

Religious use of visual imagery is not necessarily "imagistic," in Whitehouse's sense, as he himself acknowledges. In Asian religions the use of rich visual imagery—anthropomorphic statues and paintings but also aniconic idols and magical and esoteric diagrams and drawings—is often associated, it is true, with practices of highly emotional devotion, trance or possession, self-mortification, frenzied ecstasy, and in tantric traditions, sexual rites. But such practices also exist in the absence of visual imagery and just as commonly that imagery is used, at the heart of literate doctrinal traditions, as foci for meditation, or the memorization and rehearsal of sacred texts and prayers, and thus for the transmission of logically ordered doctrine. Its use is governed by elaborate techniques and protocols that tend to ensure reliable transmission of doctrine.[9] The visual imagery, and the affecting experiences that worshipers and celebrants derive from its use, contribute to this by making the meaning of doctrines seem vivid and personally consequential.[10] Certain uses of imagery, particularly the worship of statues that are said not only to represent but to embody divinities, have aroused controversy, and there are traditions within Jainism that oppose this. And the more extreme view that use of visual imagery is in general somehow fundamentally inimical to the reliable transmission of doctrine is one that does arise repeatedly within many religious traditions. The mission-inspired movements Whitehouse has studied in New Britain of course inherit an extreme distrust of visual imagery and a fear of "idolatry" from Protestant Christianity. He is perhaps too influenced by such theological views in treating visual imagery, analytically, as a sign of the imagistic rather than the doctrinal mode, and indeed in his use of the term "imagistic" to designate that mode.

Popular Buddhism and Jainism do, it is true, include instances of ecstatic practices that are likely to give rise to vivid and compelling episodic memories, but for the most part these lack the sociopolitical features Whitehouse ascribes to the "imagistic mode." They do not give rise to small, tightly knit groups of people bound together by shared memories of traumatic rites (as in the Baktaman case), nor do they give rise to convulsive political movements or epidemics of imitation, in which neighboring groups adopt similar rites and undergo similar sociopolitical dynamics (as in the Taro Cult). On the contrary, the striking features of these spirit religions are pervasiveness and stability across very wide expanses of space and time. And the vast majority of the ideas we find expressed in them are not the kind of "revelation" that Whitehouse sees being transmitted by imagistic cults. Instead, for the most part, they are ideas that are virtually ubiquitous in all human societies: common "superstitious" ideas of gods, ghosts, ancestors, and witches, who may be bargained with, propitiated, or scared away, together with commonsense ideas of supernaturally sanctioned just deserts and ideas of moral purity, pollution, and contagion. These ideas of supernatural beings and processes are so widespread in human societies that Boyer and others have described them as being in a sense "natural" or "intuitive" for human beings to hold (Boyer 1994, 2001; see also Atran 2002). To use the epidemiological idiom recommended by Sperber (1996), they are so easy to catch and so easy to transmit that human beings more or less everywhere have caught them. The unusual thing is to find people who are free of them.

Whitehouse nowhere claims, I think, that his doctrinal and imagistic modes are exhaustive of human religion. What they explain, insofar as they do, is the transmission and spread of historically specific religious revelations through distinctive patterns of ritual practice and institutionalization. The more or less universal ideas of "intuitive" religion do not need such specifically sociopolitical dynamics. Such ideas are endemic. If Boyer and others are correct, they have been selected for over a very long period of human evolution because although they may or may not be so now, they have been adaptive for human beings in the past. Whitehouse's concepts of imagistic and doctrinal modes aim to describe dynamics of much shorter duration, and how ideas that may well never have contributed to reproductive fitness—that might indeed be dramatically self-destructive and ordinarily rather hard for human beings to "catch"—can nevertheless be spread and reproduced. If this is so, then despite initial appearances, despite the apparent fit between Whitehouse's theory and some indigenous ideas, and contrary to what Whitehouse has himself occasionally implied, the popular spirit religions with which Jainism, Buddhism, and other great doctrinal traditions have been historically in relatively stable synthesis are not "imagistic."

For Jainism in particular, and renouncer religions in general, this does not end the matter. I shall suggest that something that resembles Whitehouse's imagistic mode does occur in these religions: not at the popular periphery or among those who do not have access to the doctrinal tradition, but at its center and among its most religiously informed and educated members. Indeed I shall suggest that a very close integration between this phenomenon and the doctrinal tradition, which Whitehouse, as we have seen, has conjectured ought not to be possible, is central to the structure and dynamics of renouncer religions. I shall begin my attempt to show this by describing the process whereby new Jain renouncers are ordained.[11]

Jain renouncers live and travel continuously in small single-sex groups of a guru and his or her disciples, or sometimes two or three disciples of the same usually deceased guru, together with their disciples. The size of these groups varies between two and a dozen or so people in total. Women renouncers are much more numerous than men, and for this reason—since the process is essentially the same—I shall describe the ceremonies as for a female ordinand.

She will typically be a young woman of marriageable age, and will usually have been living, for several months at least, with her guru's traveling group. She will have shared many aspects of their daily routine—their quarters, their hours of rising and sleeping, their daily periods of meditation and confession, and many of their dietary restrictions. And she will at the same time have performed some of the menial tasks that are required to sustain the renouncers' regime, but which they themselves cannot undertake, such as boiling water for them to drink (see Laidlaw 1995: 154–66, 307). And perhaps most of all, she will have spent long hours studying Jain scriptures and memorizing ritual texts. She will have proved her readiness by demonstrating knowledge of these texts, and by practice of the most important doctrinally sanctioned ascetic practices. The most important of these is *pratikraman* (see Laidlaw 1995: 195–98, 204–15), a long, formal, collective rite of confession and penance that involves extended recitation that renouncers, though not lay people, are expected to be able to do from memory. And she will have completed several periods of extended fasting: either restricting her diet in one of various ways or going without food altogether for periods of one, eight, fifteen, or perhaps thirty days at a time (Reynell 1991). Only when her guru is convinced that she will be able to be permanently bound by her vows will the ceremony be authorized and organization for it begin.

There are two ceremonies that have to happen in series, referred to respectively as the Lesser or Incomplete and Greater or Complete Ordination (*choti* or *kacci diksha* and *bari* or *pakki diksha*). In terms of the size of the crowds that gather and of the splendor of the ceremonial, the former is by far the more magnificent. The latter is "greater" in the sense that it is the theoretically irreversible culmination of the process, when the initiate takes life-long vows, but in practice the first initiation is final. Both are relatively infrequent rituals. Perhaps no more than once every couple of years are they performed anywhere in India in any one of the main traditions within Jainism. And of course it does not occur regularly, but only when the need arises. Even though they draw huge crowds of spectators, from all over the subcontinent, most ordinary laypeople will witness at most two or three in a lifetime.

Nevertheless, this ceremony qualifies unambiguously as being within Whitehouse's doctrinal mode. It is composed of versions, albeit amplified, of rituals that are repeated frequently and regularly in every local Jain community, and that are heavily dependent of the rehearsal of the content of doctrinal texts.[12] These include the ritualized confession mentioned above, which contains a range of standard prayers and recitations of cardinal elements of Jain metaphysics and ethics. In traditions which uphold the veneration of idols of the Jinas (this includes the great majority of Jains in India), expanded forms of rites of worship—called *puja*—which again are performed by most observant Jains daily, are also a central part of the ceremony. The expansion of these regularly repeated rites is achieved partly by adding extra elements, such as additional offerings and more songs, but essentially it is achieved by repetition. A common technique is for prayers to be recited many times over, in each case with the lines being recited in different orders, in various inversions and combinations, according to numbered diagrams in printed pamphlets (Humphrey and Laidlaw 1994: 193–95). By all these means rites of worship that may be completed, at their shortest, in several minutes, are expanded to hours or even days.

These events also show their inclusion in the doctrinal mode by the prevalence of seemingly endless lectures that reiteratively summarize and expand on elements of Jain doctrine. There are lengthy speeches by lay worthies—politicians, bureaucrats, and businessmen-patrons—on the importance of Jainism and its contribution to the public good in India, to the spread of vegetarianism and other moral virtues, and in general to "World Peace." The themes, the phrases, the examples, the stories are all repeated tirelessly. And there are equally lengthy sermons by all the leading renouncers who are present. Invariably these are organized using two basic techniques: narrative and tabulation. A well-known religious story is told, and there follows an exposition of the main points of religious doctrine that the preacher considers to be illustrated by the narrative. Or a numbered list is expounded. There are scores of these in widespread use: the 5 great vows, the 6 obligatory actions, the 8 auspicious signs, the 12 restraints, the 14 stages of enlightenment, the 14 disciplines, 21 types of water for drinking during fasts, 36 illustrious persons, 64 royal gods or Indras, 84 ritual infractions. The formalization and numbering are aids to memorization. The preacher will expound the list, and explain the meaning of the terms on the list, and how they differ from each other. Then each item is expanded on with instructions as to the conduct that is required of an observant Jain, in the light of the concept and its meaning. These meanings may then be illustrated with stories of people (or gods or animals or demons) who did or did not follow the relevant injunctions. These sermons may be longer than usual, but they take the same form and draw on the same repertoire as those given daily by renouncers wherever they are staying.

Thus both in terms of liturgical action, which includes summary of and invites and requires reflection on doctrine by ordinary celebrants, and also in terms of formal speeches and lectures, these events are settings for extended and repetitive rehearsals of Jain doctrine.

The organized nature of the event itself, and the large-scale, widely spread, and formal institutional structure that is needed to put it into effect also belong to Whitehouse's doctrinal mode. A plethora of lay associations, overlapping and competing in membership and purpose, some at the level of the town or city, others regional or national, each with formal membership, constitution, committee of management, and so on, will typically be involved. Shared and explicitly standardized doctrine is the basis for an "imagined community" of millions who of course have no personal knowledge of each other; but as many as tens of thousands of them may gather together for one of these events.

But at the heart of all this standard, indeed textbook, doctrinal religiosity something altogether different is going on. A small, tightly knit group of women (or men), bound together by privations and privileges that cut them off from everyone else, and by the experience of having gone through just this ceremony, organize the highly emotional and indeed traumatic process whereby a young person casts off all substantial connection with her former family and friends, and changes her name, identity, and appearance forever, so that she is said to have died to the world. She is in effect reborn as part of a small and tightly knit group, a powerful example, although little that relies on visual imagery is involved, of the kind of social dynamics Whitehouse describes as arising from infrequently repeated traumatic rituals in his imagistic mode.

This happens, in the Jain case, by dramatic reversal. In the days before the rite much that is done resembles preparation for a particularly lavish wedding ceremony. The ordinand dresses each day in a new set of the most expensive and highly decorated clothes, her hands and feet are painted with henna, her face made up, and she is weighed down with expensive jewelry. For several days she undergoes an overwhelming and exhausting round of social visits (*bindauri*) at which she is almost literally force-fed with the richest possible food (see description in Vallely 2002: 87). As at a lavish wedding, she rides in a procession (*varghora* or *julus*) and, from the back of an elephant, showers the watching crowd with coins and sweets.

The formal rites begin in a similar vein: all color and noise and rich celebration. The turning point comes toward evening, when the initiate takes her last food as a layperson and embarks on a total fast. Next day, during the ceremony, she is called upon to dance. She is still dressed in colorful clothes, but takes up as a prop an *ogha*, which looks like a short-handled version of an old-fashioned mop, the cords in the head being made of wool. Renouncers use this to sweep the ground before they walk or sit or lie down, gently to remove any insects that might be there, so that they do not crush and kill them. It is of course an emblem of the perpetual restraint she will be required to exercise. Her dancing, in front of an audience including men, would ordinarily be a breach of everyday sexual taboo. Here, it is also a final expression of sensuality, (highly circumscribed) sexuality, and emotion, a final exercise of freedom of bodily movement, and a paradoxical celebration of the fact that she is giving these things up.

She then disappears behind a screen, away from the sight of all laypeople, away from her family, and into the care of her fellow renouncers, into the only area of the ritual arena that is bare and free of decoration. There, her laywoman's clothes are removed for the last time and, also for the last time, she is bathed, to remove the cosmetics, perfumes, and oils with which her body has been decorated.

Then all the hair is removed from her head, a process that will be repeated regularly for the rest of her life. The founding renouncers of the Jain tradition are all said to have done this themselves, by tearing it out in just five handfuls. Normal practice today is for one renouncer to pluck another's hair, a few strands at a time, but even this is still very painful, and protracted, and results in unsightly wounds. For this first time, and for some renouncers also subsequently, much of the hair will usually be shaved off, with what remains being plucked thereafter. Renouncers and laity alike assured me that this was to spare the feelings of the laity outside, especially the initiate's family, and not for lack of ascetic prowess in the new renouncer. However that may be, the process nevertheless remains a renunciation of bodily adornment and female sexuality, and an emblem of the ascetic life to come. Some strands of her hair are distributed among the congregation, the rest is thrown into a river.

She is then dressed and for the first time appears in her renouncer's plain white cotton unstitched clothes. From now on she will not bathe. The most she may do is occasionally wipe herself with damp rags. She will drink only water that has been boiled in advance, and eat only alms collected from lay families under highly regulated circumstances. She may never choose or prepare her own food, nor may she own property, wear shoes, or travel in any vehicle. As well as studying scriptures and, in due course, giving sermons, she will undertake regular fasts.

Appearing again now before the lay congregation, the initiate takes an oath to observe monastic vows from her teacher and superior and in turn receives her new name. She continues to fast until the next day, when she will receive alms for the first time. Conventionally, this should be from her parents: an honor for them all, although also an ordeal, because they must behave toward each other in an entirely formal and impersonal manner, as if meeting for the first time, the kinship relations that existed between them having now been broken.

The second ordination, usually some weeks or months later, is a private, indeed in details a secret affair attended only by the renouncers. For this she again fasts, her hair is again plucked, and she takes a second set of monastic vows, which mark her final and irreversible incorporation into the order.

Thus the ordination process, which from the outside and from the point of view of the laity in particular, is a recognizably doctrinal rite, is at the same time, for the initiate herself and for the small group of renouncers she is joining, equally paradigmatically a traumatic rite of the kind that is central to Whitehouse's imagistic mode. It is an intense and traumatic experience, unique for the initiate, but something that she will later, though at infrequent intervals and at one remove, experience again at others' initiations, as part of the small group of renouncers conducting the most important, intimate, and hidden parts of the ceremonies. The rites are infrequent, traumatic, personally consequential, and experienced under testing emotional and physical conditions. They will certainly give rise to episodic memories, if not quite "flashbulb" memories, since most of what happens is not unexpected. It plays a crucial part in constituting a very tightly bound small group of religious agents.

The significant element of the imagistic mode that is not present in all this, or is present only in attenuated form, is one that is not stressed as such but is instead implicit in Whitehouse's accounts. The tortures suffered by young boys in the classic Melanesian examples were the subject exclusively of episodic memory only because everyone involved was forbidden from discussing them openly. No one talked about their experiences, compared notes, or speculated in calm and unthreatening circumstances, and no one simply told the victims what it was all for, or what it all meant. It is this that inhibited the incorporation of episodic memories into semantic schemas. Such taboos were perhaps endemic in traditional Papua New Guinea, which may explain why Whitehouse does not much comment on them, or on their role in sustaining the "divergence" of religious modes there. There must have been some minimal discussion, when the same men subsequently took part in staging the initiation of younger generations, but otherwise they had to rely on their own episodic memory and imaginative resources to make sense of what they had gone through (see persuasive comments on this in Barth 2002: 16). These conditions for what Whitehouse calls "spontaneous exegetical reflection" are absent in the Jain case. Instead, Jain renouncers' memories of initiation are informed and shaped by their continuing education within the group that shares them, and in the light of doctrinal tradition. So instead of giving rise to unconnected and spontaneous "revelations" (or even, which is at least more plausible, ideas that may be touted as such), these memories and reflections endow individuals' understanding of inherited doctrine with personal experience and conviction. Thus they inform change and development of and within the tradition.

The first ordination is a public event, and although certain crucial elements happen in private, among the renouncers only, what goes on is well known and its importance and symbolism are openly discussed. The second ordination is clearly a more esoteric affair, but even it is a perfectly legitimate subject for discussion among the renouncers, indeed for religious instruction of juniors by seniors. Each renouncer regards it as a religious duty to discipline the thoughts they have while fasting or undergoing other austerities, in the light of Jain teaching. The tradition has developed techniques that help them to do this, and it is a skill they deliberately cultivate. Whatever they felt about it and however they remember their initiation, there are powerful narrative conventions into which they are expected, over time, to fit any personal recollections or revelations. This is true also of the experiences that led them to their decision to renounce lay life in the first place.

So personal episodic memories of initiation are treated subsequently rather differently from those in the Melanesian and other similar cases. Certainly, people's reflection on the meaning of their experiences is not properly speaking spontaneous. But I doubt in fact that "spontaneous" is really an accurate description of what occurs in Papua New Guinea either. The contrast with the doctrinal mode is too polar. There will always be a set of occasions and relationships that will be reasonably reliable prompts to future reflection, which will therefore be shaped by patterned circumstances as well as by the generally shared cultural resources that are available to people. But in the Jain case this subsequent reflection will also be actively and openly collaborative.

In other respects, however, the afterlife of the memories of initiation is likely to conform to Whitehouse's model for traumatic rituals. It is impossible to doubt that these shared experiences bind the group together and color their religious sensibility, their thinking, and their teaching. This would appear then to be a sufficient cluster of features to qualify as an instance of what Whitehouse calls the imagistic mode. If this is so, however, it is embedded in a doctrinal tradition, and the same individuals are at the same time part of both.

In the Jain ordination we have a single ritual that is classically doctrinal, when considered from the point of view of the mass lay congregations who attend, yet it is equally clearly imagistic, when one looks at the social dynamics that take place for the small group of renouncers at its core. This small group, formed around shared traumatic ritual experience, is crucial to the reproduction and transmission of the doctrinal tradition. In fact, in terms of religious value as well as sociologically, it is at its center, and its members are endowed with an axiomatic religious authority. Whitehouse's prediction notwithstanding, at the heart of this religion there is an enduring equilibrium between imagistic religious dynamics and the doctrinal tradition in which they are embedded, and which they play a crucial role in transmitting.

So renouncer groups would have to be seen, if we use Whitehouse's categories, as both imagistic and doctrinal. But the implied presence here of his two different politicoreligious dynamics does highlight a pervasive duality in the institutions of organized Jainism. The renouncers are organized in highly fissiparous and independent segmentary groups of quasi kin. They may come together on occasions, for rituals and for summer retreats, and they recognize links between them and the paramountcy of the most senior renouncers, but each small group is for all practical purposes autonomous, and bonds of personal loyalty within them are enduring and intense. The "imagined community" of the doctrinal tradition is divided, too, but into a very much smaller number of formal, large-scale, and impersonal organizations of laity. The two kinds of structure are connected, because schisms among the laity are always expressed as being a matter of which groups of renouncers conform to Jain teachings in their ascetic practice, and which therefore to support. The drawing of boundaries between distinct sects and schools onto the nested segmentary structure of renouncer lineages is a process that is largely driven by the laity-dominated formal organizations (see the interesting discussion in Banks [1986]).

So rather than it being the case, as one might have expected at first sight, that renouncer religions can be thought of simply as doctrinal traditions, interacting with popular cults in the imagistic mode, it is instead more accurate to think of the distinction between renouncers and laity within the tradition as key to a more complex structure.

Popular spirit religion includes many "imagistic practices," but much the greater part of it is "intuitive" religion and on the whole it is quite routine and undramatic and does not involve rare, climactic rituals or traumatic personal experiences. Only occasionally in the spirit religions do we see evanescent cult phenomena comparable to Whitehouse's imagistic mode. But the groups of renouncers around which the tradition is organized are structured by "imagistic" dynamics, because of the role played in their constitution by episodic memories of traumatic rites. My conjecture would be that the original *sramana* movements from which these are descended were rather distinctly imagistic cult groups, and that these features have remained embedded in the doctrinal traditions to which they have given rise.

It is quite possible that this complex embedded structure helps to explain the remarkable dynamic force that renouncer movements have represented in Indic religions. Whitehouse conjectures (2000: 128–29) that without "sporadic outbursts" of imagistic religiosity, in the form of schismatic movements and messianic cults, doctrinal traditions will inevitably succumb to the "tedium effect" and eventually die out. Perhaps the structure that embeds "*sramanic*" dynamics at the center of a tradition has the same preservative effect as imagistic dynamics. If so, then perhaps this is really the "secret" of these religions, of which Dumont famously spoke.

There is certainly dynamic tension in this structure. To what extent does the doctrinal tradition "domesticate" the *sramanic*, by moderating the traumatic experiences around which it is formed? In Jainism this has undoubtedly occurred, but the fact that renouncers remain itinerant and mendicant and do not control property keeps them distinctly separate from the larger and looser membership of the doctrinal religion. Becoming a renouncer remains an extreme experience, by any standards, even if it is not focused on one short instance of physical torture, as it may have been to a greater extent around the hair-plucking in the past. And charismatic renouncers regularly make their name by insisting on reinstating lapsed austerities. To what extent, on the other hand, do renouncers diverge from the faithful transmission of doctrine, inspired by their own experiences and reflections to unpredictable behavior and doctrinal invention? They do so routinely, as is well documented in the ethnography of renouncers in all these traditions. Indeed, unpredictable, unorthodox, and often downright scary behavior, as well as innovative religious insight, is stereotypical of ascetic renouncers, and part of their ambiguous prestige. There is great emphasis within all these religions on the revelatory power of fasting and other physical austerities and of meditation carried out during such extreme physical trials.

I do not think that this structure in itself disproves the thesis that the modes are dynamically divergent. What I have described is not an intermediate case, it is not a point on a continuum between the doctrinal and imagistic modes, and it is not an unstructured mixture of their respective features. It is instead a patterned coexistence, and a partial integration of the two modes, embodied respectively in formal lay sectarian organizations and in renouncer lineages. It may indeed be that the divergence thesis explains how these two sets of politicoreligious dynamics could have remained for a very long period embedded one within the other and both contributing to the shaping of the same rites and ceremonies, and yet have remained discernibly distinct: divergent if not ever actually breaking apart.

And it is in fact going too far to say not "ever" breaking apart. There have been movements within Jainism that have sought to dispense with the institutions of renouncer lineages altogether and to reconfigure the religion as a doctrinal tradition. It is possible that the fifteenth century lay reformer Lonka Shah may have begun in this vein (on Lonka Shah see Dundas 1992: 246–51). He is said to have declared, on the basis of his own reading of canonical texts, that many practices performed and condoned by the renouncers of his time were nondoctrinal. Chief among these was worship of images of the Jinas. Commentators have detected Muslim influence, which was comparatively recent at that time in the area of India where Lonka Shah lived, in his iconophobia. Perhaps if this is so, it is also evident in his assertion of his own authority, as a layman, to interpret scripture. In any case, if that is so, he was ultimately unsuccessful, because the movement he began developed into a traditionally structured Jain sect, the Sthanakvasis, with lineages of renouncers supported and venerated by a lay following. It is perhaps too early to say whether the same will happen to a twentieth-century movement, the Kanji Swami Panth. Kanji Swami (b. 1889) was a renouncer who, in 1934, repudiated his monastic vows, left his order, and set up as a lay preacher whose charismatic sermons (many recorded on tape) attracted a considerable following. The sect that now bears his name does not have renouncers and is led by educated laymen. Its main activities are publishing didactic digests of Jain doctrine; organizing classes, complete with regular tests; and giving proselytizing sermons to attract new followers from other Jain traditions. It does not abjure all sensory ritual or even the use of temple images, because these, it holds, can be aids in learning doctrine, but it does without renouncers and is decidedly unenthusiastic about traditional Jain asceticism (see Dundas 2002: 265–71). Perhaps then it is the exception that proves the rule: a purely doctrinal variant of Jainism.

The Kanji Swami Panth is a small and marginal movement within Jainism. There is evidence that similar movements have occurred recently in Theravada Buddhism and have been much more far-reaching in their effects. Gombrich and Obeyesekere's magisterial study of the development of Sri Lankan Buddhism during the twentieth century (1988) includes an account of how the traditional position of authority of

Buddhist monks came to be challenged by what they call "Protestant Buddhism." This closely resembles Whitehouse's account of "splintering" in doctrinal religions. Responding to the challenge and emulating the methods of Christian missionaries, Buddhist reformers sought to purge the religion of traditional popular spirit religion, and at the same time to diminish the importance of monks and encourage educated laity to adopt prestigious practices—notably the study of ancient texts and meditation—that had formerly been reserved for monks alone. These changes all brought Buddhism closer to the doctrinal mode. It is interesting to note, then, that at the same time the spirit religions became more apparently imagistic, with greater emphasis on emotionally extreme practices and including more cohesive and dynamic cult organizations. Where the traditional embedding of the imagistic, in the form of *sramanic* renouncer lineages, in the Buddhist doctrinal tradition has been broken down, we see the occurrence of "modes dynamics" rather like those described by Whitehouse for New Britain. We see schismogenesis, with the doctrinal tradition and the spirit religions becoming more unlike each other, and the latter taking on the characteristics of spasmodic imagistic cults, something that had been very rare when the "traditional synthesis" was intact.

Notes

I am grateful for helpful comments on earlier drafts of this chapter from Susan Bayly, Caroline Humphrey, Jonathan Mair, and Harvey Whitehouse.

1. Illuminating discussions of early *sramana* movements include Basham 1951; Thapar 1978; Carrithers 1983; and Gombrich 1988, 1996.

2. For excellent general studies see Dundas 2002 and Jaini 1979. The anthropology of Jainism is more recent than that of Theravada Buddhism. More or less the first fieldwork was carried out independently by scholars from a number of different institutions in the mid-1980s, and most of the principal ethnographies have appeared since the landmark edited collection by Carrithers and Humphrey (1991). The principal ethnographic works, drawn upon here, are Reynell 1985; Banks 1992; Folkert 1993; Humphrey and Laidlaw 1994; Laidlaw 1995; Babb 1996; Cort 2001; Kelting 2001; and Vallely 2002.

3. See Burghart (1983), the essays collected in Madan (1982) and Ishwaran (1999), Strenski (1983), and Van der Veer (1987).

4. Until recently this has almost entirely been the anthropology of Theravada Buddhism, and this is what I shall be concerned with here.

5. An important exception is Southwold 1983.

6. This is true even of those, such as Spiro (1967, 1970), who have argued for a clear analytical distinction between them.

7. For Jain cases, which are comparatively mild, see Cort 1997; Humphrey and Laidlaw 1994: 230–32. For much more extreme Buddhist cases, see especially Obeyesekere 1978 and 1981.

8. See Whitehouse 2000: 150ff, where the term is used to refer to "pilgrimages, carnivals, witch-hunts, folk religions, and agricultural festivals"; Whitehouse 2000: 155–56, where it refers to all use of images in religious practice, as opposed by extreme iconoclasts during the Protestant Reformation; Whitehouse 2002b: 48–49, where it refers to sectarian marching, funerals, and ritualized violence in Northern Ireland.

9. A Jain example is the Naupad Oli Puja, where the nine segments of a magical diagram, or *yantra*, each of which represents an important category in Jain doctrine, are worshiped in turn, with series of songs and prayers relating to the category in question. Worshipers recite these texts while meditating on the visual image (Laidlaw 1995: 220–28; see also Cort 2001: 118–19, 162–63).

10. A Jain example is the use of large cloth paintings representing Jain pilgrimage sites, usually holy mountains, which are worshiped by imagining (or remembering) one's own experience of visiting those places (see illustration in Cort 2001: 178).

11. For other description and analyses of this see, Agrawal 1972; Fischer and Jain 1977; Laidlaw 1995: 334–38, 343–44; Shanta 1997: 444–72; Dundas 2002: 150–86; Vallely 2002: 77–114.

12. So although ordination ceremonies are only infrequently performed, a great deal of what goes on in them is, in Whitehouse's terms, subject to "frequent" repetition. For a discussion of the relation between frequency of repetition and the "compositionality" of ritual, see McCauley and Lawson 2002.

References

Agrawal, B. C. 1972. "Diksa Ceremony in Jainism." *Eastern Anthropologist* 31: 12–20.
Atran, Scott. 2002. *In Gods We Trust*. New York: Oxford University Press.
Babb, Lawrence A. 1996. *Absent Lord*. Berkeley: University of California Press.
Banks, Marcus. 1986. "Defining Division: An Historical Overview of Jain Social Organisation." *Modern Asian Studies* 20: 447–60.
———. 1992. *Organizing Jainism in India and England*. Oxford: Clarendon.
Barth, Fredrik. 2002. "Review of Whitehouse, Arguments and Icons." *Journal of Ritual Studies* 16, no. 2: 14–17.
Basham, A. L. 1951. *History and Doctrine of the Ajivikas*. London: Luzac & Co.
Boyer, Pascal. 1994. *The Naturalness of Religious Ideas*. Berkeley: University of California Press.
———. 2001. *Religion Explained*. London: Heineman.
Burghart, Richard. 1983. "Renunciation in the Religious Traditions of South Asia." *Man* (NS) 18: 635–53.
Carrithers, Michael. 1983. *The Buddha*. Oxford: Oxford University Press.
Carrithers, Michael, and Caroline Humphrey, eds. 1991. *The Assembly of Listeners*. Cambridge: Cambridge University Press.
Cort, John E. 1997. "Tantra in Jainism: The Cult of Ghantakarn Mahavir, the Great Hero Bell-Ears." *Bulletin d'Etudes Indiennes* 15: 115–33.
———. 2001. *Jains in the World*. Oxford: Oxford University Press.
Dumont, Louis. 1960. "World Renunciation in Indian Religions." *Contributions to Indian Sociology* 4: 33–62.

Dundas, Paul. 2002 (1992). *The Jains*. 2nd ed. London: Routledge.
Fischer, Eberhard, and Jyotindra Jain. 1977. *Art and Rituals: 2500 Years of Jainism in India*. New Delhi: Sterling.
Folkert, Kendall W. 1993. *Scripture and Community*. Atlanta: Scholars Press.
Gellner, David N. 2001 (1990). "What is the Anthropology of Buddhism About?" In *The Anthropology of Buddhism and Hinduism*. New Delhi: Oxford University Press.
Gombrich, Richard. 1971. *Precept and Practice*. Oxford: Clarendon Press.
———. 1988. *Theravada Buddhism*. London: Routledge.
———. 1996. *How Buddhism Began*. London: Athlone.
Gombrich, Richard, and Gananath Obeyesekere. 1988. *Buddhism Transformed*. Princeton, N.J.: Princeton University Press.
Hume, David. 1976 [1757]. *The Natural History of Religion*. Oxford: Clarendon Press.
Humphrey, Caroline, and James Laidlaw. 1994. *The Archetypal Actions of Ritual*. Oxford: Clarendon Press.
Ishwaran, L., ed. 1999. *Ascetic Culture*. Leiden: Brill.
Jaini, Padmanabh S. 1979. *The Jaina Path of Purification*. Berkeley: University of California Press.
Kelting, Whitney M. 2001. *Singing to the Jinas*. New York: Oxford University Press.
Laidlaw, James. 1995. *Riches and Renunciation*. Oxford: Clarendon Press.
McCauley, Robert N., and E. Thomas Lawson. 2002. *Bringing Ritual to Mind*. Cambridge: Cambridge University Press.
Madan, T. N., ed. 1982. *Way of Life: King, Householder, Renouncer*. Delhi: Vikas.
Obeyesekere, Gananath. 1978. "The Firewalkers of Kataragama." *Journal of Asian Studies* 37: 457–76.
———. 1981. *Medusa's Hair*. Chicago: University of Chicago Press.
Reynell, Josephine. 1985. "Honour, Nurture and Festivity." Unpublished Ph.D. diss., Cambridge University.
———. 1991. "Women and the Reproduction of the Jain Community." In Carrithers and Humphrey (eds.), *The Assembly of Listeners*. Cambridge: Cambridge University Press.
Shanta, N. 1997. *The Unknown Pilgrims*. Delhi: Sri Satguru Publications.
Southwold, Martin. 1983. *Buddhism in Life*. Manchester: Manchester University Press.
Sperber, Dan. 1996. *Explaining Culture*. Oxford: Blackwell.
Spiro, Melford E. 1982 (1970). *Buddhism and Society*. 2nd ed. Berkeley: University of California Press.
———. 1996 (1967). *Burmese Supernaturalism*. Expanded ed. New Brunswick, N.J.: Transaction Books.
Strenski, Ivan. 1983. "On Generalized Exchange and the Domestication of the Sangha." *Man* (NS) 18(3): 463–77.
Tambiah, S. J. 1970. *Buddhism and the Spirit Cults in North-East Thailand*. Cambridge: Cambridge University Press.
———. 1976. *World Conqueror and World Renouncer*. Cambridge: Cambridge University Press.
———. 1984. *The Buddhist Saints of the Forest and the Cult of Amulets*. Cambridge: Cambridge University Press.

Thapar, Romila. 1978. *Ancient Indian Social History*. Hyderabad: Orient Longman.
Vallely, Anne. 2002. *Guardians of the Transcendent*. Toronto: University of Toronto Press.
Van der Veer, Peter. 1987. "Taming the Ascetic." *Man* (NS) 22: 680–95.
Whitehouse, Harvey. 1995. *Inside the Cult: Religious Innovation and Transmission in Papua New Guinea*. Oxford: Oxford University Press.
———. 2000. *Arguments and Icons: Divergent Modes of Religiosity*. Oxford: Clarendon Press.
———. 2002a. "Modes of Religiosity." *Method and Theory in the Study of Religion* 14: 293–315.
———. 2002b. "Conjectures, Refutations, and Verification." *Journal of Ritual Studies* 16, no. 2: 44–59.

7

Conceptualizing from Within: Divergent Religious Modes from Asian Modernist Perspectives

SUSAN BAYLY

THIS CHAPTER FOCUSES ON TWO IMPORTANT ELEMENTS of Whitehouse's theory. The first is his concern with historicity, most notably in his account of imagistic modes of religion as having been historically prior to doctrinal forms of faith, then subsequently challenged or supplanted by routinized word-based and argument-centered religious modes. The second—despite or perhaps because of what he sees as the emergence of doctrinally based transmissive modes as a dominant force in world religion—is Whitehouse's exploration of enduring interactions between image- and word-centered religious experience, most notably in his account of "splintering" as a recurrent energizing of otherwise routinized forms of religious life.

My aim then is to explore the implications for Whitehouse's theory of the existence of "native" analytical categories that correspond either closely or more distantly to the categories that he employs in distinguishing between word-based and imagistic religious modes. In the Asian settings discussed here, we find believers applying models and categories that invite comparison with those of Whitehouse's divergent modes of religiosity (DMR) theory to account for the decline, renewal, or progressive transformation of their own and other people's spirituality. Such analytical thinking about divergent or plural religious modes has been a notable feature of many modernist religious movements both within and beyond Asia, including the Vietnamese Cao Dai religion and India's most important Hindu revivalist movement, the Arya Samaj. In the case of these and other self-professed religious reformers, this type of reflective analysis has entailed a process of classifying and sequencing that in some cases has become in itself a distinctive mode of religious experience.

What is proposed here is that the reflective self-consciousness that has been a hallmark of modernist Asian religious movements is in itself an important dimension of the divergent religious modes that are considered in this volume. But

I also wish to argue that we can identify a third distinct mode of religiosity operating in these Asian cases, and perhaps more widely. In this third mode, such people as Cao Daiists and Arya Samajis actively assimilate a process of comparative analysis into the experience of their own religion. This involves an insistence on historical change, and even a kind of anthropological vision of their own and other people's religious life. And I do see this as an actual "mode" of religiosity in Whitehouse's sense of the term, rather than simply an ideology or belief system. One key justification for this would be that even within the original DMR scheme, there is necessarily a process of reflection by which the experience of the second or doctrinal mode identifies and relativizes the forms of religiosity that are defined as inherent in the first mode. The distinctiveness of the third mode is thus that it involves an understanding of spiritual practice as inherent in a separately demarcated domain of culture, and is thus central to the emergence of this quintessentially "modern" understanding of religion as a nameable isolate, that is, something set apart from other elements of cultural life.

The cases discussed here thus have important implications for the applicability of DMR theory to situations in which believers themselves recognize and reflect on the existence of cognitive bimodality in the experience of faith. This is because each of these traditions of spiritual renovation has offered adherents something akin to a grand theory of divergent or bimodal religious experience, differentiating between superior and inferior forms of spiritual attainment in both Western and "native" faiths, and making such distinctions a critical element in their own ordering of faith and practice. The idea then is that it is not just "us" who may fruitfully apply a particular social science theory to "them": From the nineteenth century onward, there were people both within and beyond Asia who actively disseminated their own ideas about the ordering and sequencing of religious modes. This gave rise to what was in effect an array of indigenous religiosity theories emanating from within the modernist forms of Asian religion, with far-reaching effects for those involved.

These reflective intellectual processes have been central to the building of dynamic religious revitalization movements in many colonial and postcolonial societies. In proclaiming the dawning of a new spiritual age both within and beyond their home societies, their adherents built on both Western and "native" theories of inspiration, degeneration, and spiritual progress in the attempt to identify an appropriate mode of renovated religiosity for their own nation, and ultimately for all humanity. We may therefore be able to enhance the scope and value of DMR theory by recognizing the ways in which believers have both theorized and actively reordered the components of their religious life in terms that either echo or diverge from those of the Whitehouse model. One particular area of divergence to be explored here is the fact that the idea of bimodality arising in these Asian renovation movements has entailed for many a vision of the imagistic and inspirational as succeeding and depending on a prior reflective knowledge of the word, the book, and the doctrinal. What is of interest here, then, is not so much the analytical tools generated by Western social scientists, but the evidence that there is in many societies a more universal sensibility by which people come to know their own religiosity.

The Hierarchical and the Historical

One of the great features of Asian life, both during and since the colonial period, has been the rise and continuing appeal of large-scale movements of spiritual renewal with avowedly modernist aims. South Asia specialists have attached particular significance to the activities of contending Hindu, Sikh, Buddhist, and Muslim reformists in the nineteenth and early twentieth centuries. Hindu revivalists like the founder of the Arya Samaj, Swami Dayananda Saraswati (1824–1883), and Ceylon's so-called Protestant Buddhist reformers have been widely represented as radical innovators whose conception of religions as mutually exclusive faith communities marked a radical departure from older and more fluid understandings of divinity.[1]

Their effectiveness in inspiring campaigns of militant social activism has had far-reaching political consequences, both in the colonial period and more recently. The revivalist agitations powerfully affected the thinking and policy-making of the colonial authorities: Both local and foreign commentators saw these activities as a sign of far-reaching social transformation in Asian religious and cultural life, treating the rise of such movements as the Arya Samaj and Theosophy as evolutionary developments with profound and even threatening racial overtones for their own societies (Morris 1888; Bayly 1999: 465). In India especially, the reformers' thinking engendered new and more aggressive forms of nationalism in which nationhood was equated with the achievement or recovery of purified religiosity.

As has been widely recognized, these Asian modernists directed much thought and anxiety to the process of defining and classifying the qualities, defects, and virtues of their own and other people's religions. This inclination to see the world as an arena of opposed and mutually exclusive religious allegiances is often thought of as a defining feature of modernity both within and beyond the colonial world (Van der Veer and Lehmann 1999). At the same time, however, many of them also thought in anxious and often confrontational ways about religiosities. What aroused particular anxiety in their thinking was the existence of multiple modes or registers of religious experience, both in their home societies and in the wider world. Thus for many of Asia's self-professed religious reformers and revivalists, distinctions much like those defined in Whitehouse's scheme were a matter of active discussion and reflection, with religiosity in forms corresponding to the imagistic being widely associated with the alien, the inferior, and the primitive.

The distinctions made in these cases were therefore not so much—or not only—a means of differentiating between one religion and another, though in the subcontinent they often did inform the ideas of so-called communalists. But what they also entailed in many instances was a fearful recognition that both one's own and other people's religious life could involve modes of experience which were dark, dangerously uncontrolled and sensual, inspirational, and visceral rather than reflective and disciplined. It was religiosity in these forms that came to be widely thought of as an emanation from some historically prior stage in the development of human religious insight.

As will be seen below, this kind of theorizing led to many possible responses, including those of south Asians who feared that either personally or collectively they might be degraded and damaged through the allure of the imagistic. The common thread here was that these ideas rested on historical thinking, and in particular on an understanding of religious modes as the products of sequential, evolutionary, or degenerative historical processes. In some cases this could lead to the stigmatizing of the imagistic as either a cause or a consequence of the downfall of peoples, races, and whole civilizations. Such thinking often identified particular categories of people—sometimes women, and also members of alien races or communities—as possessing an innate or atavistic predisposition toward the imagistic.

Before exploring further where such thinking led Arya Samajis and other Asian religious modernists, it is important to note that these historicizing and evolutionist ideas differ quite considerably from older Asian understandings of religiosity. Asia's "world" religions have always made implicit statements about the existence of divergent religious modes, but they have done so in ways that have suggested a hierarchical and relativizing relationship between them. This is the implication of the concept of Hindu *rasas*, moods and colorings appropriate to divergent aspects of experience in different moments of cosmic and mundane time. The theory of *rasas* thus suggests that particular beings may apprehend the world in different ways in accordance with their own divergent responses to cosmic and other configurations.

There were comparable understandings in east Asian religion. In Vietnam, certain kinds of temple iconography convey implicit classifications of divergent religious modes associating less-refined forms of religiosity with alien peoples and races, and attributing a purer and superior religiosity to the native Kinh/Viet. Such images may be seen in spaces where deified heroes, ancestral spirits, and divinities from Vietnam's distinctively pluralized religious landscape share composite temple sites, drawing on an extensive repertoire of Buddhist, Taoist, Confucian, and sometimes Hindu representational forms.

One such site is the Bach Ma temple, a tenth-century dynastic foundation located in Hanoi's Old Quarter. In past centuries the temple was a major center of imperial worship and benefaction; it was closed after independence but has recently been reopened. The divinities that it houses include personifications of the city's White Horse protector deity, together with altars of the past, present, and future Buddha, and of the tutelaries known as the Holy Mothers (Thanh Mau). In addition, a pair of nearly life-sized clay sentinels stand at the entrance to the White Horse protector's inner sanctuary. Local scholars and others associated with the shrine's recent renovation refer to them as the Cham guards, thus identifying them with the brown-skinned Indic people who founded the ancient imperial polity known as Champa, and were subsequently reduced to the status of a marginalized "tribal" minority by the expansive Vietnamese dynastic polities of the precolonial period (Whitmore 1997).

These clay figures are distinctly un-Vietnamese in appearance: they have bare torsos, dark skins, strong features, and protruding bellies, and thus contrast dramatically with the pale, decorously draped figures to be seen elsewhere within the enclosure. As a presence in the temple, the Cham sentinels thus embody something that is unmistakably potent yet set apart from the other religiosities and dispositions that may be approached and transacted with inside the temple. The precise nature of their otherness is left undefined, but it is nevertheless of a kind that has been widely thought of in Vietnam as a predisposition to forms of religion which are strong, dark, and sensual—"imagistic" rather than doctrinal. Champa and the Cham are still often referred to by Vietnamese in terms associating them with Indic Hinduism, with the Theravada Buddhism of the precolonial Khmer/Cambodian polities with which the Champa rulers sometimes allied, and also with Islam. Today most members of the small Vietnamese Cham minority are Muslim; they are Indochina's only "native" Muslim population.[2]

The Cham sentinels can thus be seen as embodiments of a mode of religion that is sensual, unverbalized, inspirational, and thus imagistic. The implication here is that these qualities characterize the modality of rough and unrefined people, meaning those other than the Kinh/Viet who experience religion in a higher or more refined mode. The figures and their qualities are nevertheless of value. With their potency ordered and contained, they have a recognized place within the shrine, though it is one that is hierarchically related to the more refined Buddhist and Confucian religiosities that are represented and invoked within the temple space. Indeed even in the period of high Confucian revival that immediately preceded colonial conquest, Vietnam's rulers created religious forms that ordered and disciplined this kind of difference. Thus rather than rejecting or attacking them, the Emperor Gia Long (1802–1820) and his successor Minh Mang (1820–1840) enjoined their subjects to honor the capricious spirits of land and locality. They were to be kept at a distance, but through a variety of bureaucratic devices, these embodiments of unrefined religiosity were to be incorporated and granted legitimacy within the imperial scheme (Marr 1981: 48; Whitmore 1997: 673–74).

In the Indian context, too, there are powerful indigenous traditions that involve the recognition and hierarchical classification of divergent religious modes. A case in point is the influential Advaita Vedanta school of Hinduism. In the teachings of the ninth-century Advaita philosopher Sankara, the divine in its truest and highest form is to be apprehended as an impersonal absolute. The austere and demanding Vedanta path—realization of a featureless inner self without recourse to rituals or devotional communion—is an exaltation of the doctrinal (Flood 1996: 238–49).

Yet at the same time, in older Vedanta teachings, and in many contemporary formulations, *bhakti*—adoration of god with form and sensory capacities—is a lesser but still legitimate spiritual path. The *bhakta's* worship requires both the personification of divinity and the existence of an individuated self with faculties attuned to experiencing something very different from the Vedantist's cosmic enlightenment: a form of communion achieved through the senses, and above all through sight (Eck 1985; Fuller 1992: 59–62). According to a modern manual for pilgrims to the temple of Lord Krishna of Guruvayur in Kerala, this kind of theistic devotion is suitable for "the common man" and "the easiest path to realise God in this degenerate age of Kali." Both statements are attributed to Sankara himself (Vaidyanathan 1977: xiii; compare Madan 1987: 38). Thus once again we see an account of divergent religiosities that classes the different modes in hierarchical terms, associating the imagistic with persons of lesser or lowlier apprehensory faculties, but still conceding its worth and legitimacy.

Historicizing Divergent Religiosities

It is true of course that even in these older analytical schemes, there were some forms of religiosity that could not be easily absorbed or accommodated hierarchically. Even before the rise of nineteenth- and twentieth-century "modernist" forms of religion, there were some Asian thinkers for whom certain named religions were either unassimilable, or were to be regarded as modes or paths (dharmas) that were appropriate to entirely separate geographical settings —Christianity in Vietnam, and both Christianity and Islam for some traditional Hindu pandits (Young 1981).

Yet it is still in the great Asian renovation movements that one can identify a new and more consistently hard-edged conception of divergent religiosities. One key manifestation of this is to be seen in the historicizing claims of many south Asian religious purifiers. According to the Arya Samaj's founder Swami

Dayananda Saraswati, the Hindu faith in its original pure form was a religion of the word and the book (Dayananda 1970 [1908]; Llewellyn 1993). The sacred task for all Hindus is therefore to reinstate this lost perfection. The true source of Hinduism is its sole authoritative scripture, the Vedas, a divine text imparted to man at the dawn of time; the knowledge it contained prefigured all the scientific and technological achievements of the modern West.[3]

Thus in Arya teachings, the subsequent history of the Hindus has been degenerative. Echoing the historicizing logic of nineteenth-century European race theorists, Aryas are still taught that the key moments in this decline from the vedic golden age were the events of India's subjugation, first by Muslims, and then by the British. These degenerative processes were made manifest in the embrace of nonauthoritative scripture—for Aryas, this means the puranic texts that enjoin the idolatrous worship of deities in impure and degraded forms, that is, in iconic modes ascribing personification and sensuality to the divine (Dayananda 1970 [1908]).[4]

Arya Samajis have thus embraced a theory that classes the lower and alien religious modes as survivals from a shameful past that should be expunged by the soldierlike religious purifier. This clearly contrasts with Cao Dai, whose adherents are taught to treat the lower modes as remnants of a past and fragmentary truth. As will be seen below, Cao Daiists are therefore to absorb, rank, and sequence the lesser imagistic religiosities: controlling and disciplining them, but still making contact with the spirits and other beings from whom these potent but imperfect truths have emanated. Thus for Cao Daiists, modes or registers of religious experience that can be placed in the category of the imagistic are contained and neutralized, rather than confronted and expelled.

Broadly speaking, however, both the Arya Samaj and Cao Dai were book- and word-revering movements, with a unitary and depersonalized understanding of divinity. Furthermore, for both groups the issue of plural religiosities has been a matter of deep and enduring concern. It has been the recognition that this heterogeneity includes forms of experience involving the lower apprehensions and faculties that revivalists have thought of as an especially problematic aspect of contemporary existence. Thus in colonial India as well as Indochina, reformist thinkers directed a great deal of systematic reflection to the issue of how religious life might be both purified and rationalized in an age of decadence and spiritual impropriety.

For self-styled Hindu and Muslim reformers, and for other proponents of religious regeneration both at home and abroad, the idea of one's own and other people's religions as being luxuriant, diverse, and uncodified has been a spur to self-reproach and social activism. The characteristic model for these reformers was and still is a religion of doctrinal coherence whose prevailing mood or disposition was one of reason, sobriety, and selfless service. Much emphasis was placed on the authority of the codified word; a key goal has been the displacement of those forms of experiential faith and worship that can be seen as corrupting the higher human faculties through the arousal of degrading lusts and sensory responses.

For both Indian and Vietnamese modernists, the exaltation of reason and science has had important practical manifestations. They have all tended to be keen users of modern communications media, especially newspapers and magazines; in more recent times Cao Daiists have become particularly enterprising Internet communicators. The thrust of Arya self-presentation has been strongly statistical. In the face of colonial census-taking and other forms of official knowledge-gathering, the Arya Samaj developed its own enumerative strategies. Like other Indian modernist religious movements, its self-representations were framed as statements of demographic health and vigor (Jones 1976). Cao Daiists on the other hand have been great issuers of bulletins, declarations, and circulars. The formal creation of Cao Dai as a movement took the form of a documentary pronouncement issued by the recipients of the Supreme Being's initial revelatory messages and conveyed to the French authorities by means of a treatylike declaration announcing the dawn of mankind's final age of revelation.[5]

In south Asia, the teachings of both Hindu and non-Hindu reformists have consistently extolled a model of religious life involving both personal and social activism rather than inner contemplative striving. Those who have disparaged the experience of religion in an identifiably imagistic register have also tended to embrace exemplary social activism as a defining feature of their religiosity. Such goals thus bore fruit in a variety of campaigns launched by Hindu revivalists and other south Asian religious reformers. These took significantly different forms from their Vietnamese and other east Asian counterparts, yet here too they provided a predominantly hierarchical account of this divergence. Arya Samajis made particular efforts to discourage the use of pictorial images in domestic Hindu worship. Other preoccupations for reform-minded south Asian campaigners were the forms of ecstatic communion pursued at the shrines of Sufi *pirs* (Muslim cult saints) and in Hindu *bhakti* (theistic devotional Hinduism). The idea that what is experienced at this level of religious understanding is to be seen as indecent and indecorous, and furthermore that it has particular dangers because of its appeal to and power over women, is an important dimension of revivalist concerns, as will be seen below.

First though, it should be noted that such movements as the Arya Samaj attracted many of the same Western-educated professional and commercial people who took a key role in the shaping of south Asia's contending nationalist ideologies. Indeed, few if any educated Asians would have been untouched by these organizations' campaigns, either as supporters or as recruits to the neotraditionalist groups that opposed them. Thus when such groups as the Arya Samaj battled with the neotraditional activists who are known in north India as *sanatan dharmis*, their adherents were divided on important doctrinal matters, but still tended to organize and communicate in much the same word- and text-centered mode, and with much the same vision of religion as an essence to protect and promote in the face of competition from other faith communities.

Cao Dai's founders and early leaders were of similar background. Most were francophone landlords and petty officials; they thus belonged to that important class of colonial subjects for whom the French coined the neo-Darwinian term *évolué*, and they too often linked their spiritual reformist aims to ideals of prophetic nationhood. Equally important, however, has been the appeal of these renovatory spiritual movements to people far removed from the world of the colonial intelligentsias. Soon after their foundation, both the Arya Samaj and Cao Dai acquired mass followings. By the late 1930s, Cao Dai had attracted millions of Vietnamese peasant adherents who were concentrated primarily in the southwestern provinces, with its Vatican-like headquarters at Tay Ninh as their spiritual focus. During the 1940s, Cao Dai was armed and trained as an insurgent militia by the Japanese and became in effect a kind of militarized supermodernist phantom state in one of the most turbulent periods of Vietnam's troubled colonial history.[6] The Arya Samaj also acquired a mass peasant following, primarily among the middling-caste Hindi speakers who formed a large component of the colonial army; the movement also recruited successfully among the plantation labor force in the overseas diaspora, most notably in Fiji (Kelly 1991; Datta 1997).

"Communal" Understandings of Divergence

Within south Asia, the Arya Samaj and other Hindu revivalist organizations have operated in ways that have been widely seen as confrontational and threatening to the people whom they define as of unlike or inferior religiosity. As was noted above, their views were consistently given concrete practical expression; they systematized and proselytized, and their transmissive mode was both consciously expansive, and explicitly critical of other people's religiosities. Such calls by competing proselytizers for the exaltation of scripture and the repudiation of "syncretistic" religious practices thus went hand in hand with the assertion of mutually exclusive confessional allegiances—so-called communalism. One key expression of these confrontational attitudes can be seen in the case of cow protection, a cause vehemently promoted from the 1890s onward through the activities of the north Indian organizations known as Gaurakshini Sabhas or "save Mother Cow" societies (Yang 1980; Robb 1986; Pandey 1989).

Cow protectionists are still active in many parts of India. During fieldwork in the 1990s, I often saw cow protection slogans daubed in public places. In the old royal city of Udaipur, I observed demonstrators exalting a living cow as an embodiment of the perfected spirituality that Hindu supremacists claim as the essence of their own superior religiosity.[7] The demonstration's focus was a garlanded calf being offered for *darshan* (auspicious sighting) in a processional chariot, attended by lay activists and *sadhus* (monk-ascetics) playing recorded devotional hymns (*bhajans*) to a crowd of onlookers.[8]

Performances of this kind might appear to suggest a clear divide between the "polytheistic" and image-centered religiosity of Hindus and the word- and book-revering faith of Muslims. But this is not necessarily what one encounters among cow protectors, either today or during the colonial period, when these organizations received strong support both from the Aryas and from opposing neotraditionalist *sanatan dharm* ("defense of tradition") activists. What proponents of cow protection have imputed to Muslims is not what one would expect as a characterization of Islam: a representation of the Muslim faith as an arena of the imagistic, with Hindu reformists claiming for their own worship the superior qualities of book- and word-revering religiosity.

It is true that militant cow protectors have sponsored campaigns to "reform" lower-caste Hindus who allegedly ate beef or sold cows for slaughter. The possible existence of such people within the Hindu fold was clearly problematic. Yet in the eyes of Aryas and other cow protectors, these were people who could be elevated above brute animality, and for many north Indians of nonelite peasant caste, the cause of cow protection was an attractive path to social and spiritual uplift (Pinch 1996).

In contrast, what Gaurakshini Sabha adherents have said about Muslims is that they are a people predisposed by their innate and inferior religiosity to be meat-eaters and killers of Mother Cow. Hindu campaigns against cattle slaughter have thus vilified Muslims as practitioners of a violent religion that can only be experienced at a lowly and inferior register, by way of the passions and the lower sensory faculties.[9] Thus when Aryas and other Gaurakshini Sabha adherents have enjoined Hindus to adore the cow, and even when they perform public rituals honoring cows adorned in the manner of living divinities, they deploy categories of analysis that tend to repudiate any notion that these are imagistic forms of experience.

Certainly for Arya supporters of the Gaurakshini cause, the cow is a manifestation of a higher word- and reason-centered form of religiosity, and an embodiment of the future pure India that was to be created through the efforts of the virtuous Hindu nation-builder (Bose 1998). Mother Cow has thus been associated with highly abstract notions of science and modernity in Arya writings. Even Swami Dayananda mixed eugenicist ideas and arguments with more traditional references to the Vedas in his discussion of the cow cause. Thus for the cow protector, the issue is not so much or at least not only the veneration of the cow as a deity, but rather the embodiment of an abstract and depersonified goal, that is, the modern nation-builder's path toward refined and transcendent spirituality. This does tend to complicate the two categories of the imagistic and the doctrinal, in a way that perhaps more accurately reflects the complex ways in which these differentiations are made in practice by Asian believers.

The Allure of the Imagistic

Elsewhere in the subcontinent, most notably in colonial Ceylon, calls from competing proselytizers for the exaltation of scripture and the repudiation of "syncretistic" religious practices have gone hand in hand with the assertion of mutually exclusive confessional allegiances and the spread of so-called communalism. This type of interreligious conflict was far less prevalent in French-ruled Indochina, but even so the creation of the Cao Dai religion in southern Vietnam—often referred to in its adherents' writings as "Reformed Buddhism"—was in many ways comparable to the rise of the great south Asian reformist movements (Gobron 1950).

Like Arya Samajis, Vietnam's Cao Daiists have also been much concerned with situating their revelatory teachings in a context involving knowledgeable interaction with "scientific" religious modernizers both within and beyond Asia. They also resemble modernists like the Aryas in placing their emphasis on social action rather than inner spiritual striving. As will be seen below, the key difference is that they have found ways of disciplining and transcending the imagistic, absorbing rather than seeking to expunge competing revelations of the book and the word.

In south Asia, these processes are far more problematic. For both Hindu and Muslim supremacists, the imagistic was widely thought of as a defining attribute of other people's religiosities. At the same time, however, its qualities were known to be dangerously seductive to those of more refined religious orientations. Indeed, this was its great danger, and hence its importance in the thinking of many Hindu and other communalists. The idea here is that one's own faith community can be damaged or denatured through the appeal of the imagistic. For many such polemicists, the imagistic is a lower and anterior form of religious experience, hence a mode to be superseded by their own refined and purified religiosity. But what was also apparent in accounts by Hindu reformists was a sense of the doctrinal as having been only recently and insecurely achieved or embraced by one's fellow Hindus. It was a matter of particular concern that there were people of lower sensibilities—especially women, but also those of lower caste—who had an innate predisposition toward the sensual, the erotic, and the unrefined.

Such people therefore required special protection from these inferior but alluring modes of religious experience. And what this entailed was protection from the forces and sites of "syncretism," that is, from arenas like the Sufi shrines at which promiscuous mixing of religions, people, and religiosities could and did transpire. Above all, these were sites where such vulnerable people as women and low-caste men could be suborned and corrupted by the imagistic religiosity that was for many reformists a defining quality of Islam—or at least of Islam in its most dangerous and contaminating religious mode (Gupta 2002).[10]

It is this that helps to explain the highly charged nature of reformist purification campaigns, which in south Asia have often featured extreme and violent language as well as violent action. Whitehouse points to something very similar in his discussion of sixteenth-century European witch-hunts and their connection with the image-hating attitudes for which Reformation historians have coined the term iconophobia (2000: 156). The suggestion here is that the Protestant conversion process subjected Christians to a form of painful mental trauma arising from the struggle to purge both themselves and those around them of a banned but still seductive religious heritage (Whitehouse 2000: 155). Antiwitch crazes can thus be understood as expressions of the profound psychic tensions that arise when the doctrinal finds itself in frustrated opposition to the imagistic.

Whitehouse thus offers suggestive evidence on this point in the form of a quoted diatribe by a sixteenth-century Lutheran iconophobe who denounces newly converted Protestants for clinging to their former papistical idolatries, reviling their image-revering practices in revealingly vituperative terms as "seductive, ungodly and devilish" (2000: 155). While Whitehouse connects such attitudes with the fervor of Christian missionaries encountering precontact Melanesian religions, this idea of the imagistic as satanically seductive also has important implications for the Indian context. The Lutheran pastor would appear to have had precisely this fear of corrupting allure, suggesting that the imagistic is something that he has felt himself, as well as having observed its power to ensnare others. He thus has good reason to represent those who resist the authority of word-based religion as either knowingly or unwittingly in league with demonic forces; these of course are the alluringly demonic forces that Reformation iconophobes so often personified in the figure of the witch.

Violently emotional personifications of this kind have certainly been pervasive in south Asian communalist polemics. Indeed, in Whitehouse's terms, movements like the Arya Samaj are of particular interest because they have functioned primarily in a word- and scripture-based religious mode, while at the same time persistently demonizing those who do not conform to their scripturally based definitions of true faith. Thus at least some Hindu modernists—especially those expressing strongly Hindu supremacist views—can be thought of as people in pain like the witch-hunting Reformation iconophobes referred to by Whitehouse.

When the subcontinent's so-called communalists portray those of other faiths as subhuman and demonic, a source of insidious dangers to their own pure but vulnerable spirituality, they too may be experiencing a reaction against the seductive intimacies of a shared religious landscape with parallels to that of Western Europe at the time of the Reformation. Thus the equivalent of Europe's sexualized European witch-temptress in south Asia would be the personifications deployed in the battles waged by Hindu and Muslim cultural nationalists over the status of the two main languages of Gangetic Upper India, Hindi and Urdu (King 1992, 1994).

It is striking that those involved in these nineteenth- and twentieth-century Indian conflicts used provocative female imagery to denigrate each other's languages. In anti-Urdu polemics in particular, the key point about human verbal capabilities was that only some languages were to be seen as capable of embodying refined religious consciousness (King 1994). For promoters of Hindi, "Semitic" languages were defective in this regard; only Sanskrit and Sanskrit-derived regional tongues written in the Nagri script were languages in the true sense.[11] Once again, the conventional stereotype of Islam as a religion of the book and the word is reversed or inverted in Hindu supremacist thinking. The implication of the Nagri campaigners' polemics was that Muslims only seem to have a book-based faith and, by implication, that Islam embodied a deficient and indeed illegitimate form of the doctrinal. In other words, for Hindu supremacists, imagistic practices are accidental accretions in Hinduism that can be removed by reform, but they are essential to Islam.

Such polemicists thus represented "Semitic" language forms as invasive and corrupting to Hindus. What they had in mind were the dangerously attractive uses to which Muslims put language. The concerns here were with Urdu and Persian poetry, music, and dance, especially in the forms to be encountered at Sufi saint cult shrines (*dargahs*). It was in these spaces that inferior religiosities were known to find expression in such practices as hypnotic drumming, ecstatic performance of *qawwali* (devotional song), erotic versification, and the use of both chanting (*dhikr*) and intoxicants to induce states of mystical self-annihilation.

In polemical writings as well as visual iconography, Hindi campaigners often represented the two languages as contrasting female personifications: Hindi as a pure but vulnerable maiden, Urdu as a whorish temptress (King 1992). The goals of the religious purist and the language campaigner were thus closely allied. Hindu polemicists regularly pointed to the "syncretistic" space of the *dargah* as a menace to their own pure but vulnerable spirituality. These of course were places where Hindus and Muslims—especially women—crowded dangerously together to receive amulets and other sanctified items from the hands of male shrine guardians.

This experience of the flash of miraculous curative energy or *barakat* transmitted to the female body through a scrap of written text, and the practices of ecstasy and spirit possession that often accompany these practices, are clearly imagistic deployments of language. It should therefore be noted that Muslims too often point to the *dargah* as a dangerous and corrupting space. Islamizing purists often associate Sufi shrines with themes of allure and guilty desire, often through narratives that focus on female personifications and on acts of corruption and defilement of the female body. The amulets distributed at *dargahs* often take the form of Koranic verses to be ingested or worn as a direct transmission of the *pir*'s power (*barakat*) to the devotee. This flash of curative energy entering female bodies through a scrap of written text derives unmistakably from a nondoctrinal religious mode; it is not surprising that both Muslim and Hindu purist reformers find such practices objectionable.

I have had experience of this in my own fieldwork, most notably at a Sufi *dargah* in rural Maharasthra that until quite recently was much frequented by both Hindu and Muslim women seeking cures for barrenness. In the early 1980s, the *pirzada* (shrine guardian) regaled me with a kind of smiling Nehruvian "secular" parable linking the presence of a garlanded *lingam* and *yoni* carving in the shrine's inner precinct to a mildly erotic local legend about amorous dalliance between the Muslim saint and a local Hindu goddess. All too predictably, this Hindu emblem of cosmic generative power has now become the focus of an Ayodhya-style account of historic despoliation, featuring themes of allure, corruption, and guilty desire.[12] The story has become a tale of defilement, with the goddess being raped by the saint; the *lingam* and *yoni* are now described as spoils from her ravaged temple. The narrative had therefore been reformulated to convey a historical sequence involving violent conflict and division, rather than synchronic hierarchy in the relationship between the two religious modes.

Divergent Religiosities in Vietnam

Vietnam's Cao Dai religion lacks the confrontational dimension of south Asia's reformist movements. Yet it too is a faith of transcendent and omnipresent divinity enjoining particular forms of action in the face of plural religiosities. Its moral codes are sober and puritanical; its daily regimens are disciplined and austere. Much like the Arya Samajis and other self-liberation movements that originated under colonialism, it too teaches bodily and spiritual self-regeneration, with an emphasis on sexual abstinence and vegetarianism. In contrast to the Arya Samaj, however, Cao Dai was created in the 1920s as a universalizing faith intended for both Asian and European adherents. Its transcendent spiritual power was to be attained through mastery of psychic clairvoyant techniques drawn from both European and Asian forms of revelatory spiritist religion that were explicitly conceived of as modern, scientific, and universally liberating (Oliver 1976; Smith 1970; Werner 1981).

At Cao Dai temples, and in particular at the great cathedral-like headquarters at Tay Ninh, much emphasis is placed on regularity and exactitude in the regimens of daily life, and in the enactment of everyday worship. This is particularly evident at Tay Ninh, where in recent years the daily noontime processional rituals have become major public spectacles attracting many outsiders. Foreign visitors are particularly welcome. They are ushered by shrine attendants into the shrine's upper gallery to observe the massed ranks of officiants garbed in their color-coded robes of office performing rigorously synchronized altar prostrations to an accompaniment of choral hymns and orchestral music. The orchestrated precision of these daily rites is a key manifestation of the Cao Dai lifestyle, with its emphasis on propriety, austerity, and sober regimens of bodily and spiritual self-cultivation.

These occasions are also important transmissive opportunities. Lay volunteers, predominantly mature Cao Daiists with knowledge of foreign languages, seek out individual visitors to whom they deliver oral synopses of Cao Dai doctrine. My own experience of this took the form of an approach from a smiling francophone woman in the white garb of a lay Cao Dai adherent. She was a retired teacher, and her quietly voiced commentary corresponded closely to the textual accounts of the movement's history and doctrines that have been promulgated by Cao Daiists since the movement's foundation (with many now available online). I was told that the Cao Dai Supreme Being is father and creator of all humankind. His teachings are the perfection of all preexisting faiths of revelation and spiritist insight; humanity is one within his embrace, and in delivering his final revelatory truth (his Third Amnesty) to humankind, he has merged all preexisting religious systems, thus returning the world to its original primordial unity. I was further directed to observe that the Supreme Being's only iconic representation is the conventionalized image of a numinous, all-seeing eye, which is depicted on Cao Dai texts and on the walls of Cao Dai temples, including the many overseas localities where expatriate Vietnamese have established expansive centers of Cao Dai faith and worship.[13]

Also conspicuous in the Tay Ninh iconography, and in Cao Daiists' verbalized accounts, are the spirit superbeings who have been the deliverers of the Supreme Deity's truth messages. These messages were attained by means of psychic mediumship techniques, which gave controlled but empowering access to the imagistic profusion of less-advanced religiosities.[14] Public séances are no longer allowed at Tay Ninh, but the pantheon of Cao Dai messengers is still known and revered. Its most prominent figures are the great Asian sages, together with personalities from the world of international politics and the arts and letters syllabus of the colonial *lycée* curriculum. Joan of Arc and the poet-novelist Victor Hugo figure prominently among these figures, as do Confucius and Lao Tse, and also Jesus, Lenin, Hitler, Winston Churchill, and the philosopher Descartes.

Cao Daiists have highly bureaucratized dealings with the spirit world; these involve an enormous ramifying system of ranks, titles, and organizational structures. These were originally modeled on the forms and hierarchies of the colonial bureaucracy and the Roman Catholic Church. The superior Cao Dai mediums were the College of Cardinals who operated from Tay Ninh. There is a Cao Dai Pope (though the office is now vacant), and a vast hierarchy of officiants and office-holders. There are also temporal ministries controlling land, property, schools, and welfare operations.

The historicizing perspective of Cao Dai is a key feature of its temple iconography. At the entrance to the Tay Ninh Holy See, a giant mural depicts Victor Hugo in his French Academician's uniform. Accompanying him are two other key Cao Dai messengers, the poet Trang Trinh (1492–1587), who is revered as an early prophet of Vietnamese nationhood, and the Chinese nationalist leader Sun Yat Sen (1866–1925). The mural has been reproduced in many Cao Dai publications and website materials, often with a caption explaining that it shows Sun Yat Sen holding an inkstone symbolizing the alliance between Chinese and Christian civilization giving birth to Cao Dai doctrine. With him is Victor Hugo and his fellow poet Trang Trinh using French and Chinese characters to write the words "God and Humanity" and "Love and Justice," "which represents law and the rule of doctrine" (Hartney 1997).

This is both the moment of the Supreme Being's revelation of his Third Amnesty to all mankind, and a representation of Cao Daiists' psychic mediumship techniques: The rules for Cao Dai séances specify the immediate written transcription of the divine message, with the words then being precisely recorded in the Cao Dai archives. Well into the twentieth century, Victor Hugo was known both in the West and in French-ruled colonial societies as a keen proponent of psychic spiritism; like many other antiestablishment French leftists, he extolled spiritist techniques as an advanced mode of insight that was rational, scientific, and inherently anticlerical (Weber 1988: 400).[15] In Cao Dai, his spirit was vested with high rank in the movement's cosmic bureaucracy as the Supreme Being's messenger of compassion to foreign lands. Both these bureaucratized dealings with the spirit world and its expansionist thrust were important dimensions of Cao Dai's modernism.

The vesting of Republican China's first President, Sun Yat Sen, with spirit messenger status is also an important feature of Cao Dai religiosity. By origin a Western-trained medical doctor, Sun is remembered as a revolutionary, a man of science, and the architect of China's key early modernist institution, its republican reunification army. When he died in 1925, Sun's followers reportedly made pioneering use of film and recording technology to perpetuate his message, playing records and showing film clips of his speeches to young acolytes gathered at his mausoleum in Beijing (Spence 2002). Early Cao Daiists were highly knowledgeable about radical nationalist movements in Japan, China, and India. Sun was readily identifiable as a prophetic personage who spoke from the beyond through the particular media—radio and modern broadcasting—that Cao Daiists saw as critical for the transmission of cosmic truth in an age of perfected reason and scientific modernity.

Like Arya Samajis, Cao Dai adherents have been assertive and activist in their engagement with divergent religiosities. Their Holy See at Tay Ninh is close to an array of mountain shrine sites that have long been associated with apocalyptic Buddhist and Taoist occult traditions. The area is also associated with traditions of mystical kingship, which make it a place of both power and danger for those on both sides of the shifting and problematic Vietnam-Cambodia border. It is therefore instructive to observe the ways in which Cao Daiists have used Tay Ninh as an arena both to reflect on and publicly control and discipline this profusion of lesser religious modes. Indeed, it is this process of collective reflection which I see as a third distinct mode of religiosity involving significant acts of self-awareness on the part of those involved in modernist debates about the nature of human religious consciousness both within and beyond Asia.

Visualizing Spiritual Evolution

Though certainly not unique to Cao Dai, this reflective mode or register can be observed with particular clarity in one particular area of Cao Dai life. This is the invention of large-scale public rituals involving the display and personification of both the imagistic and the doctrinal in the form of elaborate processional tableaux representing the progress and historical development of the world's religiosities. It may seem surprising to find Cao Daiists expending so much creative energy on the invention of novel ritual forms. After all, Asia's other modernist religious movements have tended to disparage most rituals as survivals of "tradition" that fossilize faith and rob believers of agency and responsibility (Humphrey and Laidlaw 1994; Laidlaw 1995).

Yet to Cao Dai leaders, the staging of these displays was progressive, a taking of initiative and an affirmation of Cao Dai's mastery of time, space, and history. Those involved in the tableaux were garbed as soldiers, sportsmen, and modern technocrats, that is as doers and actors in a world of service and achievement. Furthermore, during the colonial period the movement's spokesmen put much effort into negotiating with the French authorities over the staging of these rituals; they also went to great lengths to create a documentary record of each performance. Thus in the planning and enactment of these displays, Cao Daiists were behaving as purposive and creative actors, makers of dynamic happenings in the world, both spiritually and politically. Indeed French officials found these schemes alarming precisely because they were political initiatives; without being any less meaningful as spiritual acts, they had the effect of forging new and assertive political relationships both with the colonial authorities and with Cao Dai's foreign admirers and champions. This purposiveness through the making and remaking of ritual is still a key feature of Cao Dai life today. And during the colonial period, French commentators were deeply divided about Cao Dai: To its admirers it was much like the Arya Samaj, an expression of progress, rationalization, and racial awakening in Asia, but at the same time, to fearful colonial officials, Cao Dai was subversive and sinister, its rituals a conspiratorial burlesquing of reason, science, and the *mission civilisatrice* (the French civilizing mission).

From this perspective then, those Cao Dai rituals that the French refused to sanction were just as important as the ones they allowed. In 1932, the colonial administration turned down a plan for a rite of commemoration honoring yet another important Cao Dai spirit-messenger, the French disarmament activist Aristide Briand (1862–1932).[16] It is clear why the idea was alarming to French officials, and also why Briand was meaningful for Cao Dai. This visionary French socialist was cofounder of the leftist newspaper *L'Humanité*, and also a celebrated orator (Oudin 1987). Thus, like Victor Hugo, Briand was both a hero of progressive political causes and a master of language, a deliverer of compelling messages in both written and oratorical form about the future of humanity and its evolutionary attainments, in forms that compelled and inspired the enhancement of human insight.

Five years after the banning of the Briand commemoration, and having enlisted the support of French literary and political luminaries, the Cao Dai leadership succeeded in inducing the French authorities to permit the staging of an even more ambitious ritual. This was the establishment of an opulent new Cao Dai temple in Pnomh Penh; it was celebrated with a massive public display that featured the processing of a portrait of Victor Hugo and a statue of Joan of Arc in a gleaming American motorcar (Gobron 1950: 88–97).

This 1937 celebration was Cao Dai's greatest prewar achievement, in effect an inner colonial conquest of the Khmers by the massed forces of modernist enlightened Cao Dai spirituality. It had been allowed to go forward after a long period during which the colonial authorities had pressed hard for the curtailment of Cao Dai activities in Cambodia, regarding these initiatives as deeply subversive to the colonial political order.[17] For Cao Dai, this was at least implicitly an assertion of the triumph of the doctrinal over the imagistic, with the Theravada Buddhism of the Khmer kingdom being treated as an arena of lesser or unrefined religiosity, and the installation rite providing a reflective account of humanity's progress toward ultimate enlightenment.

During the Second World War, the recruitment and training of the Cao Dai military by the Japanese occupation forces paved the way for the movement's emergence as an important political force in Indochina's postwar decolonization struggle. In 1946, the Cao Dai hierarchy created an official propaganda bureau. This *Service de Propagande* used sophisticated photographic and communications techniques to tell the world about Cao Dai doctrines and rituals, as well as documenting the movement's growing involvement in the escalating war between the French and the revolutionary nationalist Viet Minh forces (Gobron 1949).

In 1948, this propaganda service staged a large-scale public exhibition at Tay Ninh featuring an array of strikingly dramatic documentary photographs of contemporary Cao Dai religious and military life. This event closely resembled the many government-sponsored expositions that have been widely portrayed as exercises in orientalist governmentality on the part of hegemonic colonial regimes. Yet in this case, it was Cao Daiists who were deploying these tools of power in a situation that was characteristic of many turbulent colonial societies after the Second World War—volatile, violent, and politically fluid, thus full of opportunities for those with the ability to disseminate strong images of a new political and moral order.[18]

The exhibition pictures show Cao Dai dignitaries and their vestments, as well as everyday life in Cao Dai communities in the Tay Ninh region. They include scenes of productivity in a Cao Dai sawmill and a Cao Dai marketplace, diligent Cao Dai schoolchildren, and the white-uniformed male and female personnel of the Cao Dai medical service. Especially compelling are the pictures of the Cao Dai military filmed in a variety of dramatic action poses. There are also striking shots of Cao Dai boys in Western-style sports uniforms performing mass gymnastics and paramilitary exercises for an audience of Vietnamese and French spectators. These displays are much like the mass youth spectacles that were a hallmark of modernist political life in Europe and many colonial societies from the mid-1930s onward.[19]

The message is clear: As with their rituals, so too in everyday life—Cao Daiists were responsible agents in a world of struggle that demanded dedicated selfless service and feats of soldierlike moral and bodily purification in the national cause. There are close parallels here with India's nationalist traditions: an ideal of self-sacrifice and moral self-cultivation as a path to national liberation, with divine purpose imagined as the liberation of homeland—but in this case through the creation of a Cao Dai parastate.

The images that point most persuasively in this direction are those that document yet another remarkable Cao Dai ritual, the festival of the Cao Dai Holy Mother, which took place in September 1948.[20] At this 1948 Cao Dai Mother festival, large crowds assembled to watch a grand procession passing in review before the Cao Dai Pope and other dignitaries, together with a party of uniformed French officials. Highlights of the procession included festival floats bearing a variety of symbolic items: a dummy Joan of Arc bearing a banner and riding a white horse, an armored car, a mock-up naval vessel, a giant book symbolizing knowledge and enlightenment, and a montage of three sacral personages, referred to as "saints" in the captions: Confucius, the Buddha Sakyamuni, and Jesus.

The most striking of all these components of the festival—and the most disturbing to a contemporary eye—is the photograph of a troupe of fifteen barefooted Cao Daiist boys. Their torsos are bare, and their faces and bodies have been artificially blackened; they wear grass skirts and ankle bracelets. The boys appear to be dancing; at their head is a youth in a grass skirt bearing a mock sword. The caption reads: "Les petits vietnamiens déguisés en nègres simulent une danse fantastique" (Little Vietnamese boys dressed up as "nègres"—blacks—performing a "danse fantastique," that is, an exotic or savage dance) (Gobron 1949: figure 154).

This is a remarkable expression of Cao Dai imagination. The boys dancing in fancy dress were very clearly to be taken as simulating the undeveloped or unevolved spiritual and political state of true "primitives." The ambiguity may be intentional: The boys could be thought of as both pseudo-Africans and "Canaques," a colonial term for "warlike" and "unevolved" islanders from French-ruled Melanesian territories. They could also be thought of as members of Indochina's indigenous ethnic minority populations, that is, the highland and forest peoples who are still often referred to by the demeaning Vietnamese term *moi* ("savage") (Salemink 2003).

Thus in this ritual, what can be seen is a paradigm of the broader Cao Dai project, which is to reflect on the historical evolution of religion toward a universalistic spirit. This vision represents symbolically, though definitely not imagistically, a rationalistic understanding of the progression of human religiosity from the "primitive" to the universal, and thus by implication, from the imagistic to the doctrinal. Such representations are still a muted but nevertheless significant feature of Cao Dai self-representations today, and in a less dramatic way this notion of progress is reflected in the structure and rituals of contemporary Cao Dai life both within and beyond Vietnam.

In their different ways, then, both Cao Dai and the Arya Samaj exemplify the features of many modernist religions in which adherents reflect upon themselves, and on the development of human spirituality, in ways that parallel the external observations of Western academic commentators. In this respect, what has been argued here is that a third modernist and evolutionary mode of religion may be a useful addition to the other two proposed and explored in this volume.

Notes

For incisive comments on earlier drafts of this chapter I warmly thank Caroline Humphrey, Leo Howe, Sugata Bose, Maya Warrier, Magnus Marsden, Christopher Bayly, and the editors of this volume. I thank Christ's College, Cambridge, for grants in support of my recent fieldwork in Vietnam.

1. See, for example, Farquhar 1967 [1914]; Gombrich and Obeyesekere 1988; Van der Veer 1988.

2. See Cabaton 1901; Maspero 1928; Dharma 1987; Bayly 2000.

3. Arya Samaj teachings exalt rationality, restraint, and austerity. The movement is radically monotheist, abhorring priestly authority and elaborate ritual. Its experience of Hinduism is action-centered, soldierlike, and explicitly masculinized. Celibacy, bodybuilding, and chastity belts for men are all extolled; allegiance is exclusive, with much insistence on the policing of boundaries and the maintenance of clear distinctions between proper and improper forms of religiosity.

4. For a present-day version, see, for example, http://www.world.std.com/~aditya/dham.html.

5. As confirmed in their publications and present-day websites. It is notable that the mechanism of embracing Cao Dai allegiance was the inscribing of one's signature on a printed membership document, rather than a process of ritualized initiation or religious instruction. See Marr 1984: 51.

6. Fall 1955; Smith 1970; Oliver 1976; Werner 1981; Blagov 1999. On Vietnam's other mass "syncretizing" faith, Hoa Hao, see Tai 1983.

7. As a long-standing dynastic center, Udaipur has strong traditions of lordly benefaction and public piety. On cow protection, see Van der Veer 1994: 86–94; Pandey 1989; Yang 1980.

8. This was a notably low-key occasion; demonstrations of this kind do not necessarily become confrontational or violent, though they are often seen as dangerously provocative.

9. Cow protectionists also denounced the British as consumers of beef and leather; Christianity too was decried in Hindu supremacist polemics as a faith of disorder and carnal license (Jones 1992).

10. Ironically, Wahhabis, Salafiyyas, and other Muslim purists have disparaged *dargahs* in much the same terms.

11. Many of these campaigners were concerned mainly with such practical goals as the securing of public employment. The campaigns sharpened divisions between the languages, identifying Hindi as a "Hindu" tongue, and Urdu, once a meeting point for a composite Hindu and Muslim gentry culture, as the speech of Muslims (King 1994).

12. On the use of the contested terms "Nehruvian" and "secularism," and the so-called Ayodhya conflict (involving a disputed shrine site where, in 1992, Hindu zealots demolished an ancient mosque to avenge the alleged razing by a precolonial Muslim ruler of a Hindu holy site), see Hansen 1999.

13. See http://www.caodai.org/ and compare the Sydney Centre for Studies in Caodaism website: http://www-personal.usyd.edu.au/~cdao/tam.htm.

14. Cao Dai practices draw on Vietnamese traditions of occult divination and ancestral spirit religion, and on writings by Western spiritists who inspired movements synthesizing positivistic science and such techniques as séances, table-rapping, and spirit-writing. Cao Dai publications make much of celebrity clairvoyants and psychics including Allen Kardec, the founder of Kardecism, a movement of science- and philanthropy-loving spiritism with a large following in Brazil (Gobron 1950: 111; Werner 1981; Hess 1990: 410–11; folder marked "Caodaisme," Carton 273, INDO/NF/2409, Centre des Archives d'Outre-Mer, Aix-en-Provence [CAOM]).

15. See also Simon 1923 and de Mutigny 1981.

16. Report from Résident Supérieur (Cambodia) to Gov. General, 11 April 1932, Carton 273, INDO/NF/2409, CAOM.

17. Pres., Ligue Français pour la Défense des Droits de l'Homme et du Citoyen, to Col. Minister, 28 Dec. 1931, in folder marked "Caodaisme"; also "Situation du culte caodaiste [1935]," Carton 273, INDO/NF/2409, CAOM.

18. Marguerite Gobron, the widow of a key French Cao Daiist, published 167 of the photographs in her book *Le Caodaisme en images* (Gobron 1949). Topics covered in the exhibition include the creation of the Cao Dai army as an act of God's will and an embodiment of sacred mission.

19. Arya Samaj schooling also emphasizes bodily regimentation and physical training, including marching, gymnastics, swordplay, and wrestling (Datta 1997; compare Marr 1984: 79–82, 97 and Larcher-Goscha 2000).

20. This ceremony had some of the features of fabricated folk spectacles such as the *fetes populaires* of 1930s France. Other elements clearly derived from processional festivals staged to venerate Buddhist relics and the chariot-borne images of Hindu deities.

References

Bayly, S. 1999. "The Evolution of Colonial Cultures: Nineteenth-century Asia." In Andrew Porter (ed.), *The Oxford History of the British Empire. Volume 3, The Nineteenth Century*, pp. 447–69. Oxford, New York: Oxford University Press.

———. 2000. "French Anthropology and the Durkheimians in Colonial Indochina." *Modern Asian Studies* 34: 581–622.

Blagov, Sergei. 1999. *La Cao Dai: Un nouveau mouvement religieux*. Moscow: l'Institut des Etudes Orientales.

Bose, Sugata. 1998. "Nation as Mother: Representations and Contestation of 'India' in Bengali Literature and Culture." In Sugata Bose and Ayesha Jalal (eds.), *Nationalism, Democracy and Development: State and Politics in India*, pp. 50–75. Delhi, Oxford: Oxford University Press.

Cabaton, Antoine. 1901. *Nouvelles recherches sur les Chams*. Paris: Ernest Leroux.

Datta, Nonica. 1997. "Arya Samaj and the Making of Jat Identity." *Studies in History* (NS) 13: 97–199.

Dayananda Sarasvati. 1970 [1908]. *An English Translation of the Satyarth Prakash [Light of Truth] of Maharshi Swami Dayanand Saraswati*, ed. Vaidyanath Shastri, Jagdish Vidyarthi, and Bharatendra Nath. New Delhi: Jan Gyan Prakashan.

Dharma, Po. 1987. *Le Panduranga. (Campa), 1802–1835. Ses rapports avec le Vietnam*. Paris: Ecole Française de l'Extreme Orient.

Eck, Diana. 1985. *Darshan, Seeing the Divine Image in India*. 2d ed. Chambersburg, Pa.: Anima Books.

Fall, Bernard B. 1955. "The Political-Religious Sects of Viet-Nam." *Pacific Affairs* 28: 235–53.

Farquhar, J. N. 1967 [1914]. *Modern Religious Movements in India*. Delhi: Munshiram Manoharlal.

Flood, Gavin D. 1996. *An Introduction to Hinduism*. Cambridge: Cambridge University Press.

Fuller, Chris J. 1992. *The Camphor Flame: Popular Hinduism and Society in India*. Princeton, N.J.: Princeton University Press.

Gobron, M. G. 1949. *Le Caodaisme en images* [Paris: Dervy] http://pandora.nla.gov.au/pan/10190/20010608/ www-personal.usyd.edu.au/_cdao/frames1/main1.htm.

Gobron, Gabriel. 1950. *History and Philosophy of Caodaism. Reformed Buddhism, Vietnamese Spiritism, New Religion in Eurasia*, trans. Pham Xuan Thai. Saigon: Tu Hai Publishing House.

Gombrich, Richard, and Gananath Obeyesekere. 1988. *Buddhism Transformed: Religious Change in Sri Lanka*. Princeton, N.J.: Princeton University Press.

Gupta, Charu. 2002. *Sexuality, Obscenity and Community: Women, Muslims and the Hindu Public in Colonial India*. New York: Palgrave Macmillan.

Hansen, Thomas Blum. 1999. *The Saffron Wave: Democracy and Hindu Nationalism in India*. Princeton, N.J.: Princeton University Press.

Hartney, Christopher. 1997. "Performing Dualism: Experiences of Caodaism." Paper presented to the Annual Conference of Australian Association for the Study of Religions, University of Queensland, 10–13 July 1997, available at http://pandora.nla.gov.au/pan/10190/20010608/www-.usyd.edu.au/_cdao/dualism.htm.

Hess, David J. 1990. "Ghosts and Domestic Politics in Brazil: Some Parallels between Spirit Possession and Spirit Infestation." *Ethos* 18: 407–38.

Humphrey, Caroline, and James Laidlaw. 1994. *The Archetypal Actions of Ritual: A Theory of Ritual Illustrated by the Jain Rite of Worship*. Oxford: Clarendon Press.

Jones, Kenneth W. 1976. *Arya Dharm: Hindu Consciousness in 19th-Century Punjab*. Berkeley and Los Angeles: University of California Press.

———. 1992. "Swami Dayananda Saraswati's Critique of Christianity." In his *Religious Controversy in British India: Dialogues in South Asian Languages*. Albany: State University of New York Press.

Kelly, John D. 1991. *A Politics of Virtue: Hinduism, Sexuality and Countercolonial Discourse in Fiji*. Chicago: University of Chicago Press.

King, Christopher R. 1992. "Images of Virtue and Vice: The Hindu-Urdu Controversy in Two Nineteenth-Century Hindi Plays." In Kenneth W. Jones (ed.), *Religious Controversy in British India: Dialogues in South Asian Languages*. Albany: State University of New York Press.

———. 1994. *One Language, Two Scripts: The Hindi Movement in Nineteenth-Century North India*. New Delhi: Oxford University Press.

Laidlaw, James. 1995. *Riches and Renunciation: Religion, Economy and Society among the Jains*. Oxford: Clarendon Press.

Larcher-Goscha, Agathe. 2000. "The Development of Sports in Colonial Vietnam: A Modern Rediscovery of the Body and the Affirmation of National Strength, (1918–1940)." Paper delivered to Association for Asian Studies, San Diego, unpublished manuscript.

Llewellyn, J. E. 1993. *The Arya Samaj As a Fundamentalist Movement: A Study in Comparative Fundamentalism*. New Delhi: Manohar.

Madan, T. N. 1987. *Non-Renunciation: Themes and Interpretations of Hindu Culture*. Delhi: Oxford University Press.

Marr, David. 1981. "Sino-Vietnamese Relations." *Australian Journal of Chinese Affairs* 6: 45–64.

———. 1984. *Vietnamese Tradition on Trial, 1920–1945*. Berkeley: University of California Press.

Maspero, Georges. 1928. *Le Royaume de Champa*. Paris, Brussels: Vahoest.

Morris, Charles. 1888. *The Aryan Race: Its Origins and Achievements*. Chicago: S. C. Griggs and Co.

Mutigny, Jean de. 1981. *Victor Hugo et le spiritisme*. Paris: F. Nathan.

Oliver, V. 1976. *Caodai Spiritism: A Study of Religion in Vietnamese Society*. Leiden: E. J. Brill.

Oudin, Bernard. 1987. *Aristide Briand: la paix, une idée neuve en Europe*. Paris: R. Laffont.

Pandey, Gyanendra. 1989. "Rallying Round the Cow: Sectarian Strife in the Bhojpuri Region, c. 1888–1917." In Ranajit Guha (ed.), *Subaltern Studies II.* Delhi: Oxford University Press.

Pinch, William R. 1996. *Peasants and Monks in British India.* Berkeley, London: University of California Press.

Robb, Peter. 1986. "The Challenge of Gau Mata: British Policy and Religious Change in India, 1880–1916." *Modern Asian Studies* 20: 285–319.

Salemink, Oscar. 2003. *The Ethnography of Vietnam's Central Highlanders: A Historical Contextualization, 1850–1990.* Honolulu: University of Hawaii Press.

Simon, Gustave, ed. 1923. *Chez Victor Hugo: Les Tables Tournantes de Jersey. Procès-verbaux des séances.* Paris: Louis Conard.

Smith, R. B. 1970. "An Introduction to Caodaism." *Bulletin of the School of Oriental and African Studies, University of London* 33: 335–49; 33: 573-89.

Spence, Jonathan D. 2002. "Sun Yat-sen." Available at http://www.time.com/time/asia/asia/magazine/1999/990823/sun_yat_sen1.html.

Tai, Hue-Tam Ho. 1983. *Millenarianism and Peasant Politics in Vietnam.* Cambridge, Mass.: Harvard University Press.

Vaidyanathan, K. R. 1977. *Sri Krishna: The Lord of Guruvayur.* Bombay: Bharatiya Vidya Bhavan.

Van der Veer, Peter. 1988. *Gods on Earth: The Management of Religious Experience and Identity in a North Indian Pilgramage Centre.* London: Athlone.

———. 1994. *Religious Nationalism: Hindus and Muslims in India.* Berkeley: University of California Press.

Van der Veer, Peter, and Hartmut Lehmann, eds. 1999. *Nation and Religion: Perspectives on Europe and Asia.* Princeton, N.J.: Princeton University Press.

Weber, Eugen. 1988. "Religion and Superstition in Nineteenth-century France." *The Historical Journal* 31: 399–423.

Werner, Jayne Susan. 1981. *Peasant Politics and Religious Sectarianism: Peasant and Priest in the Cao Dai in Viet Nam.* New Haven, Conn.: Yale University Press.

Whitmore, John K. 1997. "Literati Culture and Integration in Dai Viet, c. 1430–c. 1840." *Modern Asian Studies* 31: 665–87.

Yang, Anand. 1980. "Sacred Symbol and Sacred Space in Rural India: Community Mobilization in the 'Anti-Cow Killing' Riot of 1893." *Comparative Studies in Society and History* 25: 576–96.

Young, Richard Fox. 1981. *Resistant Hinduism: Sanskrit Sources on Anti-Christian Apologetics in Early Nineteenth-century India.* Vienna: Indological Institute of the University of Vienna.

Late Medieval Christianity, Balinese Hinduism, and the Doctrinal Mode of Religiosity   8

LEO HOWE

IN TWO RECENT WORKS, HARVEY WHITEHOUSE (1995, 2000) distinguishes two fundamentally different types of modes of religiosity, the imagistic and the doctrinal. In the latter, doctrine is defined as orally transmitted, argument-based rhetoric that facilitates the spread of religious ideology. He claims, "In such [doctrinal] traditions, the persuasiveness of ethical and cosmological representations depends to a large extent on their overall coherence, achieved through the ordering of dogma in strings of implied questions and answers" (2000: 14). Further, "words are powerful in Christianity because they are used rhetorically to bind together a set of absolute presuppositions through the logic of question and answer" (2000: 35). Whatever theological question we ask, there is a ready-made answer, and all questions in the end "lead us back to absolute presuppositions beyond which further enquiry is impossible" (2000: 35).

This description of doctrinal religion is modeled on Reformation theology, which in one guise or another was the form of missionary Christianity introduced into Papua New Guinea (PNG). It differs markedly from indigenous PNG religions, which are imagistic. The doctrinal and the imagistic modes depend on different kinds of memory operation, schematic memory and episodic memory respectively,[1] which in turn create quite different kinds of trajectories for forms of social organization, solidarity and leadership, size of membership, strength of emotional commitment, and so forth (Whitehouse 1995: chapter 8, 2000). Briefly, doctrinal religion, transmitted through frequent and highly repetitive sermonizing, can spread rapidly, building up large, anonymous, imagined communities that tend to have hierarchical structures bent on disciplining their members. They are often unemotional, and are therefore prone to the tedium effect, which causes members to drift away or revert to more ecstatic rites. Imagistic religion, by contrast, relies on nonverbal, infrequent, highly arousing, sometimes violent rituals that create specific episodic memories that bind together the small number of participants in very cohesive, face-to-face groups, leading to an elaboration of local differences rather than extensive homogeneity. While conceiving of these modes as ideal types, though in reality they are only tendencies and often aspects of both can be found in any particular religious tradition, Whitehouse also notes that imagistic and doctrinal modes can be treated as discrete domains of operation (2000: 145).

Although still very much a theory in its infancy, it brings considerable order and clarity to a number of difficult problems in the anthropology of religion. Nonetheless it has evolved from fieldwork in PNG and been tested against PNG material. Given that missionary Christianity and indigenous religions in PNG mirror the ideal types very closely, it is not surprising that the fit between theory and data is pretty good.

When Whitehouse moves away from PNG, it is to write a chapter on the European Reformation because reformed Christianity, based on the Word, is seen as the precursor of the form of doctrinal Christianity introduced into PNG (2000: chapter 8). While pre-Reformation religion is broadly described as doctrinal at the top (priests, theologians, monks) and imagistic at the bottom (the ordinary population), post-Reformation churches "attempted to marginalize the imagistic domain of operation within Christianity" (2000: 150). This is an oversimplified account of late medieval Christianity that, once seen through a different perspective, suggests two things. First, the differences within the category of doctrinal religiosity are as great as the differences between imagistic and doctrinal modes, and second, that late medieval Christianity, which I claim is basically doctrinal, nevertheless exhibits some of the social correlates that Whitehouse's theory associates with imagistic religiosity. The main theme of this chapter is thus an examination of the concept of the doctrinal mode. The first half discusses the nature of pre-Reformation religion in Europe, and explores the relation between doctrine and practice. The second half suggests that similar arguments can be made for the varieties of Hinduism in Bali, Indonesia.

Late Medieval Christianity as a Doctrinal Religion

I argue that a description of pre-Reformation religion in Europe as doctrinal at the top and imagistic at the bottom is inadequate. This perspective perpetuates the view that a gulf divided popular and elite religion, and that orthodoxy was the preserve of the affluent and well-educated while the masses were steeped in magic, superstition, ecstatic rituals, and heresy. Eamon Duffy (1992: 1–2) points out for example that historians, such as Keith Thomas (1973), who have written about the religion of the majority "have been skeptical about or uninterested in the interconnections between 'elite' or clerical culture and that of the people at large," and goes on to say, "It is an extraordinary feature of Thomas's work . . . that there is in it virtually no sustained discussion of the liturgy and its effects on the religious world-view of ordinary men and women." For his part Duffy is keen to reconnect the elite with the masses by showing that the liturgy was "the principal reservoir from which the religious paradigms and beliefs of the people were drawn" (1992: 2).

For the masses, while religious traditions were magically oriented and occasionally evoked extreme emotions, much of this magic emanated from orthodox doctrines and practices such as the miracle of the Mass (Rubin 1991), forms of fasting (Bynum 1987), the cult of saints and relics (Duffy 1992: chapter 5), and the church-provided sacramentals (exorcisms, blessings, etc., for the problems of everyday life) from all of which diverse material and spiritual benefits accrued. For the most part this religion consisted of periodic rituals (baptism, confirmation, marriage, confession, penance, extreme unction, death, the Mass, etc.) sanctioned and structured by orthodox church doctrine (Muir 1997). It is stretching things to describe this religion, even for the ordinary laity, as imagistic, and to argue that such a tradition entailed social processes similar to those produced by the violent and infrequent rituals of PNG imagistic cults, which had no verbally expressed doctrine at all. In this sense, there seems to be some slippage in the meaning of the term "imagistic" when used for both late medieval religion and PNG cultic religion. In the latter, violent rituals ensure shock and high emotional arousal leading to enduring episodic memories that cement face-to-face relations among the participants. Iconic imagery is vital, but its ritual meanings are secret and usually the opposite of their ordinary ones (Barth 1975, 1987). In the former, by contrast, the cross, the saints, the altar, and all the rest of the paraphernalia of church ceremony, are ever present and have stable and public meanings sanctioned by doctrine, and church rituals only occasionally led to ecstasy. One might wonder who was being imagistic: the frenzied mobs who destroyed, often ritualistically, the icons of the Catholic church in many towns of northern Europe in the sixteenth century (Eire 1986; Duffy 1992), or those who wished to preserve them.

Religion on the eve of the Reformation was doctrinal, but it was ritually doctrinal. By this I mean that the Latin liturgy and associated doctrines were converted into performative ritual, the doctrine being embedded in the ceremonies. Cameron puts it well: "All the most popular activities of late medieval religion were based on *doing* something, on participation, activity, movement, essentially on experiencing an event more than on understanding a message" (1991: 16, his emphasis). The laity might be uninformed about the niceties of theology, but they knew how to do the rituals, or at least how to behave when they were being performed by the priest. Such rituals shared some, but obviously not all, of the characteristics Whitehouse associates with verbal doctrine. Like the latter they were frequent, repetitive, and routinized, subject to hierarchical authority and discipline, and had relatively stable meanings. They were unlike verbal doctrine in that, as we shall see, they produced fairly intense social cohesion within the local community despite the fact that the rituals and the embedded messages were universalistic, and their revelatory potential was more likely achieved through emotional and sensual stimulation than intellectual persuasion (Whitehouse 1995: 197). It is therefore difficult to identify a religious tradition based on such ritualization in any unambiguous way, a difficulty that will recur elsewhere in this chapter, because these rituals are very different to those of PNG cultic religions. Reformed religion was doctrinal in a more straightforward manner, since it was verbally codified in the vernacular, and ritual was banished.[2] Pre- and post-Reformation Christianities entailed clearly very different forms of religiosity and have quite different implications for forms of social organization, but neither, it seems to me, is imagistic in the same way that PNG cults are.

I now want to discuss one way of describing late medieval religion. While this doctrinal religion evinces certain aspects of the form of social organization Whitehouse sees as stemming from imagistic religions, it also shows clear differences to reformed Christianity. In short, the conceptual distinction between doctrinal and imagistic is blurred not sharp. To do this I draw on John Bossy's excellent book *Christianity in the West, 1400–1700* (1985). Bossy's work is rather different from many who write about pre-Reformation religion and its reformed varieties, because he finds many positive things to say about the former. When reading about the Reformation it is often difficult to avoid taking sides since many writers appear to give the impression that in parts of Europe in the sixteenth century a bad old religion was replaced by a good new religion. This is not surprising since much of our knowledge of pre-Reformation religion is colored by the contemptuous evaluations of the reformers themselves. After all it was Luther who began talking of the pope as the anti-Christ and cartoons of the period show the devil giving birth to the pope and devils defecating monks into a cess pit (Scribner 1987b). I emphasize that the following is only one possible description because there is considerable controversy about the issue, and Bossy probably provides an overidealized perspective (Scribner 1986: 9, 74), but anything more comprehensive cannot be attempted here.

The main thrust of Bossy's argument is that pre-Reformation Christianity was highly social in nature. And by this he has something very specific in mind. He means that Jesus came into the world with a full complement of kin. Mary's mother was Anne (later to become, as St. Anne, the center of an important fifteenth-century cult). After Anne's husband, Joachim, died, she married twice more and as grandchildren (i.e., stepcousins to Jesus), she had James, Simon, Jude, and John the Evangelist, while on the paternal side Mary's cousin was John the Baptist. This extended family acted as a kind of template for local Christian communities and for axioms of kinship, friendship, and charity that Bossy sees as the hallmark of late medieval religion. The maternal line of Anne, Mary, and Jesus was only replaced much later in reformed religion (Protestant and Catholic) by the nuclear family of Joseph, Mary, and Jesus, with the rest of the kinship connections largely disappearing from view. I will briefly describe three examples of this Christian kinship: baptism, death, and confraternities.

Baptism was strongly influenced by axioms of kinship. Original sin was removed by a rite of exorcism at the church door in which the Devil was expelled from the child. Then came the rite of baptism proper in which the child was incorporated into the Christian community through the institution of godparenthood. We see the child acquiring several godparents who became kin not only to the child but to his natural parents as well, thus creating a bar to intermarriage between those involved. And, at least for the ordinary masses, this was a kinship of equality, binding together people of roughly equal standing (Bossy 1985: 15–16). Often godparents were already kin of some sort, and since the godparental relation took precedence over the natural kin relation, it was hoped that tense kinship could be converted into peaceful friendship. Here then is the basic kinship axiom, the extension of kinship into the wider, but nonetheless local, Christian community.

Kinship and family also figured prominently in death rituals, which were highly elaborate in the fifteenth century. A huge amount of filial piety was unleashed at death, much of it by family members trying to fulfill their charitable duties to each other and to the deceased. However, much of this lay ritual (cleansing the body, vigil, mourning, feasts, and the Mass for the dead) was at odds with church liturgy, which emphasized the separation of the dead from the living rather than their continuing interrelation. For example, by this period, it had become established teaching, if not formally codified in doctrine, that the destiny of the soul was settled by a divine judgment immediately after death, rather than delaying it until the Last Judgment. This inhibited the living from righting the wrongs done to the deceased by which they might ease his troubles in the afterlife. Bossy's point, however, is that the church found it had to accommodate itself to lay practice by allowing priests to say Masses for the dead so that the living could discharge their charitable duties. This institution became quantitative since the more Masses said the shorter the period spent in purgatory (Bossy 1985: 28). Masses also decreased the likelihood that ghosts would return to avenge injuries (Thomas 1973: 712–17). Since priests were paid for saying Masses, the church quickly recognized the advantages of conformity (Bossy 1985: 26–33). It is also possible to understand the increasing importance of the doctrine of purgatory from the twelfth century onward as part of this accommodation of orthodox doctrine to lay practice. If the older orthodoxy only provided for the dead to go to heaven or hell, both domains being radically separated from the living, purgatory allowed family and community life to continue after death (Le Goff 1984). Purgatory was visualized, or specialized, as the local churchyard where people were buried in a kind of undifferentiated collectivity (often headstones were not used; bones were later dug up and mixed with those of others in the charnel house), where festivities and commerce took place, and where therefore the living and the dead could continue to interact. In short, the elaborate ritual, the Mass for the dead, and the notion of purgatory combined to ensure that the dead remained part of the kith and kin of the social community. What we can discern in these practices are the boundaries of small communities, living, worshipping, and dying together, under the watchful eye of priest and doctrine, communities that strove for internal peace through orthodox commitment to the rituals and sacraments of the church.

The final example has to do with the institution of confraternities. At least as much as compaternity via baptism, confraternities were associations embodying sacred Christian kinship as opposed to profane consanguinity. They espoused the principle that "we are all brothers in God" (Bossy 1985: 58) and obliged members to keep the peace and to be charitable at all times. People voluntarily took on extended forms of social kinship, that is, Christian brotherhood, as an antidote to the problems of hierarchical natural families, lord–vassal relationships, and family feuds. If there was "a desperate recognition of the primacy of hatred among the natural passions" (Bossy 1985: 60), then confraternities were an attempt to imitate the Christian life by turning the other cheek: members competed amongst themselves to be the first to give "the kiss of peace to him by whom he had been offended" (quoted in Bossy 1985: 60). The point was not that peacekeeping was something one did after war or feud, but rather something much more active, the "creation of bonds of Christian kinship" to prevent enmity and feud in the first place.

In each of these three examples, ideas of kinship, family, and community are firmly Christian practice: the extension of kinship bonds within the local community so that conflict could be supplanted by the peace that flows from familial duty and charity. These are small-scale, face-to-face communities defined by local practices. Even if some of these practices were not necessarily orthodox doctrine, they tended to become so because the church had to accommodate to them if it was to retain authority over its flock. We see how the church had sometimes to catch up with lay practice, altering doctrine as needed. Characterizing the situation thus makes it seem problematical to label this religion imagistic rather than doctrinal.

I insert here a few words about the notion of charity. Keith Thomas tends to see medieval charity as somewhat impersonal, the gifts and help of the affluent to the less well-off and to beggars. Even when it was more personal it tends to be explained as a defensive act, witchcraft being a powerful incentive for maintaining charity when social and economic changes were undermining it (Thomas 1973:

672). No doubt this is true, but it misses a different aspect of charity. For Bossy, charity was usually exclusive rather than inclusive, and thus intensely personal and social. Charity was largely confined to those belonging to one's own group: one's wider kin network, both natural and godparental, the dead of the local community, comembers in one's confraternity, and so on. Because friendship with some entailed enmity with others, general charity was exceptional, which is why Bossy equates charity with social integration. Much of the time one could only practice "partial, segmental or occasional" charity. Moreover, charity was not just about saving one's own skin. Fulfilling familial duties to the dead meant more than keeping vengeful ghosts at bay. It was also because death was a pitiable condition and deserved a charitable disposition on behalf of the living (Bossy 1985: 33, 57, 60–61), that is, it was a Christian act rather than simply a defensive one. Charity as the central Christian act reinforces what has been said about the essentially social and kinship nature of late medieval religion, which helped both to bind people together into communities and to bind these communities to the church. For example, charity was crucial to the Mass, which was not simply about individual salvation. Before receiving the host people were required to practice charity, that is, obtain forgiveness for their sins and redress the wrongs done to their neighbors, for one had to be in a worthy state before receiving communion, otherwise the Lord would be profaned. The Mass was therefore symbolic of the peaceful bonds uniting the community (Bossy 1983; Holt 1995: 19–20).

Now one of the most momentous things that Reformation theology taught, especially through Luther, was that almost all of this structure of Christianity, built upon kinship, community, charity, and obligations, had no scriptural authority. When Luther read Erasmus's translation of the Bible from Greek, he noted that while the Latin Vulgate had Jesus say: Do penance, for the Kingdom of Heaven is at hand, the Greek should really be translated as: Repent, for the Kingdom of Heaven is at hand. Where the Vulgate indicated an outward practice, Erasmus insisted on an inner psychological attitude, that of being repentant (McGrath 1999: 55; Dickens and Jones 2000 : 104). Similar new readings were made for many other parts of the Bible. This eventually led Luther, following St. Augustine, to his doctrine of the justification by faith alone, and therefore away from the Pelagian doctrine of salvation through good works, which underpinned the Catholic sacraments. Simply, what this means is salvation cannot be achieved by doing good works. It is not even the case that by developing faith you can be saved, because this implies human action or work, and so reverts back to the Pelagian view. Rather, according to Luther, God provides everything necessary for justification by the boundless grace that he gives freely, and all the sinner has to do is receive it (McGrath 1999: 113). Once grace is received, good works follow; good works are therefore the outcome of salvation, not its precondition. Much of Reformation theology flows from insights of this kind.[3]

Since there can be no quid pro quo with God, the Catholic sacraments lose their basic point, and the whole edifice comes under siege. The kinship template falls away, the reformers paying virtually no attention to Jesus's wider kin network; social relationships based on exchanges necessary for atonement are no longer meaningful, only the relationship to God is necessary; ritual, at best, is seen as meaningless performance, at worst the work of the devil; the focus on images is condemned as idolatrous; saints became otiose; charity becomes more impersonal and anonymous. In short, we see the almost "instant dissolution of the multitude of relationships" (Bossy 1985: 97) that late medieval religion had endorsed. In its place we have the layman's guide to scripture in such works as Erasmus's *Enchiridion* and Calvin's *Institutes of the Christian Religion*; the large-scale and anonymous community of believers and the priesthood of all believers (at least in theory if not in practice); whitewashed churches and repetitive sermonizing that induces boredom (Burke 1987: 230; Cameron 1991: 412). Even community came under pressure since, in some places, "unnecessary 'company keeping' and 'good fellowship' were construed as vices" (Collinson 1997: 281). This is a drastically different religion, built on the individual rather than the social and communal, and based on inner attitudes, the Word, and the sense of hearing, rather than on ritual, images, and the sense of vision (Muir 1997: 193). But these social changes in part flow from changes of doctrine. Both were essentially doctrinal religions, but with almost diametrically opposed social practices.

Doctrine and Practice

If imagistic religiosity implies an absence of verbal doctrine, then it is difficult to see how late medieval religion, even for the ordinary laity, can be so described, since the relationship between lay practice and doctrine was tight if not straightforward. Whitehouse's definition of doctrine seems too narrow to do justice to this complex relationship. Characterized as a closed loop of rhetorical questions and answers deriving from absolute presuppositions, it appears static and unresponsive to change. So to conclude this section I discuss the essentially dialectical relationship between practice, criticism, and doctrine, taking the Eucharist as my example.

From the very beginning the Eucharist was a central rite binding the Christian community together by commensality. But just how Christ was present in the bread and wine did not become an issue until about the tenth century, after which a variety of views were aired. By the time of the fourth Lateran Council (1215), however, the majority view of both laity and theologians was codified as the dogma of transubstantiation (Bynum 1987: 50). After consecration, while the bread and wine retained their physical appearances and properties (the Aristotelian "accidents") Christ, by a miracle, was really and substantially present in the Eucharistic elements. From this point on there is a massive elaboration of the Eucharist: the proliferation of Eucharistic miracles, the multiplication of paraphernalia surrounding the Eucharist, the adoration of the host, the increasing separation of priest from laity, the institution of the Corpus Christi feast in 1264 (followed by Corpus Christi plays, processions, and confraternities), multiple sequential Masses, and so on. There is in all this an intense preoccupation with the carnality of Christ, his actual bodily presence, and with the eating of his body in a reenactment of the sacrifice on the cross. The Eucharist was not interpreted in any of the ways that reformers such as Luther, Calvin, and Zwingli would later advance; it was Christ actually and bodily there.[4] But as the Eucharist became the most important of the sacraments, Eucharistic doctrine gave rise to complex theological problems. It is a history of what Miri Rubin, from whose work the following material is taken, calls "designing the eucharist" (1991: 34).

One problem was that the Mass was an invisible miracle. The bread and the wine changed, but the changes could not be seen. Some of the most important medieval heresies (see Lambert 1992 for a discussion) revolved around this issue. Their arguments were that the change does not happen and, prefiguring Reformation thought, claimed that the words of Jesus at the Last Supper should be understood figuratively not literally. The church's answer was to say that since Christ was made flesh in Mary's womb by the Holy Spirit, the bread can be turned into Christ's body by the same miracle.

The exact moment when transubstantiation occurred also created difficulties. Since the priest had to consecrate the bread and wine in two separate acts, did the bread change before the wine was consecrated, or was there a delay while the wine was being consecrated? This mattered because gazing at the host in adoration before it changed constituted idolatry while gazing at it after consecration conferred great benefits. A related issue was this: If the change occurred all at once after everything was done and said, what was the status of the host if the priest fell ill or died between the two consecrations? The church finally decided that transubstantiation had fully taken place (including wine into blood) after the first consecration. This decision helped to solve another problem. The laity were typically given only the host and not the wine, but it was commonly believed that the bread changed into flesh and the wine into blood. This meant that the laity only consumed the bloodless flesh. Doctrine was established therefore that decreed that at the moment of consecration both the blood and flesh were present together in both the bread and wine.

One of the most intriguing problems was raised by people wondering about what happened to the host once it was eaten. This was given urgency by reports that people had visions of the host turning into flesh and blood as it was being consumed, of how their teeth tore into the flesh, and of experiencing the taste and texture of real flesh and blood. The reality of eating Christ, while a reenactment of the sacrifice, was also to some an act of cannibalism.[5] More to the point was that when one consumed the host, Christ was in the stomach and even worse, excreted through the anus. Such a mixing of the sacred and the profane was abhorrent. One doctrinal solution was to decree that the divine food was entirely absorbed in the stomach with no residue left for the intestines. Another was that a period of fasting should precede the Eucharist so that the host would not get mixed with ordinary food.[6]

These are a sample of the problems raised by the Eucharist. Others revolved around whether the rite was an instance of automatic magic or dependent on God's will, whether the status of the priest affected the consecration, what should happen if the host, being administered to a dying person, was vomited up, and whether the rite would fall into disrepute if done too frequently. In light of these examples, doctrine is not closed but responsive to various influences and lay practice, and its presuppositions, while vigorously defended, are not unquestionable. From a wider perspective most lay religious practices eventually came under the scrutiny of the church and were either approved or rejected, thus continuing the process of Christianization through the construction of orthodoxy (Asad 1993), but while the church had the last word, it did not have the only word.

To summarize so far: Whitehouse writes that in "the doctrinal mode, much of what defines one's religious identity . . . constitutes a set of representations encoded in semantic memory producing imagined, anonymous religious communities" (2000: 11–12). I suggest this is much more the case for reformed Christianity than late medieval Christianity, it being much easier to spread the Word than diffuse a ritual. Medieval Christianity, although a doctrinal religion, produced "enduring and particularistic social bonds" (Whitehouse 2000: 12) of a kind not qualitatively different from those usually associated with imagistic religions, only in this case they were not forged through intense, infrequent, violent, life-changing episodes as in PNG cults, but gradually over a lifetime through kinship, community, charity, and collective, repetitive ritual. And while the tedium effect may have been a serious problem for the reformed churches, it was not nearly so important in pre-Reformation Christianity.[7]

Varieties of Balinese Hinduism and the Doctrinal Mode of Religiosity

Perhaps 90 percent of Balinese are Hindus, or at least this is how they presently describe themselves. However, while the forms of Hinduism to which they now adhere are diverse, these are all doctrinal since they evince very few imagistic aspects. In none of these Hinduisms are there violent, shock-inducing rituals comparable to those experienced by members of PNG imagistic cults. Nonetheless, these various forms of Hinduism generate social relationships that range from small-scale, face-to-face communities at one end of the spectrum to large, anonymous, imagined communities at the other end. Thus within the doctrinal mode of religiosity one also finds social relationships broadly characteristic of the imagistic mode. A brief description of the three most significant forms of Hinduism in Bali suggests not only that the doctrinal mode is a very broad category indeed but also that these different forms have quite different implications for scale, forms of social organization, identity, and degrees of emotional commitment.[8]

These three Hinduisms can be labeled *adat*, *agama Hindu*, and devotional Hinduism. *Adat* is the "traditional," ritual-based, priest-dominated religion of most Balinese, which, while it has undergone many changes since the nineteenth century, is still assiduously maintained in modern Bali. While it has many indigenous elements, foremost of which is an ancestor cult, it has been strongly influenced by ideas and practices imported from India millennia ago. These include a castelike system of descent groups ranked hierarchically, idioms of divine kingship, *brahmana* priests using a Shivaite liturgy, endogamous or hypergamous marriage, many Sanskrit words in the Balinese language, and so forth. This is a highly communal religion founded on elaborate ritual, in which households and descent groups appease divinized ancestors and placate demons in order to ensure the fertility of crops and the safety and prosperity of people. During the late nineteenth and early twentieth centuries, this religion was deemed to be hardly a religion at all by Javanese Muslim clerics and some Dutch colonial officials, since according to them it lacked a high god and a holy book and practiced indiscriminate spirit worship, and thus was inferior to Islam and Christianity. These criticisms were taken to heart by some Balinese intellectuals in north Bali who began to ask the same sorts of questions of their religion as were being posed by outsiders. The debates which ensued (What was Balinese religion? Who was its high god? What was all this ritual for?) also included arguments between elites and commoners about the link between religion and caste, the former wishing to preserve hierarchy since it bolstered their privileges, the latter wishing to eradicate it by ethicizing religion, simplifying ritual, and basing status on wisdom and achievement rather than ascription by birth.[9]

When Indonesia gained its independence in 1950, the first principle of the constitution proclaimed belief in one god but without specifying which god. Indonesia was to be neither a secular nor an Islamic state but to be based on broad religious values. The Ministry of Religion, staffed mostly by Muslims, insisted that only religions (*agama*) that were monotheistic, possessed a holy book, and were not restricted to a single ethnic group were eligible for state support and protection. Initially this limited the field to Islam, Protestantism, Catholicism, and Buddhism, and Balinese religion, classified as "tribal" and thus not an *agama*, was excluded. Since members of these *agama* could actively proselytize, while it was illegal for others to do so, Balinese viewed this as a disastrous situation. Throughout the 1950s, Balinese carried on a campaign for their religion to be classified as an *agama*. To do this Balinese scholars studied in India and Indian scholars were invited to Bali (Bakker 1993: 2–3); promises were made to rationalize religion by simplifying ritual, stressing doctrine, and translating Indian religious texts into Indonesian; a high god was identified; and in the Bhagavad Gita, Balinese asserted they possessed a sacred literature. In 1958, this religion gained state recognition as an *agama* and after several name changes became known as *agama Hindu*. Today its affairs are administered by a state agency called the Parisada Hindu Darma Indonesia, and membership of the religion is open to any Indonesian. Since that time the Parisada has published numerous books in Indonesian, on sale all over Bali. These specify and explain core religious doctrines, many of which are standard Indian ideas such as samsara, *moksha*, karma, dharma, and so on, and these teachings form the basis of the school curriculum in Hindu religion.

The relationship between *adat* and *agama Hindu* is ambiguous and tense. In one sense the new religion is supposed to underpin *adat* by providing theological substance and philosophical justification for traditional ritual practices. However, many of the doctrines are abstruse and largely unknown to ordinary Balinese, so that to some extent *agama Hindu* stands apart from *adat* and has its own distinctive mode of knowledge. If *adat* is an orthopraxy, *agama Hindu* is an orthodoxy (Geertz 1973: 186). For example, *agama Hindu* is highly intellectualized, presenting its material in codified lists, such as the "five gods," types of sacred places, the "five techniques of self control," the "seven darknesses or evils," and so forth, which have virtually no relevance to village life, while the main religious activity of village women and girls, the making of offerings, is hardly mentioned at all (Parker 1992: 11).

An unintended outcome of this attempt to impose a state-sponsored religious orthodoxy in Bali has been a grassroots response, especially by urban-based intellectuals and the middle class, to introduce other forms of Hinduism. By conceptualizing religion in terms of *agama*, the state forced Balinese to align *adat* with more "authentic" forms of Indian Hinduism. However, once this contemporary dialogue with India opened up, it became obvious that Indian Hinduism was not a unitary religion. Those Balinese not content to let the state dictate the manner in which religious reform was to proceed exploited the opportunities that then became available and began to select forms of Hinduism more in tune with their particular interests and sentiments. Into the space created by the separation of *adat* and *agama Hindu* erupted more radical movements. The one I wish to describe is the devotional movement centered on the Indian god-man Sri Sathya Sai Baba.[10]

Worship of Sai Baba began in Java in 1980 and was quickly introduced into Bali, where there are now centers all over the island with a small but growing total membership of about 10,000 people. Initially thought to be communist and subversive, it was almost banned, but has over the last five years become respectable. It is radically different from both *adat* and *agama Hindu*. It preaches a universalistic message of love, charity, and salvation through devotion to Sai Baba, denies any role to priests, is relatively egalitarian, uses only a few simple offerings, enjoins the spiritual development of the individual, and imposes few burdens of time and money on its members, who are free to come and go as they please. Its services are conducted in Indonesian not Balinese, and members dress in ordinary white clothes rather than the traditional dress required for Balinese ceremonies. Its central act is the singing of devotional hymns alongside prayers, meditation, a sermon, and the distribution of holy water and holy ash.

One of the main reasons people give for joining the movement is that they are unsatisfied with *adat* ritual traditions, which some find increasingly difficult to understand. Many Balinese now ask questions of their traditional religion to which they cannot get answers. They are perplexed by mechanical and excessive ritual and when they ask parents, teachers, and priests to explain the point and purpose of these ceremonies, they are usually given the standard Balinese answer: *"mula keto,"* that's how it is. Many accuse priests of being unable or unwilling to divulge the sacred knowledge that they are supposed to obtain from immersion in the palm leaf texts. Consequently more and more Balinese view *adat* as having strayed from the path of true religion, as being mired in incomprehensible ritual, and as having been exploited by the venal motives of greedy priests. Devoting oneself to Sai Baba and imbibing his messages of simple love and charity seem to provide an emotional attachment and a spiritual understanding that cannot be obtained from either *adat* religion or the abstruse doctrines of *agama Hindu*.

These forms of Hinduism are all doctrinal but in different ways. *Adat* is ritually doctrinal in the sense in which I described late medieval Christianity. It is a highly collective religion revolving around the performance of frequent, repetitive, and routinized ceremonies presided over by priests who, in their religious texts, are supposed to be the holders of doctrinal knowledge. This knowledge, however, is less about ethics and the right way to live, and much more about how to enact the ceremonies. There is no loop of rhetorical questions and answers, and traditionally priests are not sermonizers. Priests make sure the correct offerings are made and placed in the appropriate positions and that the correct prayers are uttered. Many of these ceremonies cannot be performed without considerable assistance from kin, neighbors, friends, and clients, and it is the mutual reciprocal obligations of labor and materials that produce small and cohesive communities. Attempts to simplify and reduce the costs of such ceremonies by using small amounts of offerings and limited outside labor, which other forms of Hinduism encourage in their desire to ethicize religion and free it from excessive ritual, lead to accusations of meanness and an uncaring attitude to those the rituals are supposed to benefit. With the possible exception of tooth filing, which most Balinese describe as only mildly distressing, there are no violent rituals to provide the episodic memories that cement participants together; there are in fact no initiation rituals that have a wider participation than the members of an extended family. While this religion is hierarchical, not particularly emotionally satisfying, and highly repetitive and possesses fairly uniform beliefs and practices, all of which Whitehouse associates with the doctrinal mode, it also evinces aspects that are supposedly characteristic of the imagistic mode, such as small-scale and particularistic face-to-face communities, high social cohesion, and an absence of proselytization (Whitehouse 1995: 197), features that are forged through regular social contact throughout a lifetime of living together.

Agama Hindu is obviously doctrinal since it consists of strings of verbal dogma that are internally consistent and coherent. And true to the notion of doctrinal religiosity, it has helped forge a sense of an imagined Balinese community that is much wider than anything that existed hitherto (Picard 1999, Vickers 1987) and that supersedes the much more traditional and parochial identities founded on village, caste, and occupation. As this new religion took shape in the 1920s and was elaborated from the 1950s onwards, priests, intellectuals, and religious leaders constructed a discourse that placed Hindu religion at the base of Balinese culture. In one botanical metaphor, religion is the root, *adat* (customary knowledge and ritual practice) is the trunk, and the plastic and performing arts are the leaves and branches (Picard 1999:17). In trying to embed *agama Hindu* into Balinese society, the Parisada attempts to homogenize religious belief and practice across the island, and encourages priests to sermonize and instruct the population on right belief. One outcome of this is that, at least for urban intellectuals and the middle class, *agama Hindu* has come to be seen as the symbol of a collective Balinese identity (*kebalian*), which differentiates Balinese from Muslims and Christians. In this sense *agama Hindu* typifies Whitehouse's doctrinal religiosity better than any other Hinduism in Bali.

The issue of identity is interesting. Whereas *adat* tends to facilitate multiple and narrow identities based on local allegiances, and *agama Hindu* facilitates a broader Balinese identity based on a homogenizing state-imposed orthodoxy and difference from members of other *agama*, devotion to Sai Baba has tended to produce an even more inclusive identity. Sri Sathya Sai Baba is an Indian man whom most Balinese devotees have never seen in the flesh. Yet they have an intense emotional commitment to him, yearning to see and touch him, dreaming of him, carrying pictures of him everywhere, and sometimes on the verge of tears when they speak of his place in their lives. Moreover, during the singing of devotional hymns many devotees appear transfixed and in a trancelike state. Meetings at the center in Bali's capital Denpasar are attended by Balinese from all over south Bali, who often do not know each other. Quite regularly there are members attending from overseas, and Balinese give talks about their visits to Baba's ashram in which, amongst other things, they speak of their meetings with devotees from Africa, Australia, the United States, and elsewhere. For many long-time devotees the attachment to Baba becomes so strong that it encourages the formation of an identity that is removed from concerns that are peculiarly Balinese. The acceptance of a universal message marks out devotees as increasingly committed to a global world. This new identity is about the individual in his or her specific relationship to the universal God. Through a quest for personal realization devotees procure the conditions for establishing new spiritual relationships with others from very different cultural backgrounds, with Baba acting as the fixed center drawing them all into a community of equals.

One especially interesting facet of the worship of Sai Baba is that this intense emotional devotion, focused also on iconic imagery of Baba, especially his feet, and which could be seen as characteristically imagistic, is not accompanied by bonds of fellowship with other members, as one might expect of such an apparently imagistic practice, possibly because each devotee undertakes his or her journey of spiritual development independently of others. When devotees attend the meetings they come individually or in small family groups, immediately sit down in regimented rows of segregated men and women, meditate silently, and engage in very little conversation with neighbors. When the service finishes some ninety minutes later, most simply get up and return to their neighborhoods and villages where they may be the only representatives of the movement. While clearly some friendships are made, the organization is based essentially on each individual's dyadic tie to Sai Baba, and not to other devotees. There is no social organization to speak of, no dues payable for membership, no register of members, and no duties to perform. Such high emotional stimulation is not therefore associated with cohesive face-to-face communities. Nor is it particularly associated with stability of membership or an absence of the tedium effect: Several apparently dedicated members I met in 1997 did not appear at any service during the months of July and August in 1999.

Conversely, despite its repetitive and routinized rituals, and the distinct lack of the kind of emotional arousal associated with Sai Baba, boredom with *adat* religion is rarely mentioned and rarely on display. Women who have to produce offerings on an almost daily basis often hint at the burden, and may be scolded should they complain, but the majority of Balinese, while sometimes voicing discontent about the mechanical nature of this ritual, thoroughly enjoy their ceremonies. Ceremonial days are very lively, boisterous, fun affairs, with evening entertainments in which the whole village engages, producing the highly valued atmosphere the Balinese call *rame*.

These different forms of Hinduism are not exclusive. Indeed, according to members, devotion to Sai Baba provides a rational justification for participating in village *adat* rituals because the love of Baba and the simple philosophy he expounds supply a meaning to the ceremonies that is otherwise lacking. Devotees say that they therefore become more diligent in their *adat* religious obligations. Moreover *agama Hindu* and devotionalism aver that they are true to the ancient Hindu religion from which *adat* has deviated through overreliance on ritual, and hence their aim is to return *adat* to its more authentic form. From an outsider's point of view the three forms of Hinduism are different, but to a Balinese there is often little contradiction in adhering to all of them.

This short survey of Balinese Hinduisms suggests that any association between the doctrinal mode, types of social organization, degrees of emotional arousal, and forms of identity is difficult to make. *Adat* is characterized by high social cohesion in small, face-to-face communities and by multiple, parochial identities, but also by highly repetitive and routinized rituals with little evidence of a tedium effect. Conversely, Sai Baba devotionalism is characterized by high emotional arousal but also by large-scale, anonymous, imagined communities and a globally constituted identity.

Conclusion

I have tried to show that the nature of the doctrinal religiosity cannot be specified with any great precision. In some forms many of the characteristics Whitehouse identifies as social correlates of the doctrinal mode are clearly present, but in other forms they are not, and such latter forms may exhibit features more appropriate to the imagistic mode. One reason for this may be that in many religious traditions doctrinal and imagistic practices coexist, as Whitehouse (2000: 1) notes. But this is where the problem lies. In a table Whitehouse (1995: 197) summarizes the characteristics of each mode that then delineate the two ideal types. However, if a social correlate supposedly intrinsic to the imagistic mode is found within what is otherwise a doctrinal religion, how do we know this is an instance of coexistence rather than a problem with the theory? For example, in Sai Baba one finds high emotional and sensual stimulation (imagistic mode) both in personal devotion to Baba and during the singing of devotional hymns. However, this is not accompanied by an enduring and intense face-to-face community, which is almost absent, but rather by a diffuse, large-scale, anonymous, and imagined community (doctrinal mode). A different way of conceptualizing the coexistence of doctrinal and imagistic practices is to argue that, because of the tedium effect to which doctrinal religions are prone, religious fervor needs to be periodically renewed through imagistic practices (Whitehouse 2000: 126). In PNG this is often the case, but usually in the form of splinter groups breaking away from the mainstream and recodifying dogma in iconic imagery (Whitehouse 2000: 128–29). However, this is not what happens in Sai Baba, where the intense emotion of singing devotional hymns is at the very core of the movement and a constitutive part of the process of building the broad imagined community.

There seems therefore to be an intractable problem in how to identify particular practices as imagistic or doctrinal. Thus, the singing of devotional hymns, while emotionally arousing, is also a highly repetitive and routinized activity. Is it therefore imagistic or doctrinal? While Whitehouse (2000: 125) justifiably denies that he is concerned with a typology by which different religions may be classified, it is hard to resist the impression that he typologizes memory operations, practices, and social processes, and without providing many clues as to how to identify these as belonging to either imagistic or doctrinal modes. One might argue that it is not the activity itself that should be classified, but the disposition of the individual to the activity. In other words for those who find the singing boring, and there are some, it is doctrinal, while for others it is imagistic. I am not sure if this is a productive solution because dispositions change and are difficult to specify, and it still puts the stress on typologizing.

Such problems may arise because the theory seems burdened by an overemphasis on the logical connections between biological, psychological, and social processes, leading to a somewhat deterministic view of the relationship between kinds of memory operation and forms of social organization that, as a by-product, underestimates the significance of immediate social contexts. Whitehouse (2000: 4, 10) is surely correct to challenge Durkheim's devaluation of the influence of psychological processes on social processes but in doing so removes the contingency from this relationship that anthropologists have so often argued for. Part of the difficulty here concerns the very particular circumstances in which the theory has been worked out. In PNG the ideal types fit very closely to the empirical religions on the ground, missionary Christianity being very doctrinal and cultic religion being very imagistic, but conditions in Bali and elsewhere are quite different.

A further problem with the category of doctrinal religiosity is that it is very broad and heterogeneous, and thus cannot be reduced to a series of specific correlated themes. If it is problematic to identify a particular practice as imagistic or doctrinal, it becomes doubly hard to identify which practices cohere together. As I have tried to show, different forms of social organization, different kinds of identities, and different degrees of emotional arousal are associated with religions that, while basically doctrinal, are so in different ways. If doctrinal religions can vary so much, is that also the case with imagistic religions? But that is a problem for others to explore.

Notes

I wish to thank Stephen Hugh-Jones, Susan Bayly, and the editors for their perceptive comments and helpful suggestions on earlier versions of this chapter.

1. In fact, as Whitehouse explains, schematic and episodic memory are universal features of cognition, but they have different ramifications in doctrinal and imagistic modes of religiosity.

2. This is not strictly true since many writers (for example, Muir 1997: chapter 6; Scribner 1987a) have pointed out how ritual came in through Protestantism's back door.

3. For general surveys of the Reformation, see Dickens (1989), McGrath (1999), Cameron (1991), and Scribner (1986); for an excellent overview of the Humanist background to Reformation thought, see Nauert (1995).

4. On the diversity of Reformation views of the real presence, see McGrath (1999), Karant-Nunn (1997), and Cameron (1991).

5. It would be a mistake to think of this "cannibalism" as entirely negative. In the early Christian church, notions of the body, nutrition, digestion, change, and identity were central theological issues surrounding the problem of the resurrection of the body. How could the body be resurrected, and retain its identity, if it decayed and was eaten by beasts, birds, and fishes, whereupon its constituent elements would be scattered. According to Bynum (1995: 41), "the final victory must be the eating that does not consume, the decay that does not devour, . . . The fact that we eat God in the eucharist and are truly fed on his flesh and blood is a paradoxical redemption of that most horrible of consumptions: cannibalism." For a literary scholar's perspective on cannibalism in Eucharistic debates in early modern Europe, see Kilgour (1990).

6. It should be noted that if some of the criticisms of Eucharistic ritual raised crucial and difficult doctrinal problems, they could also be useful in removing skepticism. Exempla (moral tales) abounded in which those who doubted transubstantiation were visibly shown the miracle; in taking communion a doubter suddenly found himself gaping at a miniature Christ all bloody and wounded, or eating the wafer and suddenly tasting real blood. The tales end with the doubter convinced and chastened.

7. While the "tedium effect" no doubt played some part in the loss of commitment to reformed churches after the early phase of enthusiasm, it is not always clear whether it was boredom (because of the lack of images) or other factors that accounted for why people began to lose interest in reform from the middle of the sixteenth century. One such reason was the condemnation of the sacramentals on which the ordinary masses often relied. Another was the unfulfilled promises of reformers and preachers for social justice and social renewal. Scribner (1986: 32) notes that in the Zurich countryside peasants applied for remission of the tithe since it had no scriptural authority. When this was not granted the peasants began to hate their preachers.

8. For a considerably more detailed description and analysis of these forms of Hinduism, see Howe (1999, 2001).

9. For further background on these issues, see Picard (1990, 1999), Vickers (1989), and Bagus (1975).

10. For a stimulating discussion of Sai Baba devotionalism in India, see Babb (1986).

References

Asad, Talal. 1993. *Genealogies of Religion: Discipline and Reasons of Power in Christianity and Islam.* Baltimore: Johns Hopkins University Press.

Babb, Lawrence. 1986. *Redemptive Encounters: Three Modern Styles in the Hindu Tradition.* Berkeley: University of California Press.

Bagus, Gusti. 1975. "Surya Kanta: A Kewangsan Movement of the Jaba Caste in Bali." *Masyarakat Indonesia* 2: 153–62.

Bakker, Frik. 1993. *The Struggle of the Hindu Balinese Intellectuals: Developments in Modern Hindu Thinking in Independent Indonesia.* Amsterdam: VU University Press.

Barth, Frederik. 1975. *Ritual and Knowledge among the Baktaman of New Guinea.* New Haven, Conn.: Yale University Press.

———. 1987. *Cosmologies in the Making: A Generative Approach to Cultural Variation in Inner New Guinea.* Cambridge: Cambridge University Press.

Bossy, John. 1983. "The Mass as a Social Institution, 1200–1700." *Past and Present* 100: 29–61.

———. 1985. *Christianity in the West, 1400–1700.* Oxford: Oxford University Press.

Burke, Peter. 1987. "The Repudiation of Ritual in Early Modern Europe." In his *The Historical Anthropology of Early Modern Italy: Essays on Perception and Communication*, pp. 223–39. Cambridge: Cambridge University Press.

Bynum, Caroline Walker. 1987. *Holy Feast and Holy Fast: The Religious Significance of Food to Medieval Women.* Berkeley: University of California Press.

———. 1995. *The Resurrection of the Body in Western Christianity, 200–1336.* New York: Columbia University Press.

Cameron, Euan. 1991. *The European Reformation.* Oxford: Clarendon Press.

Collinson, Patrick. 1997. "From Iconoclasm to Iconophobia: The Cultural Impact of the Second English Reformation." In Peter Marshall (ed.), *The Impact of the English Reformation, 1500–1640*, pp. 278–307. London: Arnold.

Dickens, A. G. 1989. *The English Reformation.* London: Batsford

Dickens, A. G., and Whitney Jones. 2000. *Erasmus the Reformer.* London: Methuen.

Duffy, Eamon. 1992. *The Stripping of the Altars: Traditional Religion in England, 1400–1580.* New Haven, Conn.: Yale University Press.

Eire, Carlos. 1986. *War against the Idols: The Reformation of Worship from Erasmus to Calvin.* Cambridge: Cambridge University Press.

Geertz, Clifford. 1973. "'Internal Conversion' in Contemporary Bali." In his *The Interpretation of Cultures*, pp. 170–189. London: Hutchinson

Holt, Mack. 1995. *The French Wars of Religion, 1562–1629.* Cambridge: Cambridge University Press.

Howe, Leo 1999. "Sai Baba in Bali: Identity, Social Conflict and the Politics of Religious Truth." *Review of Indonesian and Malaysian Affairs* 33: 115–145.

———. 2001. *Hinduism and Hierarchy in Bali.* Oxford: James Currey.

Karant-Nunn, Susan. 1997. *The Reformation of Ritual: An Interpretation of Early Modern Germany.* London: Routledge.

Kilgour, Maggie. 1990. *From Communion to Cannibalism: An Anatomy of Metaphors of Incorporation.* Princeton, N.J.: Princeton University Press.

Lambert, Malcolm. 1992. *Medieval Heresy: Popular Movements from the Gregorian Reform to the Reformation.* Oxford: Blackwell.

Le Goff, Jacques. 1984. *The Birth of Purgatory.* Chicago: University of Chicago Press.

McGrath, Alister. 1999. *Reformation Thought: An Introduction.* Oxford: Blackwell.

Muir, Edward. 1997. *Ritual in Early Modern Europe.* Cambridge: Cambridge University Press.

Nauert, Charles. 1995. *Humanism and the Culture of Renaissance Europe.* Cambridge: Cambridge University Press.

Parker, Lyn. 1992. "The Quality of Schooling in a Balinese Village." *Indonesia* 54: 95–116.

Picard, Michel. 1990. "Kebalian Orang Bali: Tourism and the Uses of 'Balinese Culture' in New Order Indonesia." *Review of Indonesian and Malaysian Affairs* 24: 1–37.

———. 1999. "The Discourse of Kebalian: Transcultural Constructions of Balinese Identity." In Raechelle Rubinstein and Linda Connor (eds.), *Staying Local in the Global Village: Bali in the Twentieth Century,* pp. 15–49. Honolulu: University of Hawaii Press.

Rubin, Miri 1991. *Corpus Christi: The Eucharist in Late Medieval Culture.* Cambridge: Cambridge University Press.

Scribner, Richard. 1986. *The German Reformation.* London: MacMillan Press.

———. 1987a. "Ritual and Reformation." In his *Popular Culture and Popular Movements in Reformation Germany,* pp. 103–122. London: The Hambledon Press.

———. 1987b. "Demons, Defecation and Monsters: Popular Propaganda for the German Reformation." In his *Popular Culture and Popular Movements in Reformation Germany,* pp. 277–99. London: The Hambledon Press.

Thomas, Keith. 1973. *Religion and the Decline of Magic.* Harmondsworth: Penguin.

Vickers, Adrian. 1987. "Hinduism and Islam in Indonesia: Bali and the Pasisir." *Indonesia* 44: 31–58.

———. 1989. *Bali: A Paradise Created.* Berkeley: Periplus.

Whitehouse, Harvey. 1995. *Inside the Cult: Religious Innovation and Transmission in Papua New Guinea.* Oxford: Oxford University Press.

———. 2000. *Arguments and Icons: Divergent Modes of Religiosity.* Oxford: Oxford University Press.

Religious Doctrine or Experience: A Matter of Seeing, Learning, or Doing

9

GILBERT LEWIS

IN *ARGUMENTS AND ICONS*, WHITEHOUSE (2000) has put forward a theory of divergent modes of religiosity. He supports it with persuasive examples of religious experience and practice drawn particularly from Papua New Guinea. There are, he finds, two contrasting modes: the doctrinal mode, depending on frequent repetition and instruction and semantic memory, and the imagistic mode, depending on rare performance and episodic memory after the initial shock or surprise of experiencing the ritual action. The two contrasting forms are transmitted and develop in different ways, but they can occur together in a single tradition and interact with each other. He analyzes the complex connections that depend on these fundamental (cognitive) contrasts and discusses how this theory might correlate with and illuminate previous theories of religious transmission and development.

In accounts of many societies, without doubt it is possible to recognize cases that correspond strikingly well to one or the other of his two modes. But how should one test such a theory more widely against ethnographic or historical findings? There are problems with binary classifications in seeking empirical support for them. For with almost any contrasting pair that sets up two opposed or polar types (such as doctrinal/imagistic), it is possible to play a game of matching or equivalence and assign a particular test item more or less convincingly to one or the other of the poles. In that "more or less" lies the attraction and the trap of choices presented as binary oppositions—nature/culture, sacred/secular, yin/yang, ping/pong (Gombrich 1962: 312–51; Lewis 1980: 5). This potential was the principle at work in Osgood's semantic differential test in his measurements of associative meaning (Osgood, Suci, and Tannenbaum 1957). The problems come not with cases that clearly fit at one of the poles but with weak or ambiguous cases and the middle ground. I have the middle ground and mixed cases particularly in mind in this paper.

In societies without sacred texts or ordained priests to turn to, who or what constitutes the authority for religious practice or teachings? Who is to say what is or is not part of the religion or is or is not religious? For example, thinking of *Coral Gardens and Their Magic* by Malinowski (1935), what should go into an account of Trobriand religious life? It is difficult to see sharp boundaries setting off religion and religious practice from secular life. In many other places in Papua New Guinea, before colonization and missionaries came, we might well have been unsure what to include as part of their religion: should we include rites of passage, initiation into cults, taboos about certain foods and actions, ceremonies for ancestors, or certain practices associated with gardening, hunting, healing, ceremonial exchange, divination, sorcery, property protection, revenge, and redress? Should we attend to the religiosity shown in initiation and in gardening practices equally? Or should we measure religiosity by time spent or frequency? The list brings in such a mixture of activities, including ones that are exceptionally and intensely emotional and activities that are common or routine. Perhaps examples of both modes of religiosity could be found in more or less clearly typical forms, but then the empirical problem would turn on issues of distribution and prevalence, or analytically on the interpretation of patterns and salience. It might require time and historical records to see the direction and nature of changes and losses.

Should we look on the "mode of religiosity" as an attribute of the individual, the community, or the religion taken somehow as a whole? Both traditions and individuals can be mixed and inconsistent. Whitehouse notes (2002: 310), "It is precisely within those populations that lack access to the authoritative corpus of religious teachings, and so cannot be adequately motivated by those teachings, that we find the greatest profusion of imagistic practices." Without a centrally integrated religious system, people tend toward imagistic practice. In his sociology of religion, Weber (1965 [1922]: chapter 8) points out that priests, specialized in literacy, have access to the sacred scriptures and argues that priests have a vested interest in asserting their expertise and controlling religious knowledge. They tend to rationalize doctrine and make it coherent and explain or expunge contradictions.

In answer to questions about the frequency of religious experience raised by McCauley (2002: 27) and Sjöblom (2002: 35), Whitehouse takes an actor-centered view. He notes that measures of frequency should pertain only to individual participants (not populations and not mere observers). "Religious knowledge is transmitted or communicated more frequently in some societies than in others, and such variation obviously places correspondingly variable demands on memory" (Whitehouse 1992: 777). But surely the frequency of events to observe must partly depend on the size of the population under observation—the "pool" or "universe" supplying events.

Variation and innovation may be the result of failing or distorting memories. Fredrik Barth's Mountain Ok study *Cosmologies in the Making* (1987) is about processes of cultural transmission and transformation in nonliterate cultures. Those processes must include transmission, storage, retention, and repetition as Goody points out in the introduction.

When Barth first studied Baktaman religion at Bolovip, it had a population of 183 people (Barth 1975). Empirical factors to consider therefore must include: size of the group, length of time to see, intimacy and opportunity, distribution, how many observed, for how long, rules on secrecy and sacredness, public or private contexts, and frequency of repetition. In an isolated small community (e.g., of 183 people), the premature deaths of two or three senior men might be tantamount to the loss of a large part of the encyclopedia of religious knowledge if the transmission of that knowledge through practice was secret and confined to a few people at long intervals. Frankel (1986: 16–26) and Errington and Gewertz (1987: chapter I) describe Papua New Guinean examples of people explicitly aware of the risks of losing religious knowledge through premature deaths. Barth (1987: 26–27) also comments on the fear of loss that accompanies secrecy. The size of the population maintaining some practice or doctrine is presumably an important factor for religious continuity and variation.

In what follows, I try to focus on seeing, learning, and doing in the transmission of religious experience. First comes a question about the relative attention given to religious practice (orthopraxy) or religious doctrine (orthodoxy). The question was prompted by reading about Levitical sacrifice and something I noticed during a funeral at Rauit, a village in the West Sepik in Papua New Guinea. Later I wish to consider the changing nature of religious experience and action over the course of someone's life (with taboo as an example). In many cases, access to religious experience is controlled and different for men and women of the same society (e.g., in puberty ritual). I question how the difference in access to experience might affect modes of religiosity within one community.

The Big Toe Problem

Let me go straight to Leviticus and the instructions for the cleansing of the leper: "And he shall kill the he-lamb in the place where they kill the sin-offering and the burnt-offering, in the place of the sanctuary; for as the sin-offering is the priest's, so is the guilt-offering; it is most holy. And the priest shall take of the blood of the guilt-offering, and the priest shall put it upon the tip of the right ear of him that is to be cleansed, and upon the thumb of his right hand, and upon the great toe of his right foot" (Leviticus 14: 13–14). Chapter 14 states the law of the leper in the day of his cleansing. The instructions for the sacrifices are complicated, and much was needed: two clean small birds, cedar wood, scarlet, hyssop, running water, oil, three-tenths of an ephah of fine flour, two he-lambs without blemish, and one ewe-lamb of the first year without blemish, but alternative sacrificial animals and birds are then listed, "if he be poor and his means suffice not."

I had looked up Leviticus out of curiosity over attitudes to leprosy that I encountered among Gnau people at Rauit and government officials in the area (Lewis 1987). A small number of people with leprosy had been found there. The bit about putting blood on the tip of the right ear, thumb of the right hand, and great toe of the right foot caught my eye. Why that? I had seen a burial at Rauit in which a fiber string had been tied to run from a dead man's great toe to his penis to the hair on the top of his head, and from there it ran out of the earth covering his body in the grave and was tied to an upright stick. They gave no explanation for why these particular parts of the body were chosen, apart from saying that they would pull on the string to call his spirit to accompany them in a hunt to prepare for the subsequent mortuary ceremonial.

Was that burial practice something to place in the imagistic mode of religiosity? Did Old Testament sacrifice also belong in the imagistic mode? Or the doctrinal? Leviticus is not enlightening about why the ear, the toe, and the thumb were chosen. Leviticus is about the rules and the code of holiness. The sacrifices, including the identifying names for them, are part of a complex priestly system of sacrifice. The commandments of Leviticus are absolutely binding: They are in what is called "apodictic" form. The text commands what to do or not to do but does not provide explanation. The lack of explanation was stressed by Robertson Smith at the beginning of his *Lectures on the Religion of the Semites*: "Every one who reads the Old Testament with attention is struck with the fact that the origin and *rationale* of sacrifice are nowhere fully explained" (Smith 1901 [1889]: 3). He also writes, "Religion in primitive times was not a system of belief with practical applications; it was a body of fixed traditional practices, to which every member of society conformed as a matter of course. . . . Practice preceded doctrinal theory. Men form general rules of conduct before they begin to express general principles in words; political institutions are older than political theories, and in like manner religious institutions are older than religious theories" (Smith 1901 [1889]: 20). This sounds nearly tantamount to a theory of the evolution of modes of religiosity from imagistic to doctrinal.

Such a contrast between explicit rulings on practice but silence on matters of meaning also characterizes the Mishnah, a minutely detailed commentary by scholars[1] that goes into difficult points of procedure (e.g., what Rabbi Judah said about whether a man who had not a thumb on his right hand could ever have purification). Interpretation of the Mishnah was continued by later commentators such as Maimonides (1135–1204). He refused to follow symbolists in finding reasons for the details of the various sacrifices. In his *Guide for the Perplexed* (1904: part III, chapter 26), composed in Arabic in twelfth-century Egypt near Cairo, Maimonides writes, "We cannot say why one offering should be a lamb, whilst another is a ram; and why a fixed number of them should be brought. Those who trouble themselves to find a cause for any of these detailed rules, are in my eyes void of sense; they do not remove any difficulties, but rather increase them."

The position Maimonides takes is a rationalist's one. Some rules do remain perplexing. But to which mode of religiosity do the religious institutions seem to belong? The stress seems to be on practice rather than doctrine and meaning.

Ways of Alerting the Attention in Ritual

Certainly our attention may be caught by pain, by some of the strange or bloody things done in ritual. They work on the imagistic side. They may alert or provoke us to try to think of a reason for them. We may be tempted to suppose that they must be signifiers though we do not know what it is they signify. The peculiar things done in ritual thus may stimulate someone to "ungate" the way an object or action is seen so that he or she is free to look for further and further echoes to its sense (Gombrich 1965). But the stimulus does not necessarily communicate or convey a meaning, even though it may have a sharp or shocking effect.

The alerting quality in ritual varies. Many components of ritual are framing devices that identify a special arena: the aesthetic side of color, noise, and smell; the decorations; singing; the formality, stiffness, or strangeness of gesture; the tension created by anxiety or fearful expectation; excited chatter; constrained silence; awareness of the presence of rules; secrecy (Lewis 1980: 19–22, 25–32, 144). These different devices and elements can be analyzed in terms of stimulus, stimulus intensity, and sometimes communication (conveying meaning), and also in terms of their effects on performers and on spectators. As the alerting quality is variable in degree and intensity, so is the responsive effort to make any sense of them, and individuals vary in sensitivity, experience, and preparation.

"The style in ritual may tend towards clarity, overt meaning and lack of ambiguity; or for certain purposes aim to disconcert, confuse or fascinate. There are suggestive indications when the spectator is invited to 'ungate' through the isolation and situational oddity of some action or object in ritual" (Lewis 1980: 31). Thus the style of meaning (explicit or mysterious or disturbing) affects responses to different elements in ritual, including memory. If meanings are unfixed but practice fixed, that may be a factor in change and flexibility; it may be a strength for maintaining something while accommodating to change. There may be ritual occasions in which an object is held up and its symbolic meaning explicitly stated. (For example, in the Jewish Passover service text, the Haggadah, with the unleavened bread, the salt water, the bitter herbs, the roasted egg, the shankbone, etc., there is specific instruction in the text about the duty to teach and how to answer the wise son, the wicked son, the simple son, and the one who does not know how to ask.) But, as in the Leviticus example, what is clear and explicit about the ritual may be how to do it rather than its meaning. The recognition of rules or convention is a common feature that would apply to custom, etiquette, ceremony, and ritual, but these varieties of custom do not all have the quality of being peculiar or arresting to the same degree. Strikingly odd or frightening things done in ritual provoke a strong response. What I am arguing here is that there is a wide range of ways in which our attention may be caught and more subtle ways in which the peculiar quality of ritual may act on performers, participants, and audience.

Orthopraxy or Orthodoxy?

In the Leviticus example, the rabbinic authorities I quoted deliberate over questions of practice rather than questions of theological or symbolic meaning or moral justification.[2] Although the rules were fixed and explicit, problems might still come up about how to apply them in particular cases—questions of interpretation and the control of practice. Should we call this a matter of practical rather than doctrinal orthodoxy? Whitehouse contrasts the argument-centered doctrinal mode of religiosity with the imagistic iconic or nondoctrinal mode. How close is this to making a contrast between saying and doing—authoritative talking or sacred texts on the one hand and experience through practice on the other? Surely the Talmudic commentators and the rabbis must come into his doctrinal mode of religiosity. They were certainly concerned about being orthodox. But if the Whitehouse theory implies a contrast between doctrine (teachings and arguments, meaning and creed) and practice (memorable images; experience of surprise, pain, fear, trauma; effects on feelings and memory), would we need to make a further distinction between orthodoxy and orthopraxy, that is, between controls or routines about teachings and practice? Or do both belong equally in the doctrinal camp (as things to be controlled, disputed, and taught)?

The doctrinal mode depends on repetition and routine, but the imagistic mode exploits shock, exception, or rarity for its effect on memory. The difference is significant in the transmission of ritual (the "frequency hypothesis"). The contrast is striking in the examples of the imagistic mode Whitehouse cites (2002: 303)—"traumatic and violent initiation rituals, ecstatic practices of various cults, experiences of collective possession and altered states of consciousness, and extreme rituals involving homicide or cannibalism." They point to the psychological impact of shock, horror, ecstasy, or pain in ritual experience. They are linked to characteristics that he associates with the imagistic mode—nonverbal experience, first-time surprise or shock, rare repetition, flashbulb effect on memory, sense of revelation, episodic not semantic memory, lack of exegetical commentary, and motivation to spontaneous exegetical reflection.

Food Taboos: How Much of a Surprise or Shock?

Someone's attention may also be caught in more subtle ways. Certain rules may be continually present in the background of attention but jump to mind when broken. This was Radcliffe-Brown's social psychological explanation (1932: 94–97, 270–72, 276–79, 326–28) of the rules governing the period when an Andamanese boy or girl is *aka-op*: he or she must abstain for a certain length of time from each one of the more important foods of the community so that he or she will feel the moral force of the community acting on him or her. The period of abstention begins in the case of a girl at first menstruation, in the case of a boy when his back is cut. "Since the greater part of social life is the getting and eating of food, to place a person outside the social life would be to forbid him from partaking of food that is obtained by the society and consumed by it. . . . The same object is attained, however, by making the initiate abstain for a period from a number of the most important and relished foods" (Radcliffe-Brown 1932: 279). Fortes (1966) further observes how rules about food can bind a person to awareness of an aspect of his or her identity, imposing a constraint for the time the rule applies. What gives food taboos their power is the knowledge that something might be eaten and that others can eat it, but not the excluded individuals because they are who they are at that moment. If the food is there and can be eaten, though not by the excluded individuals, it thereby forces the individuals either to accept that identity and what goes with it, or to deny it or hide it, and eat.

During my fieldwork, the possibilities in food abstentions were richly exploited by the Gnau people to give a sense of sequence, succession, and pattern in ritual, and also in everyday life (Lewis 1980: 146–51): few foods were neutral, just food and always food to all persons. People generally knew the rules. Sometimes they would argue about details, for instance, what to do with a heron rarely shot, or a new variety of banana. But these were arguments about who could eat it and with which group of animal or plant to place it, not what the taboo meant. Despite the complex rules, answers about what would happen if a rule was broken were vague—premature breathlessness, decrepitude, no success in hunting or childbearing.

By this example of food taboos, I wish to suggest that religious rules can be matters of daily routine, yet still in some circumstances cause embarrassment, shock, or strong emotion. If the imagistic mode in ritual is identified with emotionally intense or traumatizing examples in mind, food taboos would be hard to place. Even though they may sometimes produce intense affective responses, they are often matters of daily routine and repetition.

The Frequency Hypothesis in Relation to Memory and Transmission

On processes in the transmission of religion, Audrey Richards (1967) suggests that the question of correlation between types of social structure and cosmology might be investigated most fruitfully in terms of differences in the social mechanisms for preserving knowledge of religious symbols, myths, and categories of experience and for passing them on to the next generation. She drew attention to institutions that provide for hereditary ownership of, or responsibility for, esoteric knowledge, making in effect groups that own and preserve *systèmes de connaissance* (as intellectual property). She noted the question of mnemonics: "Constantly repeated ritual by which ordinary members of the community acquire a knowledge of the meaning of symbols without direct instruction is one of these mechanisms, and all *rites de passage* are repeated constantly in the life of the individual. The Kriges state that a Lovedu girl is not considered fully initiated until she has witnessed the initiation ceremonies six times" (Richards 1967: 289). She notes that the use of picture designs, doggerel verse, tunes, and carvings can be understood as part of the mnemonic system of preliterate peoples. If it is true that elaborate cosmologies have a patchy distribution in Africa, we should seek explanation not only in terms of contacts with other peoples but also through study of the social mechanisms for preserving and passing on esoteric knowledge, study of the kinds of mnemonics that different peoples have been able to develop. In her study of a girl's initiation ceremony among the Bemba, *Chisungu* (1956), she analyzed the values taught by means of the songs and mimes that go with pottery emblems (she recorded forty-three of these), and how the emblems and designs acted as *aides-mémoire*.

Timing and Design in the Development of Experience and Understanding

Experience unfolds and accumulates. In ritual, the access to experience is often different for men and women. Chisungu is a purely feminine rite: "lighting the girl's fire," preparing her to receive her husband's "fire," begging for parenthood, giving the girl approaching marriage responsibility for a special pot with which she can in the future protect and purify herself and her husband, her hearth and fire. Bemba men say that, without Chisungu, a girl would be "an unfired pot;" no one would want to marry her, and she would not know what her fellow women knew. Bemba women say that it makes her grow, it teaches her, it makes her a woman. They say, with lowered eyes, Chisungu is to remove a girl's fear of blood and the danger of sex and fire. The ritual uses the device of the "marked stage," typical of all rites of role assumption (Richards 1956: 161–62): It gives the girl assurance she is fit to assume the new role; it has an element of ordeal or test about it.

Chisungu is the pivotal ritual containing a set of motifs, some of the key symbolic themes that run through other Bemba rituals (Ruel 1985). For all their major rites (including the rites of the agricultural year and the ceremonial of chiefship), Chisungu is a key. All major male ritual involving approach to the ancestors includes a formal act of sexual intercourse, which requires the controlling and purifying procedure done by the wife (taught to her in Chisungu).

In passing from infancy through childhood to maturity and on through it perhaps to old age, every person goes through considerable changes in understanding, emotional development, and social experience. With procedures that take place in adolescence such as initiation, puberty rites, and religious confirmation, we might ask whether the control and fixing of the ritual is timed to happen at that stage of life because it is most likely then to have lasting effects on outlook and feelings. Effects on the emotions and memory might well depend on the timing of exposure to initiation and other first-time critical procedures;[3] just as in matters of doctrine and responsibilities, maturity and intellectual capability might be critical to be able to take in some kinds of instruction. To form certain dispositions or habits may need repetitions of an action, particular kinesthetic experience, pain, and so forth. Social demands to take part in rituals correspond with a certain timing likely to shape certain responses. Although a single experience at a crucial stage may perhaps mark someone for life—and may be intended to—more often, I suspect, things are not so singular and lastingly critical; later experiences are likely to add to and modify first impressions and experiences. "We do not hold all our ideas with the same degree of conviction and we certainly do not do so throughout our lives" (Robertson 1996: 598). Robertson discusses the development of ideas and beliefs as an unfolding experience in which we construct understanding progressively through life through an active process of interrogation, speculation, and efforts to resolve inconsistencies.

Our interests change with our developing needs and capacities. We change from child to parent, youth to elder. The early stages of life are ones of acquisition and learning, the middle stages of consolidation, acting, and teaching, and the later stages of passing experience on. Thus Hinde (1999: chapter 7) considers religious belief from our earliest social exposure or experience under parental influence to increasingly questioned experience coconstructed as result of discourse between the child and adults. Susceptibilities vary with age as do interests and psychological dispositions. Religious experience and understanding will change over the course of someone's life. Keesing (1982: 30–39), in a chapter called "Encountering the Ancestors," introduces the reader to Kwaio ideas about their ancestors through the eyes and experience of a little girl, describing her growing awareness of rules warning her of dangers, where it's taboo for her to urinate, and the men's area which is "off limits" to her. "Why?" she asks at five years old; the answer: "Because men eat pig there." But later come her observations of adults talking to unseen presences and what her parents say about these beings, what she sees in her dreams and how her parents explain them to her, and the messages sent by ancestors. As the girl matures, so too does her grasp of differences between her own and other people's ancestors, the dangers and responsibilities that are tied to them, the differences between rules as they apply to her and to her brothers.

"What Exists, Exists in Change as Well as in Continuity"

Unfolding experience and changes in understanding and differentiation by gender are part of religious experience as well as of social practice and culture generally. At Rauit among the Gnau people, some special rules about the use of food were imposed for a boy's and a girl's puberty rites (Lewis 1980: chapter 4 and 7). I am going to focus on one motif to do with dried foods to show how the motif that appears in the puberty rites recurs in other rites, points to them, and is responded to differently by men and women. The girl's rite is set by her first menstrual period; the boy's rite is staged when he looks mature enough for the penis-bleeding he must undergo.

The Gnau understand the process of human maturing and aging through analogy with a plant growing, ripening, and withering: It involves a drying-out and toughening with age (Lewis 1980:134–40). They say fresh meat is full of water (*wor subat*): It is classed among *nem subagdem* ("fresh things," "watery things") in contrast to smoke-dried meat, which is *beirkatidem* ("dried-out").

A classification into *subagdem* or *beirkatidem* is used as the principle behind some food restrictions during the puberty rites. The things forbidden as *nem beirkatidem* ("dried-out things") are tobacco, betel nut, salt, coconut, smoked meat of any sort, and tubers or vegetables of any kind if cooked by direct roasting in a fire. All these things tend to be forbidden *en bloc* as like things. In contrast, vegetables that are boiled in water without salt and meat that is fresh and boiled in water are *subagdem* "fresh" or "watery" and permissible for the period when the *nem beirkatidem* are forbidden.

Women Tend to Stress the Nem Beirkatidem Rule at Puberty; Men Don't

In the puberty rites, the dried things are forbidden to boys and girls for a short time before the day on which their rites are done. If a girl has her first period, they must be imposed immediately; a boy is told to observe them in preparation for the day.[4] Release from the restriction comes on the day of the rites with the act of eating *teltug-nawugep* ("spinach-like leaves and ash-salt"). The girls and women who talked to me on a number of different occasions about the rites for girls always mentioned the restriction. It stood out in their accounts. With boys I did not hear of it or notice it at first but found out about the restriction because I asked. But in a different rite, the one for the birth of a first child, a very similar set of taboos is imposed on both the mother and the father of the newborn child. Both men and women spoke of it. Men made it sound a taxing and memorable feature of those rites. In the first-birth rites the restrictions are salient to both sexes, but in the puberty rites it was only girls or women who drew my attention to them.

The response of the actors to the same thing (the set of restrictions) is differently weighted, perhaps because of other things (e.g., painful penis-bleeding) that may happen in the rites. The things classed together as *nem beirkatidem* and forbidden before the day of the rites of puberty have something of the character of a recurrent motif. Restriction of the same things comes into force for a short period in the rites of puberty and for longer periods in both the Tambin rites of initiation and the rites surrounding the birth of a first child, and again, but for shorter periods, with subsequent children. The restriction on a set of things *en bloc* is what isolates them as a motif repeated in more than one kind of rite of passage, and a motif that points to a connection between the rites. For the couple's first birth, *nem beirkatidem* are restricted to the new mother and father from delivery of the first child[5] to the feast ending the pollution of birth attached to mother and child. Until then the mother and child are confined to her house and the husband cannot hold his child or touch his wife or enter her house for up to six weeks after the birth. The restriction for first childbirth thus may last up to six weeks but at puberty it lasts only a few days. On completion of the rites for the first birth, the marriage is established. The bridewealth, which had been received but stored away at marriage, was normally distributed only after the birth had confirmed the success of the marriage, together with a payment for this first birth.

The restriction observed for a short time during the puberty rites is thus repeated at childbirth, but stretched out over a longer time. The motif recurs and connects the two. From the point of view of a girl, marriage and having children are what perhaps stand out more than anything as the things in which she hopes for success and an ideal outcome. The rites to celebrate her first child's birth are longer and more magnificent than any other of the rites of passage she must undergo, and their timing is set by the birth, which is conspicuously her achievement, a climax and testing point in her life. Perhaps because the restrictions on *nem beirkatidem*, on smoking tobacco and chewing betel, provide a link to these rites marking her achievement and success, women give greater stress to them than men do when they talk about what they have to do in the puberty rites. For a woman, the restriction in the rites of puberty point forward to the rite for her first birth.

The boy's situation is different. His attention is deflected from the *nem beirkatidem* restriction to other things that happen at puberty, especially the penis-bleeding and (if it is done) the first making of his man's headdress. When as a young man, his wife bears their first child, then his attention to the *nem beirkatidem* restriction is conspicuous; it weighs on him as a privation. By association the restriction comes to be most eminently a thing attached to the rites for a new birth.

Although boys and girls must both observe the same restrictions on *nem beirkatidem*, they hold different links of significance for them. In fact, although I have discussed this restriction in isolation, there are other linked motifs that underscore and reinforce the parallels between these and other rites (Lewis 1980: 148–59).

Answers to direct questions about the meaning of the *nem beirkatidem* restriction varied with the person asked and the context in which the question was framed. If asked not in reference to a particular rite, answers were often of the nondescript sort: "It is our custom." If asked in reference to puberty, then the answer was "It is to make them grow well." If asked in reference to the first-birth rites, the most common reply was that if the mother or father broke the rule and smoked or chewed betel, the baby would cry a lot and be annoying; others said the restriction was so the baby would be well and not get sick or thin. An approach referring to the Tambin rites led most men to stress the contrasting value of *subagdem* meat for growth. The Tambin rites of initiation were perhaps the most complex and grandest of all their rites. They entailed long seclusion of young men (some of whom might be already married by then) inside the men's house. Confined perhaps for four or even six months, they said, they were forbidden *beirkatidem* meat but fed abundant boiled, fresh *subagdem* meat. As the days and weeks went by, the bones of the meat eaten were hung on a vine-rope around the men's house as a tally. This continued until they performed the series of special rites that led up to releasing them from the *nem beirkatidem* restriction and their eventual emergence from confinement magnificently decorated with headdress in a final dance and feasting. During confinement in the house, there were a whole lot of other practices in addition to eating the subagdem meat that were meant to foster good growth—avoiding fires, washing with cold water and nettles, sweating, taking certain herb preparations (Lewis 1980: 151–59). The practices as a whole were designed to benefit a young man's muscular growth and maintain the condition of his blood as full, fluid, and flowing. It was this association of good blood with growth, strength, life, and health that men tended to bring up to explain the rules in Tambin. It seemed appropriate then to learn that a sick man should refuse *nem beirkatidem* and that, in the past, a man who had killed someone was forbidden to eat anything *except nem beirkatidem* for the few days of seclusion in the rites called Lyigat, which followed immediately after killing someone.

There is a sequence in Gnau food restriction rules and a sequence in human development, and the two are linked. The motif of restriction on *nem beirkatidem* comes first as a rule for the individual alone to observe at his or her own puberty, while at the first birth the rule is binding on the couple, the husband and wife together. Marriage followed quite soon after puberty in the past, and people said that the Tambin rites often came at a time in the man's life when he had already become a father. Then in the seclusion in Tambin, the restriction on *nem beirkatidem* was necessarily an experience closely shared by a set of coinitiate men, sleeping, they said, in the spirit presence brought into the men's house, in seclusion and apart from women. Outside, the mothers, sisters, and the wives of the men who "slept in the song spirit" might avoid *nem beirkatidem* in sympathy.

The meanings connected with *nem beirkatidem* begin with a common theme, growth, given the sense of increase in size and strength, health and beauty. Then later they focus on achievement and men and women stress different things— hunting and killing came increasingly to the fore as the criteria of successful male achievement, while having children and raising a family stand out as those for a woman. People would often interpret action in puberty rites in a future light, so the significance they saw for boys and girls diverged. What is done without necessary explanation is open to comment or reflection. Experience may throw a different light on what is done, particularly when a man has learned more about the preparation and collection of herbs and materials to be used in the rites. The significance of the same motif thus may come to differ for men and women.

"What exists, exists in change as well as in continuity," writes Jack Goody in regard to the Bagre myth (1972: 14).[6] I have argued that the understanding of a ritual motif may derive from an unfolding and changing experience. It is not necessarily fixed or the same for men and women. Women are excluded from the possibility of knowing some of the experiences that men go through; vice versa, men are excluded from some of the experiences to which women have access. Forge (1966) and Tuzin (1980: 258–83) have both reported from the middle Sepik how in the view of local men (Abelam and Arapesh) full religious understanding is reached only after experiencing all the stages both as initiate and later as initiator. It is not enough to know in theory what should be done. The actual experience of going through a rite is necessary.

For a religion to be alive (and not just entombed in texts), it must be practiced. It exists in knowledge and practice. It must be present in particular people's experience. The distribution of experience and religious representations is bound to be nonuniform. Possibilities of access depend on age and sex and rules. Men's and women's experience and perspectives may then differ significantly even though we write that they have the same religion. This was already evident as a theme in Gregory Bateson's analysis of Naven (1958 [1936]), focused on the contrast between Iatmul men's and women's ethos.

The Authority of Experience

Ethnographers usually would like to hear from an authority what should be done or said—they look for orthodoxy and orthopraxy. We tend to seek out the most coherent, articulate, and experienced and, if we can, the wisest and most insightful—a Muchona, an Ogotommeli, a guru, a shaman. Perhaps then we err in searching for the expert and misconstrue order since, in Weber's view (1965 [1922]: chapter 8), the general effect of the priest in his role as religious specialist was an increasing rationalization of religion, the justification of doctrine, the ironing out of contradictions, and the making of coherence. The highest authority is not likely then to be the example to take for what is typical or common about religiosity in a particular society. However, authority may depend on various conditions: such as experience or knowledge or revelation. It requires social recognition or legitimation.

In matters of doctrine, claims to have authority turn on access to sacred texts, an original myth or charter, secret knowledge, or special qualification, for instance, a qualification by birth-right, literacy, ordination, election as Pope, infallibility ex cathedra, completion of all Tambaran stages as both initiate and initiator (Forge 1966; Tuzin 1980: 30, 268). In matters of practice a claim to authority depends on having done something or been through it (as Whitehouse's remarks on individual participation and the contrast between doctrinal and imagistic modes imply). Jackson (1983) describes the directness of knowing through personal bodily experience. By contrast with learning by observation and explanation, ritual practice imparts religious knowledge directly through personal experience. In much of our daily lives, we do things without asking explicitly what is the meaning of an act—one does not ask what is the meaning of cooking or cutting wood; one does it and experiences the effect.

Orthopraxy may entail such a claim to authority: It does not necessarily have to be formulated in words as doctrinal or symbolic meanings or moral concepts. That position comes close to an argument for the authority of revelation (which Whitehouse makes implicitly in connecting the imagistic mode with revelation). It is also quite close to a fideist position on experience: "The argument for the validity of the experience is this: you cannot understand what a certain kind of pain is except by feeling it; you cannot know what 'scarlet' means except by seeing it; you cannot grasp what belief in God means except by the grace of faith. For the fideist, to know God is to love him; there is no theoretical understanding of the reality of God; no way of grasping it by analysis and reasoning" (Lewis 1994: 581).

Mode of Religiosity: An Attribute of the Individual, the Community, or the Religion?

At the outset of this chapter, I asked whether to regard the "mode of religiosity" as an attribute of the individual, the community, or the religion. In his comments on measures of religiosity, Harvey Whitehouse emphasizes individual experience; he makes clear that the measures pertain to individuals, not populations. I have tried to bring out in this paper that individuals' attitudes and responses to their religion are likely to vary with context, age, and experience. The effects of religious teaching and practice change over the course of someone's life. That is not surprising given the regularities, the flow and accidents of life, for which religion is variously called on to provide some response. I would not therefore find it easy to say, except in approximate terms, that an individual followed the principle of the one rather than the other mode of religiosity. This is partly because dichotomies seem too convenient and simple to be adequate to the complexity of people's lives and reactions. If the mode of religiosity is, however, seen as an attribute of a community, then we need some way of assessing the distribution and prevalence of attitudes and the frequency of religious experience and practice. It is not easy to measure, and to complicate matters, we often give more weight to the unusual. We may choose the most striking religious actions or events to characterize the whole. One needs to take note (Richards 1956: 139, also 13, 61–62) that the ceremony of Chisungu witnessed in 1931 by Audrey Richards, and analyzed by her so convincingly to show its significance for Bemba women and Bemba culture more generally, had been suppressed by missionaries, as she noted, for the preceding thirty to fifty years and that Audrey Richards herself was the sponsor of the ceremony (*mwine*—the owner of the ceremony). With ethnographic accounts of major Melanesian cults or rites of initiation, it is sometimes hard to be clear what has been witnessed by the ethnographer and what has been described from a report of the past or a ceremony now defunct, whether it has been described from firsthand observation or secondhand knowledge. With male cults and initiations, it is hard to know what the other sex might see and think about them. To the extent that much significance is attributed to such rites, one is sometimes left wondering about the explanation for their loss or abandonment, and what that would imply about a mode of religiosity. In the case of the Tambin rites, which people at Rauit had tried to get going more than once around the time of my first visit, people offered a number of reasons for why they had not completed them. It seemed to me possible, reflecting on what they told me and what I had seen, that the pattern of practice in the initiation to Tambin had helped them to understand and adapt to the spells of plantation labor that young men were expected at that time to go through.

The timing, absence, and the pressures on a young man to prove himself led them to see correspondences to the seclusion in Tambin, or to mold certain actions during the plantation experience to make them so. They did something to assimilate the two experiences to a common pattern (Lewis 1980: 212–215). The new experiences and changed needs had begun to alter and substitute for the values and feelings evoked by the practice of Tambin. In considering the mode of religiosity as an attribute of the community, observations of change over time and loss—clearly historical information—would be, I think, especially revealing about the transmission and effects of religious practice. Of the third way in which we might regard "mode of religiosity"—that is, as an attribute of a religion taken somehow as a whole—I recognize that Harvey Whitehouse did not perhaps intend his theory to be understood in that way. But in practice I think many of us are liable to think of examples of "modes of religiosity" in terms of religions or religions in particular places—Baktaman religion as imagistic, orthodox Judaism as doctrinal. And if for a moment we do so, then social questions about the institutions, the nature, and size of the society; the role of literacy in it; and the organization of religious teaching and political control flock forward as part of what is needed for an understanding of the kinds of religious experience and practice that are afforded within that religion.

Notes

1. The title *Mishnah* comes from a Hebrew root meaning "to repeat" and refers to the method of teaching the Torah. Without a written text, the oral teaching had to be fixed in memory by dint of repetition.

2. There was in addition another strong tradition of exposition of Biblical texts, *Midrash* (from a Hebrew root meaning "to teach, to investigate"), which included a wide range of interpretative comments, historical, and metaphysical and ethical reflections on the text.

3. When is an impressionable age? Is the ethnologists' notion of imprinting at all relevant? Imagine, for example, the effects of experiencing circumcision as an infant a few days old or a few weeks old versus circumcision in late childhood or at puberty or at twenty-one—the contrast, for example, of Orthodox Jewish, Merina, Egyptian Muslim, and Gisu timing and procedures.

4. The restriction should be imposed as soon as the girl lets someone know she has menstruated for the first time. It is done in a curious way: a senior man of her hamlet or clan is called; a breadfruit (*genanget*) is baked, which he then breaks in half, placing the girl's great toe—the big toe again—between the two hot halves and bending her sandwiched toe sharply downward so as to make it crack. A boy is merely told to observe the restrictions.

5. The moment of delivery of the child is the moment when the cord is cut. As soon as it is cut, the placental end is tied around the mother's big toe lest, so they say, it might go back into her belly and the placenta be not expelled. Women give birth in a squatting position, and I saw that the cord was indeed tied round the toe on the few occasions when I was asked to assist at the delivery. But they did not agree, when I asked later with a direct suggestion, that this was why the action with the breadfruit was done at the time of first menstruation.

6. Goody's books on the Bagre myth of the LoDagaa of Northern Ghana (Goody 1972 and Goody and Gandah 1981, 2003) must, I suppose, constitute the most minutely detailed empirical study and analysis of memory and variation in religious performances

depending on a purely oral tradition—recitations of the same sacred narrative or myth involving thousands of short verses in ritual performances recorded at intervals over more than twenty years (see also Goody 1997: 153–81).

References

Barth, Fredrik. 1975. *Ritual and Knowledge among the Baktaman of New Guinea*. New Haven, Conn.: Yale University Press.

———. 1987. *Cosmologies in the Making: A Generative Approach to Cultural Variation in Inner New Guinea*. Cambridge: Cambridge University Press.

Bateson, Gregory. 1958 [1936]. *Naven*. Stanford: Stanford University Press.

Errington, F., and D. Gewertz. 1987. *Cultural Alternatives and a Feminist Anthropology*. Cambridge: Cambridge University Press.

Forge, Anthony. 1966. "Art and Environment in the Sepik." *Proceedings of the Royal Anthropological Institute for 1965*, 23–31.

Fortes, Meyer. 1966. "Totem and Taboo." *Proceedings of Royal Anthropological Institute*, 5–22.

Frankel, Stephen. 1986. *The Huli Response to Illness*. Cambridge: Cambridge University Press.

Gombrich, E. H. 1962. *Art and Illusion: A Study in the Psychology of Pictorial Representation*. London: Phaidon Press.

———. 1965. "The Use of Art for the Study of Symbols." *American Psychologist* 20: 35–50.

Goody, Jack. 1972. *The Myth of the Bagre*. Oxford: Clarendon Press.

———. 1997. *Representations and Contradictions*. Oxford: Blackwells.

Goody, J., and S. W. D. K. Gandah. 1981. *Une Recitation du Bagre*. Paris: Armand Colin.

———. 2003. *The Third Bagre: A Myth Revisited*. Durham, N.C.: Carolina Academic.

Hinde, Robert. 1999. *Why Gods Persist: A Scientific Approach to Religion*. London: Routledge.

Jackson, Michael. 1983. "Knowledge of the Body." *Man* 18: 327–45.

Keesing, Roger M. 1982. *Kwaio Religion: The Living and the Dead in a Solomon Island Society*. New York: Columbia University Press.

Lewis, Gilbert. 1980. *Day of Shining Red: An Essay on Understanding Ritual*. Cambridge: Cambridge University Press.

———. 1987. "A Lesson from Leviticus: Leprosy." *Man* 22: 593–612.

———. 1994. "Magic, Religion and the Rationality of Belief." In Tim Ingold (ed.), *Companion Encyclopedia of Anthropology*, pp. 563–90. London: Routledge.

McCauley, Robert N. 2002. "Theoretical Arguments Are Not Icons." *Journal of Ritual Studies* 16: 23–29.

Maimonides, Moses. 1904. *The Guide for the Perplexed*, trans. M. Friedlander. London: Routledge and Kegan Paul, Ltd.

Malinowski, Bronislaw. 1935. *Coral Gardens and Their Magic*. 2 vols. London: Allen and Unwin.

Osgood, C. E., G. Suci, and P. H. Tannenbaum. 1957. *The Measurement of Meaning*. Urbana: University of Illinois Press.

Radcliffe-Brown, A. R. 1932. *The Andaman Islanders*. Cambridge: Cambridge University Press.

Richards, Audrey I. 1956. *Chisungu: A Girl's Initiation Ceremony among the Bemba of Northern Rhodesia*. London: Faber and Faber.

———. 1967. "African Systems of Thought: An Anglo-French Dialogue." *Man* 2: 286–98.

Robertson, A. F. 1996. "The Development of Meaning: Ontogeny and Culture." *Journal of Royal Anthropological Institute* 2: 591–610.

Ruel, Malcolm. 1985. "Growing the Girl." *Cambridge Anthropology* 10: 45–55.

Sjöblom, Tom. 2002. "Review of *Arguments and Icons*." *Journal of Ritual Studies* 16: 34–37.

Smith, W. Robertson. 1901 [1889]. *Lectures on the Religion of the Semites: The Fundamental Institutions*. London: A. and C. Black.

Tuzin, Donald F. 1980. *The Voice of the Tambaran: Truth and Illusion in Ilahita Arapesh Religion.* Berkeley: University of California Press.

Weber, Max. 1965 [1922]. *The Sociology of Religion*. London: Methuen.

Whitehouse, Harvey. 1992. "Memorable Religions: Transmission, Codification and Change in Divergent Melanesian Contexts." *Man* 27: 777–97.

———. 2000. *Arguments and Icons: Divergent Modes of Religiosity*. Oxford: Oxford University Press.

———. 2002. "Modes of Religiosity." *Method and Theory in the Study of Religion* 14: 293–315.

Universalistic Orientations of an Imagistic Mode of Religiosity: The Case of the West African Poro Cult

10

CHRISTIAN K. HØJBJERG

IN TWO MONOGRAPHS AND IN SUBSEQUENT WRITINGS, Harvey Whitehouse repeatedly emphasizes that many, if not all, religious traditions incorporate both imagistic and doctrinal modes of operation (1995, 2000, 2002a, 2002b). Religions tend, however, to gravitate strongly toward one or the other of the two modes of religiosity, and the two modes interact only within readily distinguishable domains of operations. The existence of interacting modes of religiosity is demonstrated clearly in the case of the Melanesian Pomio Kivung, for instance, which is a doctrinal mode being occasionally rejuvenated by the imagistic practices of splinter-groups. I do not think that the reverse case is precluded by the divergent modes of religiosity (DMR) theory developed by Whitehouse, although it has not been described in explicit terms. From an evolutionary perspective, it is argued that the imagistic mode of religiosity is prior to the doctrinal mode, but to what extent does the imagistic mode depend on or incorporate doctrinal aspects for its survival? The aim of this chapter is to analyze the extent to which a particular West African male initiation and semisecret cult known as Poro presents an example of a predominantly imagistic mode of religiosity incorporating some elements of the doctrinal mode.

The Poro initiation cult exhibits the following key features: performance of rituals is infrequent, participants may experience a relatively high emotional arousal, and there is a focus on the use of multivalent imagery (though a number of rules of conduct and Poro "laws" are transmitted by word). Although these cognitive-psychological features suggest the presence of an imagistic mode of operation, the cult's sociopolitical dynamics are not exactly as predicted by the DMR theory. The particularistic community envisioned by the initiatory cult is hierarchically organized, and there are permanent leaders of the local Poro cults, just as initiates are differentiated according to descent. Moreover, there are several past and present examples of occasional, regionally organized Poro political or military actions, comprising an imagined community of anonymous others. The question, then, is if this scenario conflicts with the predictions of the DMR theory, according to which initiation systems like the Poro should possess a politically bounded character and are held to be incapable of rapid and wide dissemination (Whitehouse 2000: 32, 57, 122). Phrased in a more constructive fashion, this chapter seeks to establish whether the cognitive perspective put forward in the DMR theory helps to provide a more adequate understanding of the obvious—though not always well understood—sociopolitical dynamics of the Poro cult.

Cult Distribution and the Sociopolitical Context of the Poro

Imposed by outsiders, Poro is the generic term for a widespread and omnipresent male initiation cult in small-scale societies scattered over a large part of Liberia, Sierra Leone, and southeast Guinea in West Africa. Regional scholars have referred to the area as the Central West Atlantic Region, or more commonly as the Upper Guinea forest and coastal region inhabited by Mande-speaking and Mel-speaking peoples. The economy of these societies is typically based upon intensive slash-and-burn agriculture with supplementary hunting and fishing. The Poro is sometimes described as a tribal initiation institution, since membership for males is virtually compulsory. The equivalent female initiation society is generally known as Sande or Bundu. Yet the Poro is distributed among groups of people designated by varied ethnic labels (Mende, Kpelle, Gola, Loma, etc.).[1] The expression "Poro cluster" is sometimes used to refer to a considerable number of groups of people apparently sharing a similar religious institution in this particular West African culture area (d'Azevedo 1962: 516).

The role of secret societies in indigenous political organization has been a recurring focus for discussion in West African ethnology, particularly in the extensive literature on the Poro cult. The Central West Atlantic Region is commonly described as a politically ambiguous environment, characterized by the presence of numerous small, multiethnic chiefdoms with fragmented governments based on principles of kinship and territory. There seem to have been few examples of state formation or confederacies (and those that have been recorded have not endured). According to a widely accepted conceptualization, the Poro is a product of a dynamic frontier situation characterized by war and conquest, slave raiding, and control over trade routes between the coast and the interior since the fifteenth century, when the fall of the Mali empire caused large, heterogeneous groups of people to migrate toward the forest and coastal regions further south and southwest. It was during the following century that the first European merchants began to settle along the West African coast and thus contributed to the sociopolitical unrest of the region. Within this context, the "Poro appears to have emerged as a crucial institution in defense of traditional principles of ranked-lineage authority in competition with the rise of secular, individualistic political principles represented by new war lords, conquest, and immigrant populations imposed upon the older system. In a highly mobile and diversified adaptive situation, the Poro provided a sacred and secret arm of political authority and intergroup diplomacy that helped maintain stability through appeal to the gerontocratic and hierarchical principles derived from the ideal model of ranked-lineage structure of the past" (d'Azevedo 1962: 516).[2]

Despite general agreement among scholars on the presumed educational and political role of the Poro, divergent conclusions have been reached as to the sociopolitical ramifications of this semisecret cult. Some observers, including scholars and colonial and national power holders, have considered the Poro to be a politically unbounded association, capable of coordinating the actions of many communities composed of anonymous members, whereas other scholars have emphasized the Poro's capacity for sustaining only local political associations. The anticolonial rebellion in Sierra Leone in 1898, known as the Mende Rising, is an often-mentioned example of the Poro cult's presumed capacity to facilitate large-scale political activity. Despite a lack of certain evidence of the Mende Poro having been instrumental in the uprising, the authorities prohibited the cult (Little 1965: 350–51). It has been questioned whether the Poro ever possessed a centralized form of administration. This assumption relates directly to the predictions of the divergent modes of religiosity theory and is, moreover, sustained by a considerable number of regional studies emphasizing the particularistic nature of the Poro society. Even though Poro associations may fulfill sociopolitical functions at a local level, the autonomy of particular Poro ritual communities and the rivalry among leading members, as well as between Poro and local chiefs and big men, appear to conflict with a persistent, large-scale organizational structure. Cohesion and bonds of solidarity are produced only among members of small-scale communities (e.g., Bellman 1984, Højbjerg 1999). Contemporary observers continue to draw hasty inferences about the local and small-scale, or regional and large-scale, nature of the Poro male initiation society in Guinea, Liberia, and Sierra Leone. Generalizations on this topic appear most prominently in accounts of the current civil war or incidents of ethnic clashes. It is reported, for instance, that Poro has served as a basis for organizing civil defense among the Mende in Sierra Leone and the Loma and the Kpelle living in Liberia and Guinea (Ellis 1999; Højbjerg 2003, 2004; Richards 1996). As an alternative to the predominant functionalist interpretations of the Poro, the remaining part of this chapter is concerned with the issue of whether a focus on the cognitive-psychological features of the Poro initiation ritual may provide a more productive explanation for the apparently contradictory fact that Poro as a particularistic ritual practice is able to facilitate large-scale political associations, in certain situations at least.

Loma Male Initiation

The following description of Poro initiation refers to the case of the Loma in southeast Guinea. The Loma term for initiation is *pölögi* and may be associated with either earth (*pölöi*) or more likely with testicles (*pölöi*) (see endnote 1). A major theme in Loma initiation is the death and rebirth of male youth who become fully fledged members of society as their identity is transformed from that of noninitiated (*kpölöghai*) to that of initiated (*koubanumui* or *pölösinei*, i.e., "Poro man"). *Pölögi* is a rarely performed ritual. Informants indicate an interval of fourteen years between the end and beginning of two separate rituals. Irrespective of the age of entrance, the men who are initiated together belong to a distinctly named group and each *pölögi* carries an individual name. The ritual requires each initiate to undergo a period of seclusion. The period of seclusion has been reduced throughout the century. In the past, the period of seclusion is reported to have lasted seven years. Whereas the latest initiation named *bavouli* lasted for little more than two months during the rainy summer season (so as to coincide with school holidays), many elders who were initiated in the 1940s and 1950s claim to have spent from three to five years in seclusion. The initiates do not all stay for the same periods of time in the initiation camp. Whereas some initiates are present throughout the entire ritual period, small children and visiting urban residents, for instance, may be seen to spend only a few days in the initiation camp.

The first village to create a *pölögi* ritual[3] has to possess a rare object known as *ké nie yölöghöi*, which is described as a small circular wooden stool with seven legs and bounded by a chain (*yölöghöi*). The seven feet refer to the seven ranked categories of persons participating in *pölögi*, and the chain suggests unity. The stool acts as a metaphor of the *pölögi* institution as a whole in the sense that it is intended to produce cohesion among a group of socially differentiated individuals. At the entrance of the sacred groves one finds some grossly sculptured human heads that are visible to every passer-by who is familiar with the prohibitions that prevail with respect to the location. The human-like signposts are known as "ten-heads" (*umpougi*), though they exist only in the number of seven. "Ten-heads" are fabricated out of the roots of bracken. In the village where an initiatory cycle is going to begin, a greater number of *umpougi* painted in blue, white, and ochre are fabricated and thereby provide a veritable stockade in front of the sacred grove in order to mark the ritual event. Yet seven is the salient figure in this context, since it evokes a corresponding number of distinct and partly ranked categories of initiates who participate in the same ritual sequence.

The most spectacular opening performance of *pölögi* takes place in the village inaugurating a new initiatory period. Its name, "constructing-the-Poro-fence" (*pölösööi*), refers in part to a long, tall fence erected in the open at a short distance from the village and visible to anyone. *Onilégagi*, the "bird mask," plays a central part in the construction of the wall. Constructing-the-Poro-fence refers in particular to the *onilégagi's* staged killing of the neophytes. First chasing and beating the initiates as they are led toward the enclosure where the killings will take place, the masked figure then feigns the public killing of four or five initiates lying on their backs on the ground. Goat intestines twisted round *onilégagi's* short spear are exposed to the audience, situated at a distance, as a sign of the death of the boys, who are then handed over to the bush spirit *afui*.

It is said that *afui* spirit devours the initiates and that during their period of seclusion in the initiation camp the boys are in *afui's* stomach. *Afui* is represented as both a male and a female being. The male *afui* performs as a wooden mask that combines zoological and anthropomorphic features, such as ram's horns, crocodile clip, and human-like nose and eyes. The female *afui* is a harmonious sound that stems from five wind instruments (*dudegi* and *kaanivhooi*) and the regular rhythm coming from an elongated iron bell (*koli wolegi*). According to Schwab, entrance into the camp is marked by a ritual sequence of riddles. Once the novice is inside the grove and facing the forest spirit ("Big Devil"), the "masked" person asks nonsensical questions to the novice who must be "brought free," because he cannot answer (1947: 283). The same author also mentions a struggle between the "devil" and the novice before he passes to the act of scarification (*paalei* or *pölö pale*), which is probably a culminating point in the *pölögi*. Incisions are made into the torso and the back of the initiate by the means of a small hook and a knife. The scars, which in some areas are very elaborate, are the sign that a man has been devoured by *afui* and is thus recognized as a full member of the community. Shortly after the scarification the novice takes an oath upon the mask of the spirit that he will never reveal anything regarding the cult.

After the scarification, initiates are given a Poro name (*pölödaségi*) and a corresponding bush-name (*dobraségi*) chosen from among existing animal species. Whereas the Poro name may be used as a recognized public name for a person, the bush-name appears to be used only in secret communication between Poro members. A selected group of initiates receive names that are determined beforehand and which refer to the seven categories of initiates mentioned in connection with the sculptured, human-like bracken roots erected at the entrance of the sacred grove. Poro-names differ from one region to another, though the names of the leaders among the group of initiates are ascribed to the same distinct social categories. For instance, the first among initiates is invariably a member of a village's or a chiefdom's founding lineage. On the other hand, the name Köghö is ascribed to a youth from one of the latecoming lineages of the settlement and with whom the politically leading family entertains an affinal exchange. These two lineage groups are thus related in a hierarchical way as mother's brothers and sister's sons (*keke* and *daabe*).

The public appearance of the kaolin-painted neophytes named "white messengers" (*guélémanei*) is an important moment in every local *pölögi*. There are three categories of *guélémanei*: The "big shade" (*ninigolaei*), the one called *zabai* for which I possess no translation, and the "naked" (*mayakei* or *bélébélé koi*). Except for a great difference in size, *ninigolaei* and *zabai* look similar with their white-painted heads rising above large, circular raffia skirts. The naked *guélémanei* (*mayakei*), which is also named after the ant known as *bélébélé koi*, is performed by the youngest of the initiates, literally the children. *Ninigolaei*, the largest of the three *guélémaneiti* (pl.), is the one "giving birth" to all the other *guélémaneiti*. The *guélémaneiti* hide in the "great shade" cast by the *ninogolaei*, and when one of the initiators announces to the gathered women facing the strange creature "we have brought your children," the disguised novices suddenly swarm out.

As mentioned above, it is common in Upper Guinea forest and coastal ethnography to refer to male initiation as a period dedicated to learning. But what do they learn, one may ask, apart from the fact that the "devil is not a spirit, but man" (Schwab 1947: 283–84) and that one must be loyal and obey one's superiors within the Poro as well as sustain hardships? In relatively detailed descriptions of an initiation in 1995, my informants emphasized that the initiates were taught how to dance, but they were not taught anything else of significance. Dancing is usually a focal element of the coming-out ceremony of *pölögi*, and the choreography requires elaborate instruction, partly because of the encoded communication between dancers and drummers. Initiation also entailed the teaching of rules (*tögiti*) to be observed in the context of Poro rituals and methods of secret communication in the form of whistling, drumming (*kiégoi*), and metaphorical speech forms.

Activities intensify during the final stage of the *pölögi*. First, there is the appearance of the naked *guélémaneiti* who spend only a short time in the initiation camp, because of their juniority. The end of the ritual is announced by the public presentation of a painted winnower basket (*yengizazagi*) that is carried above the head by an elder man. In order to assure a safe return of the neophytes, the villagers have to carry out a "village sacrifice" (*taa zalaghai*), which is consecrated to the god-creator *gala*. Just before presenting themselves in public, the neophytes are rubbed by the Poro master (*zowoi*) with a protecting liquid (*söwöi*) belonging to the repertoire of local medicine (*sale*). Standing naked, they are ordered to jump over four branches lying on the ground and to approach a receptacle containing the liquid medicine (*söwöi sale*) upon which they take a final oath (*kpélagi*) never to reveal the "concealed things" of *pölögi*. To the rumbling sound of two large split drums (*outoukoulou*), the initiates enter the village in line, headed by Köhö, the first among initiates issuing from the "sister's son lineages" (*daabenu-*

muiti), and closed by *Kékoli*, the leading initiate issuing from a founding family (*zunumuiti*) that is known as the "mother's brother people" (*kekenumuiti*). Of special significance for the present discussion is the fact that among the Loma, as well as other Upper Guinea forest people, the order of appearance is inversely proportional to hierarchical order. Given this, it is possible to consider the coming-out ceremony as a manifestation of local political ideology, which is yet another lesson to be learned by the initiates. During the days of celebration following the return to the village, the initiates will gradually abandon an attitude of ignorance and begin to assume the status of adults.

Memory and Revelatory Knowledge

As an initiation system, Poro tends unsurprisingly to be modeled primarily on the transmissive and organizational features of the imagistic mode of religiosity although, as we shall see, some of the predictions of the DMR model with regard to the sociopolitical consequences of the imagistic mode require careful examination. Death and rebirth is the overall theme of *pölögi*, which starts by staging a public killing of the novices who, in later public ritual sequences, reappear, first as spirit-like beings called *guélémanei*, and, in the final stage of the ritual, the initiates again perform as newborn humans. Additional clusters of symbols are displayed throughout the *pölögi*, such as the sculptured fence in front of the sacred grove, or the scars left by *afui's* teeth on the bodies of the initiates. In some cases, exegesis appears rather straightforward and may even be stated explicitly, as in the case of the sculptured bracken roots (*umpougi*), the scarification (*paalei*), the sacred stool (*ké ni yölögböi*), the formation of the out-coming initiates, etc.

By contrast, the ritual demands more imaginative reflection on the part of the participants to decipher the ideas conveyed by the entrance riddles; the white-painted and raffia dressed *guélémaneiti*, including the avoidance observed between them and the bird mask; the winnower (*yengizazagi*) shown just before the closing of the ritual; the ritualized forms of address used in contact with Poro leaders; and so forth. Informants generally seem to ignore the meaning of such symbolic artifacts and actions, though it cannot be ruled out that the experience of multivocal and half-understood symbols triggers spontaneous exegetical reflections (Whitehouse 2002c). I do not, however, possess much evidence of explicit exegetical reflection on initiatory knowledge. Elder Poro members now and then state that today's initiates know very little and have been instructed only superficially compared to what they experienced themselves during former initiation rituals. On the other hand, they never provide information about the nature of the more profound knowledge they claim to possess, except from obviously performing more elegantly the dances learned during longer periods of initiation and demonstrating a more elaborate knowledge of concealed means of communication.

Ritual participants unanimously seem to consider the scarification ceremony to be a decisive step in male initiation. There seems to be evidence that acute arousal is present during the agonizing scarification procedures that Poro initiates have to endure as well as at other moments of Poro initiation. For example, initiates guard vivid memories of not only the identity of the initiators who inflict the pain on their proper backs and torsos, but in some cases also of those who perform the scarifications on fellow initiates. Moreover, the ritual participants who join the same Poro initiation camp do in general recall with great precision the identity of the other initiates as well as their positions in the organizational structure of the group of novices. This is even the case when, as often happens, a person is being initiated in a different village from that in which he lives. In later years an initiatory generation or *pölögi* age group is ascribed organizational or work tasks that relate to the entire local community. Likewise, when important decisions concerning the whole community are being taken, each age group will at first debate the issue among its own members. The fact that coparticipants sometimes develop close and lasting friendships, even when they live in relatively distant places and only see each other randomly, may be taken as further evidence that Poro initiation is a highly arousing ritual that triggers vivid and enduring episodic memories in the participants.

Before addressing the issue of sociopolitical ramifications of the Poro ritual complex, it is of interest to note one further aspect of Loma initiatory teaching. Although there is reason to doubt earlier observers' depictions of initiation as a "bush school," essential for Loma sociocultural education (for, as we have seen, there is little formalized instruction in the Loma way of life in the context of the Poro), one still encounters examples of the "doctrinal" codification and transmission of religious knowledge relating to rules of conduct and means of communication among Poro. The existence of such knowledge entails very clearly the creation of an exclusive, bounded community set apart from the surrounding village community, and from other ethnic communities and organizational forms such as colonial and national administration, missionaries, church congregations, and the Islamic religion of the coexisting Mandingo people. For instance, initiates are instructed in secret modes of communication that only Poro members are able to use and understand. During initiation, neophytes also perform ordinary tasks, such as agricultural labor, palm-wine tapping, cooking, and so forth. However, a few of the initiates belonging to the land-owning lineages are exempt from many of these duties and instead enjoy the privilege of being obeyed and entertained by common members of the initiates' cohort. In this way, initiation inculcates ideas of hierarchy that structure the relationships between Poro members, at least within ritual settings.

A Cognitive Perspective on the Sociopolitical Dynamics of the Poro

According to the DMR theory, an imagistic mode of organizing religious experience and action tends to produce highly cohesive and particularistic social ties. The assumption is largely sustained by the case of small-scale, decentralized Upper Guinea forest communities that share the practice of Poro initiation rituals. But Poro is not only a regional cult. It appears periodically to have coordinated large-scale political activity. In spite of sparse evidence, the Poro has been associated with the 1898 Mende Rising in Sierra Leone, the Gola ethnic and territorial unification during the nineteenth and early twentieth century, the Kpelle uprising in 1911 in Guinea, as well as the Lofa Defense Force and the Gilibai movement among the Loma during recent years of civil war and social upheaval in Liberia and Guinea. Some of these political projects and associations have had a politically expansionary nature, whereas others appear to have been acts of military self-defense.

A few older studies of the Poro have emphasized the possible political consequences of the "doctrinal" elements of male initiation. It is reported that initiates of the little community are taught specific modes of conduct and means of communication that may be applied at a more general level, since such rules and techniques are assumed to be shared by a large number of independent communities (cf. Little 1965: 362). This observation opens up a point of discussion of the factors intrinsic to a ritual modelled on the imagistic mode that enable large-scale political activity and the emergence of diffuse, imagined communities. It should be noted, however, that, except for the Gola case, examples of Poro unification in the Upper Guinea forest and coastal region seem always to have been circumstantial. This point may be confirmed by a very recent attempt to use the Poro as a medium for large-scale political association among the Loma in Guinea. I am going to provide only a rough sketch of this case that I describe in more detail elsewhere (Højbjerg 2003; see also Béavogui 1998: 255–57). During the mid-1980s the Loma in Guinea resumed Poro initiations. This was done discreetly at first, following the death of the dictatorial leader Sekou Touré and the gradual democratization of the country. Later, in the early 1990s, during my first period of fieldwork in the region, the frequency of secret society meetings in the sacred groves increased considerably. The renewed activity of the Poro was in part a response to a changing political situation, which comprised democratic elections to the local political administration, the presidency, and the parliament. Among the Loma and neighboring forest communities, candidates tried very explicitly to win votes by emphasizing the right to religious freedom, which contrasted with the former ban on Poro and similar ritual institutions. There are even examples of candidates joining Poro sessions and of poll stations situated in sacred groves.

More or less simultaneously ethnic tensions became more manifest, resulting in several bloody clashes between Loma and other ethnic groups identifying themselves as forest peoples on the one hand and Mandingo on the other. Violent ethnic confrontations happened especially in early 1994, when one of the factions in the Liberian civil war attacked Loma villages in Guinea, and again in 1999–2000, as the civil war became generalized in the region. In 1994, a Loma culturalist movement entitled *gilibai* ("unity") also emerged. An urban-based Christianized elite group that officially wanted to promote traditional cultural lore and crafts inaugurated the movement. Several leaders of the movement were also members of one of the country's major parties and clearly used the identity politics implied by the movement for personal purposes. Democratic elections, ethnic tensions, and the cultural movement thus constituted relevant background to the revitalization of Poro activities.

I carried out fieldwork in the area again in 1998–1999. When I look back at the events taking place in the first half of that decade, I have the impression that the local Poro associations were neither less nor more viable than they were before the politicized objectification of the Poro. On the other hand, the attempt to use the Poro as a means of promoting pantribal ethnic identity and facilitating large-scale political and military activities seems not to have had any lasting effect. For instance, there was no reaction among the Guinean Loma when the Mandingo rebel group ULIMO-K (now LURD), which was then based in Guinea, reassumed its attack on Loma settlements in northwestern Liberia. When someone finally took an initiative toward organizing civil action, it proved to be an influential woman in the town of Macenta, not a Poro leader or one of the leaders of the languishing *gilibai* movement.

Conclusion

The case of the Loma Poro cult appears to substantiate the prediction of the DMR theory that traditions dominated by the imagistic mode of religiosity are incapable of sustaining political unification at a larger scale, at least beyond instances of circumstantial political and military actions associated with the Poro. The memories generated by Poro initiation rituals tend to reinforce particularistic biases because time and place as well as the identity of actual participants are vividly specified and remembered. Repeated failure to turn the Poro into an instrument for large-scale political action is probably a result of the intensive, localized cohesion produced among participants in initiation rituals. Nevertheless, one ought not to overlook other aspects of the Poro that also seem to constrain the sociopolitical potentials of this widespread cult. The emphasis on secrecy and the pronounced competition between local Poro leaders clearly represents an obstacle to more regionally unified organizational structure. As predicted by the DMR theory, ritual communities such as the Poro are likely to be fiercely exclusivist (Whitehouse 2002a: 12–13).

Several regional scholars acknowledge the particularistic nature of the Poro in most Upper Guinea forest and coastal societies. The "Peace-Poro" assumed by many early observers to work across ethnic and community boundaries is also claimed never to have worked efficiently (Jones 1983: 181). But the same authors have never been able to resolve the apparently contradictory sociopolitical role played by a particularistic religious cult that circumstantially mediates political or military action at a regional level. Arguably, the main reason for this explanatory impasse is the functionalist bias of these studies, which focus on the social control exercised by the Poro and the counterweight it is supposed to provide vis-à-vis chiefly power. Where traditional explanations of this twofold characteristic of the Poro have failed, a cognitive approach to the sociopolitical dynamics of religion may provide the analytical tools needed by students of the Central West Atlantic Region. Such an approach allows us to appreciate that large-scale politics can depend on the imagistic practices of initiation (in combination with some doctrinal elements), even though the very same characteristics of the Poro initiation and cult organization prohibit the creation of powerful, enduring bonds between anonymous members of diffuse, imagined communities.

If generalizing theory helps to make better sense of unsolved ethnographic questions, ethnography may, as in the present case, help to inform and refine the theories in question. Whitehouse suggests that in religious traditions founded upon interacting modes of religiosity, "the cohesion of locally distinctive ritual communities may readily be projected onto the wider religious community, and such processes appear to have been crucial in many large scale and bloody religiously motivated wars" (2002a: 14). Most, if not all, interacting modes of religiosity discussed in the DMR theory are instances of predominantly "doctrinal" modes. But what are we able to say about predominantly "imagistic" modes of religiosity such as the Poro? Are regional Poro activities conditioned by the projection of local intense cohesion, or are they rather the product of "doctrinal" elements enabling rapid and large-scale diffusion? As an interacting mode of religiosity, Poro may instead be seen to depend on both, although within "readily distinguishable domains" as the DMR theory has it (Whitehouse 2000: 2, 159; 2002a: 14). So, even if I grant the last word to generalizing theory, I recommend that it consider more cases of such underrepresented interacting modes of religiosity and readily distinguishable domains about which we still know very little. Various misinterpretations noted in the extensive ethnographic literature on the Upper Guinea Poro cult prove this point all too well.

Notes

1. Local Poro names and their significance vary considerably. There is some uncertainty as to the significance of the name of the Loma initiation described in this chapter. The

term *pölöi*, from which the term for initiation (*pölögi*) is derived among the Loma, means either testicles or earth depending on the stress. It should be recalled that Loma and other Mande languages are described as tonal languages. In fact, there is no Loma term for the Poro as a cult group or as a secret association. Instead, Poro members refer to Poro-related matters as *pölövai* (i.e., *pölö* matter). A more detailed presentation of Loma Poro and male initiation will appear in a forthcoming monograph on Loma ritual and political culture.

2. For studies with a similar perspective of the Poro, see also Fulton 1972; Gibbs 1962; Murphy and Bledsoe 1987; Richards 1996; Schröder 1988; Wylie 1989. For a review of the oldest references to the Poro and Sande initiation societies in the Upper Guinea forest and coastal region, see Jones 1983: 179–82; Little 1965: 350–53; Schröder 1988: 3–12.

3. The villages that inaugurate male initiation are generally the central villages of loosely structured chiefdoms (*zui*) of the past.

References

Béavogui, F. 1998. "Le poro, une institution politico-religieuse ouest africaine: Le cas de la Guinée Forestière." In C. Coquery-Vidrovitch, O. Goerg, and H. Tenoux (eds.), *Des historiens africains en Afrique: l'historie d'hier et d'aujourd'hui: logiques du passé et dynamiques actuelles.* Paris: L'Harmattan.

Bellman, B. L. 1984. *The Language of Secrecy: Symbols and Metaphors in Poro Ritual.* New Brunswick, N.J.: Rutgers University Press.

d'Azevedo, W. 1962. "Some Historical Problems in the Delineation of a Central West Atlantic Region." *Annals of the New York Academy of Sciences* 96: 512–38.

Ellis, S. 1999. *The Mask of Anarchy: The Destruction of Liberia and the Religious Dimension of an African Civil War.* London: Hurst and Company.

Fulton, R. M. 1972. "The Political Structures and Functions of Poro in Kpelle Society." *American Anthropologist* 74: 1218–33.

Gibbs, J. L. 1962. "Poro Values and Courtroom Procedures in Kpelle Chiefdom." *Southwest Journal of Anthropology* 18: 341–50.

Højbjerg, C. K. 1999. "Loma Political Culture: A Phenomenology of Structural Form." *Africa* 69: 535–53.

———. 2003. "Tradition Invented and Inherited: A Study of Loma Cultural Identity." In T. Otto and P. Pedersen (eds.), *Disentangling Traditions.* Aarhus: Aarhus University Press.

———. 2004. "Masked Violence: Ritual Action and the Perception of Violence in an Upper Guinea Ethnic Conflict." In N. Kastfelt (ed.), *The Role of Religion in African Civil Wars.* London: Hurst and Company. (In press).

Jones, Adam. 1983. *From Slaves to Palm Kernels: A History of the Galinhas Country (West Africa), 1730–1890.* Wiesbaden: Franz Steiner Verlag.

Little, K. 1965. "The Political Functions of the Poro: Part I." *Africa* 35: 349–65.

Murphy, W. P., and C. H. Bledsoe. 1987. "Kinship and Territory in the History of a Kpelle Chiefdom (Liberia)." In Kopytoff, I. (ed.), *The African Frontier.* Bloomington: Indiana University Press.

Richards, P. 1996. *Fighting for the Rain Forest: War, Youth and Resources in Sierra Leone*. Oxford, Portsmouth: Heinemann, James Currey.

Schröder, G. 1988. "Eine Verborgene Dimension Gesellschaftlicher Wirklichkeit: Anmerkungen zur Geschichte und heutigen Bedeutung der Geheimbÿnde Poro und Sande in Liberia." Liberia Working Group Papers No. 8., Bremen.

Schwab, G. 1947. "Tribes of the Liberian Hinterland." Cambridge, Mass.: Peabody Museum (Papers of the Peabody Museum of American Archaeology and Ethnology, 31).

Whitehouse, Harvey. 1995. *Inside the Cult. Religious Innovation and Transmission in Papua New Guinea*. Oxford: Clarendon Press.

———. 2000. *Arguments and Icons: Divergent Modes of Religiosity*. Oxford: Oxford University Press.

———. 2002a. "Modes of Religiosity." *Method and Theory in the Study of Religion* 14: 293–315.

———. 2002b. "Conjectures, Refutations, and Verification: Towards a Testable Theory of 'Modes of Religiosity.'" *Journal of Ritual Studies* 16: 91–103.

———. 2002c. "Religious Reflexivity and Transmissive Frequency." *Social Anthropology* 10: 91–103.

Wylie, K.C. 1989. "From the Fountainheads of the Niger: Researching a Multiethnic Regional History." In J. P. Henderson and H. A. Reed (eds.), *Studies in the African Diaspora: A Memorial to James R. Hooker (1929–1976)*. Dover, Mass.: Majority Press.

Toward a Comparative Anthropology of Religion

11

HARVEY WHITEHOUSE

THE CONTRIBUTORS TO THIS VOLUME HAVE AT TURNS supported and challenged various aspects of the "modes theory." They have compared and evaluated it against other theories of religion and ritual. And they have advanced a range of solutions to existing problems while, in many cases, opening up a number of new ones.

In support of the modes theory, regional specialists have collectively demonstrated the global recurrence of bifurcating tendencies associated with doctrinal and imagistic modes respectively. They have done so by picking out the ebb and flow of modes dynamics across diverse populations and over substantial periods of time. Especially impressive, in this regard, are the chapters by J. D. Y. Peel, David Shankland, Jack Goody, Brian Malley, Leo Howe, James Laidlaw, Susan Bayly, and Christian Højbjerg. Although by no means straightforwardly endorsing the model, these authors have collectively demonstrated that it is fruitfully generalizable, that many of its principal predictions with regard to the broad coalescence of divergent sets of features (concerning transmission, codification, memory, and social morphology) are on the right track. Indeed, this point has been emphasized with considerable generosity throughout the book. But the theory, as expounded in *Arguments and Icons*, clearly has problems as well. These problems, it turns out, are of two main kinds.

First, as Maurice Bloch and Gilbert Lewis argue at some length, the modes theory (Whitehouse 1995, 2000) was insufficiently precise about such matters as proper measures of frequency and units of analysis. In order to be rendered in a systematically testable fashion, the theory's predictions and methods of investigation needed to be formulated more exactly and transparently.

Second, as many contributors have stressed, the modes theory at best explained only certain aspects of what we find "on the ground." Much religious activity and experience appears to fall outside the ambit of the model. We find abundant examples of religious traditions dominated by the doctrinal mode that nevertheless incorporate low-frequency, high-arousal forms of religious experience. In his discussion of various forms of Balinese Hinduism, Howe observes that Sai Baba devotionalism is characterized by "large-scale, anonymous, imagined communities and a globally constituted identity," indicative of the doctrinal mode, and yet it entails practices that evince "high emotional arousal" (p. 140). Malley makes a very similar point with regard to evangelical Christianity in North America. In the case he discusses, we find intense ritual ordeals that become the focus of elaborate, frequently rehearsed discourse. Moreover, such a pattern is found more widely. Laidlaw, for instance, reports on ritual ordeals within Jainism that, while highly arousing and personally consequential, are interpreted in classic doctrinal-mode fashion, rather than becoming a locus for "spontaneous exegetical reflection." Peel has suggested that we envisage modes of religiosity as standing in a kind of dynamic tension, prefiguring rather than merely excluding each other. This accords rather closely too with Laidlaw's suggestion that modes of religiosity can be "embedded" in one another. But such solutions raise further problems. Why would the modes neatly diverge in some cases but seemingly intermingle more closely in others? What factors drive oscillations between the two (an issue raised eloquently by Shankland)? Are there just two modes or multiple modes of religiosity (Bayly has proposed three[1])? And what are we to do about patterns of religious activity that occur (often in a very stable form) in the absence of either doctrinal or imagistic dynamics (abundant examples supplied by Lewis)?

Expressed in such a condensed form, the problems raised in response to the modes theory might seem to be overwhelming. None of these problems spells doom, however. Recall that most, if not all, the contributors acknowledge that the bifurcation is "out there." It is just that there is also a great deal more going on. The challenge is to update the modes theory so that it can capture more of the data, without (of course) foreclosing the possibility of falsification. Our starting point, I suggest, should be the fact that not all concepts are equally easy to produce and pass on.

The Cognitive Optimum Position and the Theory of Modes of Religiosity

Some cultural concepts are naturally easier to generate and to acquire than others. Learning the tune of an advertising jingle, for instance, will always be easier than learning the melody of a piece of experimental jazz. And the skill of adding up small sums is bound to be more readily acquired than that of applying the principles of calculus. And so it is also in the domain of religion. God, the gray-bearded father figure in the clouds, is bound to be more easily represented in one's mind than the notion of a disembodied, omnipresent God. These contrasts in the relative ease with which concepts of specified types can be produced, grasped, and remembered derive in large part from certain "built in" strengths and limitations of our species' cognitive architecture.

Certain systematic biases in the way we humans think persist despite all our efforts to transcend them. No matter how advanced one's knowledge becomes in the field of astronomy, for instance, one will always readily fall back on the intuitive idea of the sun moving across the sky (rather than the earth revolving around the sun) when unconsciously judging the time of day. The intuitive way of thinking, in other words, can never be eliminated but will always lurk somewhere in one's mental repertoire, ready to be called upon when the occasion allows. At the same time, however, the limitations of our cognitive apparatus *can* be progressively transformed as we undergo increasingly elaborate and advanced forms of training. The possible role of a newly discovered neurotransmitter in the onset of Parkinson's disease will be grasped and appreciated much more easily by a neuroscientist than by a musician. Both kinds of professionals have the same basic cognitive equipment, and share much the same repertoire of tacit assumptions about the world, but in certain domains of causal reasoning with regard to biological processes the neurologist has a massively richer set of mental frameworks, enabling him or her to acquire new concepts in that domain far more easily than the musician. In the domain of *religion*, experimental psychologist Justin Barrett has proposed that we refer to the expert frameworks and associated concepts as "Theologically Correct" (TC) discourse, whereas more intuitive kinds of religious thinking (such as anthropomorphic god concepts) constitute a rather more robust and ubiquitous default position. Barrett has assembled a compelling body of evidence that Christians, for instance, whether experts or novices in their particular tradition, readily slip into more intuitive ways of conceptualizing God, if the cognitive system is put under pressure. In particular, they will abandon their TC concepts of omnipresence and adopt a more humanlike notion of God, whenever the cognitive resources available for the task of reasoning about God's behavior have been sufficiently restricted (Barrett and Keil 1996; Barrett 1999). In what follows, I will refer to all aspects of religious thinking that migrate toward the intuitive end of the spectrum as *cognitively optimal*.

Cognitively optimal concepts are ones that the human mind is naturally well-equipped to process and remember, or that readily trigger exceptionally salient or attention-grabbing inferences, *in the absence of any special training or inducement to learn such concepts*. Even when people have mastered a body of difficult-to-acquire concepts (often at great cost in terms of time, energy, and training), they never outgrow their susceptibility to more natural ways of thinking. In that sense, cognitively optimal mentation might be described as a kind of "default position." Its representational content is "optimal" in the sense that it enjoys a selective advantage within human populations everywhere, all else being equal, but it is not optimal in the sense of being "truer" or more desirable, or even more adaptive, than other kinds of mental products. Concepts that human minds find easy to acquire are often false or unfalsifiable, and many have negative outcomes for the survival or well-being of the people who entertain them. Moreover, the mechanisms that cause such concepts to be easily acquired did not necessarily evolve because those concepts confer (or have ever conferred) selective advantages in biological terms. For instance, certain melodies are "catchy" because of natural human sensitivities to tonal variation. Those sensitivities probably evolved in concert with the development of language, their "proper domain" of activation; a predilection for music might very well have been a curious by-product of that, just one of the many "actual domains" for the application of our peculiarly human aural capacities (see Sperber 1996).

Cognitively optimal aspects of *religion* have received considerable attention in recent years, with the result that we now know rather a lot about the intuitive mechanisms underlying the production and acquisition of concepts of supernatural agency, ritual procedures, and mythical narratives. If we are to understand the implications of this work for the theory of modes of religiosity, and more specifically for the criticisms that have been leveled at it by some of the contributors to this volume, then we will first need to undertake a brief survey of the main findings in this area.

To begin with concepts of the supernatural, anthropomorphism is clearly part of what makes some concepts of gods, spirits, and ancestors "cognitively optimal." According to anthropologist Stewart Guthrie, there is now overwhelming evidence that humans are naturally predisposed to pay attention to the presence of potential agents in their environments, even to the extent of investing inanimate objects with human qualities on the flimsiest of pretexts. The title of Guthrie's book, *Faces in the Clouds* (1993), concisely makes the point. If the propensity to see humanlike presences helps to explain the ubiquity of supernatural beings in the world's cultural traditions, then this is, however, only part of the story. It does not, for instance, explain adequately what is so "super" about supernatural agents. This is where Pascal Boyer's work has made an especially important contribution (Boyer 2001).[2] Boyer has assembled compelling evidence that people everywhere are significantly more likely to pay attention to and to remember representations of "minimally counterintuitive" concepts than other kinds of concepts (all else being equal). By "minimally counterintuitive" Boyer means concepts that entail simple and limited violations of intuitive expectations. For instance, we intuitively expect unsupported objects to descend and for a collision of moving objects to result in breakage or displacement. And yet we readily acquire concepts of ghosts, who are construed as violating these ordinary expectations. This is precisely what makes these concepts "catchy," according to Boyer. Ghosts are minimally counterintuitive concepts in that they exhibit all the intuitive characteristics of ordinary people (e.g., intentionality and belief-desire psychology) and yet in one very simple detail they violate intuitive ontological assumptions (e.g., concerning gravity, solidity, etc.), being able to float about and pass through solid objects. Thus, *cognitively optimal* concepts of supernatural beings would be ones that are both *anthropomorphic* and *minimally counterintuitive*.

Another prominent feature of religious systems everywhere is ritualization, and this too has a number of cognitively optimal aspects. For a start, there are some compelling grounds to suppose that the urge to devise and certainly to participate in rituals is at least partly activated by mental structures that are also concerned with the avoidance of contaminants. The clinical condition of Obsessive Compulsive Disorder (OCD) would appear to be the result of overactivation of innate contamination-avoidance mechanisms (Boyer 2002) and, as such, might provide particularly revealing clues as to the compelling nature of at least some socially sanctioned, institutional rituals among people who do not suffer from the condition. Fiske and Haslam (1997) show extraordinarily strong correlations between OCD symptoms and the forms taken by ritual obligations cross-culturally, suggesting that the same cognitive mechanisms underpin both. Rituals in which supernatural beings are assumed to play some sort of role are cognitively optimal in a series of other ways as well. Whereas ordinary actions might involve agents (the person acting), patients (the person being acted upon), and perhaps also instruments (any artifacts used in the action), religious rituals often postulate a link between one of these "slots" in a natural action schema and some kind of supernatural being (see Lawson and McCauley 1990 and McCauley and Lawson 2002). So we get rituals in which a deity can be associated with the agent slot (e.g., acting "though" the priest who carries out a wedding or an ordination), or the patient slot (e.g., where the deity is construed as the beneficiary of an offering or sacrifice), or the instrument slot (e.g., where ritual artifacts are construed as somehow sacred, as for instance in the holy water used in a Roman Catholic blessing). McCauley and Lawson have developed an impressively detailed account of how intuitive (and minimally counterintuitive) thinking, based on the above kinds of considerations, might determine our implicit expectations and evaluations of rituals. This too marks off a set of features common to most religious traditions that can be described as cognitively optimal.

Finally, rituals are cognitively optimal in a sense that has been discussed at some length by several of the contributors to this volume. That is, ritualization involves a minimal violation of intuitive expectations concerning the intentionality undergirding action. As Bloch puts it (in chapter 4), rituals are special kinds of actions that "do not completely originate in the intentionality of the producer at the time of their performance" (p. 58). This argument, some key aspects of which were first identified by Humphrey and Laidlaw (1994), is central to understanding the dynamics of both doctrinal and imagistic modes. Rituals are actions that have been stipulated in advance, rather than being spontaneous expressions of the ritual actors' intentions at the moment of performance.

If there are aspects of our ideas about supernatural agency and ritualization that may be described as "cognitively optimal," this is also true of the way certain religious *narratives* are put together, for instance as more or less sacred myths, legends, and histories. We humans naturally spin yarns, and pass them on, partly because we are predisposed to represent all events in terms of simple causal stories. Cognitively optimal stories are found in all religions, and in all cultural traditions more generally. These are always stories with memorable plots and ones, moreover, that work well as parables (Turner 1996), insofar as they can provide source narratives for indefinitely many target narratives. To the extent that stories about primordial ancestors and creator beings, messiahs and prophets, and so on, are felt to provide relevant analogues and even justifications for the way things are done in the world around us, these religious narratives have great intuitive appeal and are likely to be widely recalled and transmitted.

In sum, we should have no difficulty building and passing on a religious tradition composed largely of *cognitively optimal* concepts (e.g., of saints, ancestors, gods, etc.), rituals (e.g., blessing and baptisms), and narratives (e.g., creation myths and wise sayings). Not only are such traditions hypothetically possible, they are actually very widespread.

But, and this is a big "but," cognitively optimal religious traditions are also very commonly subverted by the dynamics specified by the theory of divergent modes of religiosity. These "modes dynamics" are capable of transforming simple concepts of deities and ghosts into far more conceptually complex ideas about (for instance) redemption and the Holy Trinity. In other words, modes of religiosity provide the mnemonic infrastructure required to build *maximally counterintuitive concepts*. And these more complex religious representations, having been acquired at considerable cost, also carry *motivational force* in a way that can supercede our natural inclinations. Moreover, their mode of formation and transmission has a host of consequences for social morphology, including the scale and structure of the religious tradition and levels of cohesion among its members. Religious traditions based around cognitively optimal concepts, rituals, and narratives are not capable of generating these forms of identity and social organization.

Modes of religiosity, then, are created against a background of more intuitive, cognitively optimal ways of thinking and behaving. It is tempting to say, perhaps, that modes dynamics resolve problems that are prefigured in cognitively optimal practices. Consider, once again, Bloch's view of ritual (following Humphrey and Laidlaw 1994) as a special kind of act in which normal grounds for attributing intentionality have been removed or at least altered. If rituals are not actions authored by those who perform them, then who stipulated these actions in the first place, and why? That is a question, which, according to Bloch, may elicit three kinds of response in both ritual participants and observers.

First, people could simply ignore the problem—pretend that the question of intentional meaning is an irrelevance. As Bloch also observes, however:

> [W]e are dealing with people with human minds, that is, with animals whose minds are characterized by an intentionality-seeking device that is normally exercised ceaselessly, one might almost say obsessively, sometimes consciously but often unconsciously, and that enables them to read the minds of others and thus coordinate their behavior with them. (Bloch pp. 63–64)

As such, Bloch considers the option of *ignoring* the intentional origins of ritual acts to be "unnatural" (p. 64) and difficult to maintain. It runs against our inbuilt inclinations, which are to hunt down intentional meanings in every action we observe. Second, people might address the question of ritual meaning when pressured to do so (for instance, on the urgings of an inquisitive ethnographer)—in which case the exegetical commentaries are constructed "on the hoof," and with little consistency or conviction. Third, people might engage in a more prolonged search for "deep" and satisfying ritual exegesis:

> In rare but important moments, people are going to ask themselves, or others, why things are done or said in this way or that way, and they will not give up in spite of the apparent difficulties encountered in their search. Their mind-reading instinct will just not leave them alone. This kind of determination is what in Whitehouse's theory is deemed to cause "rich and revelatory religious experience." (Bloch pp. 65–66)

Bloch does not offer a detailed explanation for the presence of these three kinds of responses (nor of others, specified by the modes theory). Still less does he explain why some general circumstances trigger certain kinds of responses more readily than others (an issue that is, however, discussed at some length by Lewis). Bloch's arguments provide a very significant starting point, but they do not take us far enough.

According to the "modes theory," the first of Bloch's options is often associated with conditions of extensive *routinization*. The search for intentional meaning in rituals is "switched off," at least most of the time, when the actions become so familiar, so habituated, that they can be performed with little or no engagement of explicit memory, merely on the basis of implicit procedural knowledge. To put it bluntly: when actions can be carried out without any need for conscious reflection about *how* to perform them, the urge to consider *why* we perform them (i.e., to ask questions about the intentional meanings of the actions) is somewhat diminished, at least at a population level. Bloch describes this state of affairs as "unnatural" and "difficult to maintain," but it seems to me that it is rather commonplace and widespread. Fortunately, the topic is amenable to both ethnographic and experimental investigation.[3] What people genuinely find quite difficult, in these conditions, is to have to make up some kind of exegetical meaning spontaneously, on the spot (Bloch's second option). Anthropologists have often found, to their puzzlement and consternation, that people are unwilling or unable to proffer ritual exegesis, even in the face of considerable badgering to do so. It can be hard to tease apart the "can't" and the "won't" in all of this. One may readily appreciate that people are inclined to redirect questions of ritual exegesis to their leaders and experts, on grounds of deference, etiquette, politeness, and so on. But this might also be because their own thoughts on the matter are comparatively sparse and superficial. There is another very important possibility, however, that Bloch does not consider here. It is that, in conditions of routinization, people are highly susceptible to learning very elaborate exegetical concepts, transmitted verbally. Although they may be disinclined to invent their own exegesis, they might be very adept at soaking up highly *repetitive* authoritative pronouncements on the subject of what their rituals mean. Bloch's third option, the spontaneous production of elaborate, "revelatory" ritual exegesis, is most prominently associated with low-frequency, high-arousal rituals. Bloch may not agree with that claim, but he supplies no evidence to the contrary. In fact, both ethnographic and psychological data seem to me to support such a view rather strongly (see Whitehouse 2000).

According to the theory of modes of religiosity, revelations are not the outcome only of *spontaneous exegetical reflection*, as generated within the imagistic mode, they are also inherent in *verbally transmitted* religious teachings in conditions of ritual *routinization*. Heavy repetition of religious teachings can ensure the relevance of the orthodoxy for the interpretation of everyday experience, a point persuasively made by Brian Malley (p. 74):

> The repetitious and the novel portions of a sermon . . . help people connect biblical teaching to their everyday lives. The repetitive portion does this by repriming fundamental doctrines in memory: the woman who comes in discouraged is uplifted as she is reminded of God's concern for her; the man contemplating a child-care decision is reminded of his ultimate values. The novel portion of the sermon suggests new ways in which the Bible might be seen as speaking to daily life: Jesus's dining with tax-gatherers illustrates how evangelicals are to reach out to the needy; Abraham's willingness to obey God even at the cost of sacrificing his own son shows how

important faithfulness is. In both its repetitive and its novel parts, the sermon is designed to help people live in the light of the word of God.

But when a particular aspect of everyday life is illuminated by the Bible or a sermon, it is not always clear to us that we are the authors of the analogy, any more than that the preacher of a sermon is the sole author of its apparently novel elements. On the contrary, the connections we make or that are made for us in a sermon seem to have been at least partly anticipated and mapped out in advance. Such impressions also derive from *routinization*, as follows.

When standardized teachings are heavily reiterated, well beyond the point of communicative redundancy, we can describe these kinds of utterances as *ritualized*. As such, they raise all the same problems of attributing intentionality that Bloch (chapter 4) and Humphrey and Laidlaw (1994) associate with ritual in general. It is no longer clear who is speaking—is it the priest before us, or is it the countless priests whose words he is now recalling and passing on? The message clearly does not originate in the medium, but its exact origins remain mysterious. When the messages we have learned in this way are activated in our everyday activities and experiences, we cannot exactly *own* them as our thoughts, nor can we even say with confidence that the connections we make are our own inventions. An obvious (and thus a common) solution to that predicament is to attribute both the thoughts/teachings and their providential activation to a Higher Source. That is itself a kind of revelation, however commonplace.

One of the most prominent hallmarks of *both* routinized religious teachings in the doctrinal mode *and* the prolonged processes of spontaneous exegetical reflection in the imagistic mode, is that the resulting bodies of religious knowledge become extremely complex, and intrinsically hard to acquire. In the case of the doctrinal mode, learning the official teachings requires long-term training, through regular verbal transmission and through more private study and discussion with experienced members of the tradition. In the case of the imagistic mode, it generally requires a lifetime of personal reflection on matters of ritual exegesis and cosmology, accompanied by increasing responsibility for orchestrating the ritual performances themselves, to achieve the recognized position of religious "expert" (typically "elder"). Either way, we are dealing with concepts very different from those generated on the hoof in response to the badgering of ethnographers (i.e., the second of Bloch's three varieties of ritual exegesis). Modes dynamics generate intrinsically complex, difficult-to-acquire concepts. These kinds of concepts, and the forms of social morphology with which they are associated, must be systematically distinguished from those parts of the cultural repertoire that comprise more intuitive, easily transmitted ideas and forms of behavior, and which I have here described as clustering around a "cognitive optimum position."

With the above elaborations to the modes theory in place, we may be in a position to return to some of the problems and criticisms raised in this book. A major problem, of course, is empirical verification. The challenge, it seems to me, is to set out the precise conditions under which a set of ritual practices should: (a) activate doctrinal mode dynamics, (b) activate imagistic mode dynamics, (c) assume "cognitively optimal" forms, or (d) become extinct. Of crucial importance, obviously, is the exact specification of varying aspects of ritual transmission, such as frequency, arousal, codification, and so on. If all the relevant variables, and the predicted outcomes of their interaction, can be identified clearly, then we should be able to agree on what would count as confirming or disconfirming evidence, and thus to test the modes theory more systematically. Because of space limitations, I have tackled these issues in a separate book for this series, *Modes of Religiosity* (Whitehouse 2004: chapter 9), but the resulting refinements to my hypotheses owe much to the critical coaxing of contributors to the present volume.

Another major challenge, identified at the outset, was to specify more clearly the scope of the "modes theory." What aspects of religion should the theory be capable of explaining, and what is beyond its remit? Thanks to the critical observations and evidence presented by the contributors to this volume (and also to Whitehouse and Martin 2004), it is clear that the modes theory can only hope to explain the transmission of certain kinds of rituals, beliefs, and patterns of social morphology. Much of what passes as religion, however, turns out to be beyond the explanatory ambition of the theory. For this reason, I have been obliged to extend the theory, to take into account what might be called the "cognitive optimum position."

Gilbert Lewis's ethnographically rich contribution focuses almost exclusively on cognitively optimal practices rather than on the kinds of activities, among the Gnau and their neighbors, that are most clearly shaped by modes dynamics (e.g., the spectacular Tambin initiations and penis-bleeding rites, as well as the forms of religious experience and sociality stimulated by the spread of Christian traditions to the region). Focusing on the outputs of intuitive mechanisms (taboos, spittings, invocations, avoidances, etc.) was of course entirely legitimate. There is nothing to say that the latter mechanisms are more or less "interesting" or worthy of study than the modes dynamics that Lewis chose not to focus on (and justifiably so, since my earlier work had not adequately specified its scope of application). Nevertheless, while the presence of both kinds of cultural transmission can hardly be doubted, it does not (as Lewis might be taken to imply) necessarily cast doubt on the legitimacy of the doctrinal-imagistic dichotomy itself.

Some aspects of Shankland's queries concerning the scope of the modes theory invite a similar response. Shankland observes that, very broadly speaking, Turkish Islam has come to be increasingly dominated by a doctrinal mode of operation, gradually dropping its imagistic-mode dynamics. Assuming some sort of psychological "need" for a release from the excessive discipline of routinized worship, he suggests that Muslims in the region have turned increasingly to the joys of alcohol and popular music, in place of the less readily accessible euphoria promised by Sufi mysticism. But surely, Shankland muses, the "psychological roots" of both high-arousal ritual and highly drunken revelry are much the same. Moreover, they entail a common stock of activities (especially songs and dances). And, if both kinds of activity are "imagistic," then why describe that as a mode of *religiosity*? As Shankland puts it: "Why should a 'mode' stop being so when it drifts from the religious sphere?" (Shankland, p. 35).

The answer, I would suggest, is that drunken parties are not intrinsic elements of any sets of modes dynamics. Not only would the core activities have to be *ritualized*, in the sense that Bloch uses that term, but in order to contribute to the formation of an imagistic mode of religiosity, these rituals would have to drive prolonged processes of "spontaneous exegetical reflection." My understanding is that Sufi mysticism does precisely that. By contrast, there is no evidence (and no particular reason to suppose) that the consumption of alcohol and pop music in Turkey or anywhere else triggers the same psychological effects. As such, like the spittings and invocations of Lewis's Gnau informants, the drunken singing and dancing that Shankland observed in Turkey is probably beyond the remit of my theory. It too belongs to that part of the cultural repertoire that hovers around the cognitive optimum position.

I think we are now also better placed to make sense of certain aspects of the European Reformation. Howe's chapter seems to show that many of the practices of medieval Christianity were clustered around the cognitive optimum position, rather than either of our two modes of religiosity. For instance, following Bossy's (1985) account of late medieval religiosity, Howe emphasizes the extent to which basic taxonomic categories of kinship provided the main organizing principles for popular ideas concerning rites of baptism and death, as well as Christian ideals of sociality more generally. The forms of intuitive cognition supporting this kind of cultural transmission have been analyzed in particular detail by anthropologist Roy D'Andrade (1995). But there are reasons to think that ritualized expressions of kinship relations were also shaped by a pervasive concern with the avoidance of contamination/pollution and the "cleansing of the body" (Howe p. 000). Howe makes much of the contrasts between these cognitively optimal ideas of the medieval laity, on the one hand, and the more complex, "theologically correct" concepts of both the monastic tradition *and* the Reformation. The latter were expressions of a bona fide doctrinal mode of religiosity, which—in contrast with the beliefs and practices of the laity—required substantial mnemonic support in order to be transmitted intact. For the medieval church, the problem was how to reconcile maximally counterintuitive "official" concepts (for instance, about the fate of the soul), on the one hand, and more popular, intuitive notions couched in the idioms of kinship, on the other. In practice, Howe maintains, "the church found it had to accommodate itself to lay practice by allowing priests say masses for the dead so that the living could discharge their familial and charitable duties" (p. 129). By contrast, reformed thinking was less conciliatory and pursued instead the far more difficult (in fact, psychologically impossible) task of eliminating cognitively optimal versions of religious thinking from the Christian repertoire (Howe p. 131):

> One of the most momentous things that Reformation theology taught, especially through Luther, was that almost all of this structure of Christianity, built upon kinship, community, charity, and obligations, had no scriptural authority. . . . There is, unsurprisingly, not much evidence that the ordinary masses in the early stages of the Reformation understood the complexities of the evangelical message.

If monastic and reformed Christianities at the end of the European middle ages were dominated by the doctrinal mode, and lay religious life was driven more by the mechanisms of intuitive cognition, then Howe shows rather strikingly that comparable divisions are discernible in the Hindu traditions of contemporary Bali. *Adat* Hinduism is premised on much the same intuitive concepts of kinship taxonomy and contamination avoidance (in this context, caste-based) as the thinking of lay Europeans in the late medieval period. A theologically correct version of *adat* Hinduism, known as *agama*, has emerged in Bali, however, and now occupies a position somewhat resembling that of the medieval church in Europe—itself dominated by the doctrinal mode and yet obliged to reconcile its teachings, at least to some extent, with the concepts of an untutored laity. More astonishingly still, Balinese religiosity currently has the corollary of a reformed church in the guise of devotional Hinduism—essentially a reaction against the *agama* orthodoxy, much as Protestantism emerged as a reaction against the dilution of the doctrinal mode in many parts of the medieval tradition in Europe. Thanks to Howe's perceptive critique of my earlier discussion of modes dynamics in the sixteenth century, these comparative issues are capable of being framed and investigated much more profitably.

Is the notion of a "cognitively optimal position" really sufficient, though, to address all the doubts some contributors have expressed concerning the so-called "mixed-mode" problem? We still have to explain the presence of low-frequency, high-arousal rituals in traditions that lack full-blown imagistic dynamics, and that often display all the core features of the doctrinal mode. We also have to deal with growing evidence that *routinized* practices elicit very different levels of emotional arousal and motivational force in different traditions at different times. These issues might be most effectively addressed by shifting our focus onto patterns of historical transformation, an issue that has justly warranted considerable attention throughout the volume.

Implications for the Sociopolitical Dynamics of Religion

Shankland's discussion of broad historical trajectories in the Muslim world, in light of Gellner's seminal work on that topic, is one of several attempts in this book to relate the modes theory to patterns of sociopolitical transformation. Peel examines such problems in relation to the missionization of West Africa, especially by Christian denominations. Højbjerg focuses on the history of modes dynamics in a single West African case. Goody also draws on West African material but focuses primarily on the changing politico-religious climate of ancient Egypt. Malley meanwhile explores the role of doctrinal-mode dynamics in the historical development of fundamentalist Christianity in the United States. Additional trajectories are suggested by ethnographic examples from Asia, presented by Laidlaw, Bayly, and Howe. The material presented in these chapters has important implications for our understanding of the role of modes of religiosity in patterns of historical transformation.

In *Arguments and Icons* (Whitehouse 2000), I suggested that doctrinal and imagistic modes constitute major attractor positions around which religious traditions coalesce. I still think so but, as indicated above, I now think there is another attractor position, one that is even more ubiquitous and influential in cultural transmission, and that is the *cognitive optimum position*. This has important implications for the historical dynamics of religion.

In the case of the doctrinal mode, institutional stability is always the outcome of a complex compromise. If a doctrinal orthodoxy is to be preserved intact as a reasonably standardized body of meaningful and relevant teachings, then it must be subjected to a regime of heavy repetition. This is most obviously the case for the purposes of acquisition—people cannot learn a body of ideas with a heavy conceptual load unless these ideas are subject to frequent narrative rehearsal, review, and consolidation. But, as we also probably all agree, religious orthodoxies typically involve levels of repetition that are greatly in excess of the needs of learners and novices. Even after the knowledge has been quite thoroughly grasped and memorized, adherents undergo further reiterations of that knowledge (e.g., through daily or weekly sermons). When speech is *ritualized* in that way, it seems as if one's own thoughts and experiences are not entirely one's own. As Bloch and others have observed, one may come to imagine the haunting presence of Another Agent at work in all this, who is neither oneself, nor one's teacher, nor even the dimly conceived procession of teachers who have come before. That Agent at the source of it all, the Originator of the message, becomes the category of the "sacred" as Durkheim struggled to conceive of it. Thus, "intelligibility" lies not merely in a grasp of the complex chains of analogy and inference entailed by the narratives and dogmas of the doctrinal mode, it resides also in the revelatory sensation that religious knowledge makes some *special* sense of the world. What is special about it is that it comes from within, and yet it doesn't. It seems to be both internal/mental and also external/public. And in that paradox the sense that life is more than just individual experience (that a set of intentions—a plan—guides us as surely as we sometimes think that we guide ourselves) also becomes intelligible, at least to some degree.

But heavy repetition also carries risks. People can tire of hearing the same exhortations and parables. All routinized religions have ways of punishing expressions of boredom and of rewarding endurance in the face of its effects. One solution that seems to have been selected in a number of the religious traditions described in this volume is to raise levels of arousal and, in some cases, of spontaneous exegetical reflection, in the doctrinal mode. In effect, this amounts to "borrowing" some of the tried and tested techniques of the imagistic mode, but with a difference. In the case of high-arousal Jain rituals, described so vividly by Laidlaw, full-blown imagistic dynamics are prevented from taking hold because of the unrelenting emphasis on verbal rehearsal, which continues long after the ordeal has been surmounted and in spite of the fact that the ritual patients have a detailed understanding of what their ordeals will entail in advance of experiencing them. These factors might be expected to reduce the impact of episodic encoding and serve to suppress (to what extent, we don't know) processes of independent exegetical reflection. But it seems that at least some of the cohesion effects typical of the imagistic mode are present, and these may have motivational implications. Similar things may be happening among the Sai Baba devotionalists described by Howe. The truth is, there is much to find out about these phenomena, but the data presented in this volume are sufficiently rich and detailed to lead us to ask some searching questions about my original formulation of the relationship between doctrinal and imagistic modes.

Arguably, it would lead to confusion to describe most high-arousal rituals in traditions dominated by the doctrinal mode as "imagistic," at least where such practices do not generate the full complement of features that, by my definition, constitute the imagistic mode. Malley has argued that high-arousal religious experiences among evangelical Christians can have significant implications for levels of morale and commitment but, in most cases, these experiences are personal and solitary and therefore do not form the kinds of small ritual groupings we find in the imagistic mode. Nevertheless, they may have the effect of increasing the rate and volume of spontaneous rumination on matters of doctrine and exegesis. That in turn would present problems for the standardization of orthodoxy and may help to explain the relatively egalitarian and uncentralized character of such traditions (on which Malley also comments). So what we seem to have is a tradition operating broadly in the doctrinal mode but that incorporates additional features (some of which are also found in the imagistic mode) that may have the effect of bolstering levels of motivation.

Of course, not all routinized traditions are as successful as these in rousing their followers. What happens when the "tedium effect" *does* become entrenched? One possibility is that the religious authorities back off somewhat. The mechanisms used for policing the orthodoxy might be partially dismantled, as both lay and professional adherents lose heart. Unauthorized innovations may go unpunished and continued self-discipline unrewarded. Even the frequency of participation in ritual may be reduced and some of the burdens of routinization lifted. In these general circumstances, the cognitive optimum position tends to exercise a special influence.

Whenever the mechanisms for transmitting complex religious knowledge start to falter, natural mechanisms of cognition are activated by default. Hard-to-acquire concepts are increasingly reformulated as simpler, more intuitive versions. Religious ideas become the stuff of popular culture, as illustrated by Shankland's discussion of the "secularization" of certain Islamic traditions, now increasingly built around patterns of drinking and entertainment. In some populations, such a state of affairs is normalized. In others, it might trigger ambitious initiatives of reform, whereby it is felt that people should be reeducated and the "authentic" institutions reestablished. Of course, that might be more a matter of reinvention than restoration, but it is often a genuine return to the past in the sense of resurrecting the disciplines of the doctrinal mode. In much the same vein, one wonders if the iconoclastic and aniconic tendencies that Goody points to in certain periods of ancient Egyptian religiosity are really attempts to assert the dominance of doctrinal orthodoxy over cults founded on imagistic dynamics (an interpretation that might be inferred from certain parts of Goody's argument). Or, alternatively, are we dealing with periodic attempts to eradicate the images and other intuitively accessible supports of popular culture, and to replace them with the more cognitively costly concepts of a heavily policed religious orthodoxy?

Cognitively optimal concepts may impact on modes dynamics in other ways. Christian Højbjerg examines a case, that of the West African Poro cult, in which the imagistic mode provides the principal psychological and sociopolitical dynamics. Revelatory knowledge in the imagistic mode, of course, does not take the form of a doctrinal orthodoxy that must be protected from distortion and decay, nor is it vulnerable to the tedium effect. But adherents to the Poro cult obviously have the same kinds of minds as followers of a doctrinal tradition and, as such, share the same "default" intuitive assumptions about their social environments. A particularly salient assumption, Højbjerg shows, is that humanity may be divided into essentialized categories (see Hirschfeld 1996) that become the objects of coalitional thinking (see Boyer 2001). Although the doctrinal mode is capable of generating forms of political association that cut across these essentialized categories (e.g., a "brotherhood of man," or similar imagined community), that is not a feature of imagistic-mode thinking. On the contrary, as Højbjerg persuasively demonstrates, all attempts to transfer the social cohesion of Poro ritual communities to wider coalitions are highly tenuous and short-lived. The cognitively/affectively salient groupings of the imagistic mode are by their nature small-scale and fiercely exclusivist. Intuitive notions of sameness and difference, on the basis of which wider coalitions may be formed, *unless* these acquire the motivational force of attachments to imagined communities established through doctrinal-mode rituals, will *always* be overruled by particularistic bonds in situations where high-arousal, low-frequency collective rituals are performed. The ritual ordeals entailed in Poro initiations, and the cohesive groupings they create, predictably provide a much more compelling and stable foundation for collective identity and cooperation than the ever-changing regional coalitions envisaged by some observers (see Højbjerg: chapter 10).

Conclusion

Close scrutiny of a wide range of ethnographic materials in this volume has revealed that much religious thinking is an expression of natural cognition rather than of the special kinds of mnemonic and social organizational mechanisms provided by modes dynamics. Thus, drawing on a range of recent findings in the cognitive sciences, I have postulated a *cognitive optimum effect*, comprising concepts that are relatively easy to acquire and pass on, because of their intuitive (or minimally counterintuitive) properties. Most cultural concepts display those qualities and this, of course, is why people all over the world can "read" each other's intentions and cooperate successfully (at least some of the time), regardless of cultural "barriers." In a sense, most cultural differences are trivial. The overt *content* of rules and principles of politeness, decency, morality, humor, allegiance, exchange, production, consumption, love, and war certainly differ in the details, but they are generated by a common stock of underlying, largely tacit, mechanisms. As such, new "content" is far easier to learn than would be the case if the underlying mechanisms themselves differed from one population to the next. At the time of the "big debate" between rationalists and relativists (Wilson 1970), comparatively little was known about the psychic unity of our species. That situation has been changing fast, thanks to a veritable explosion of scientific research on the evolution and phylogenetic development of cognition (Barkow, Cosmides, and Tooby 1992). Most of culture requires *only* the activation of ubiquitous, "natural" mechanisms to get off the ground. That is not the case, however, in certain domains of "expert" cultural knowledge such as science, religion, and at least some forms of art (and art criticism). Although requiring natural cognition, these specialist domains also require massive investments of pedagogic labor if they are to be transmitted because the concepts they uphold and value are intrinsically difficult for the human mind to process. The mother of these expert domains is religion, and the arts and sciences her (largely ungrateful) offspring.[4] But, however advanced our expert knowledge becomes, our natural default is the cognitive optimum. At times, especially for specific practical purposes, modern astronomers will still imagine that the sun rises and travels across the sky, a child's painting will still look a bit like a Picasso, and God will still be some old bloke in the sky. No matter how fancy our theories and aesthetics become, there will always be "easier" versions of our knowledge that we fall back on as the need arises, and that threaten to spread more widely than the respectable, authoritative account.

The theory of modes of religiosity, however, is concerned with exploring how rather more variable, conceptually complex religious concepts come into being and seeks to identify at least some of the major consequences of this for the formation and transformation of religious coalitions. Despite the many constructively critical observations of contributors to this volume, those aspects of the theory of modes of religiosity that are capable of being tested by ethnographic evidence would appear to remain more or less intact. Of course, the ethnographic record is vast in scope and depth and our incursions have inevitably been localized. But this volume has had other aims as well. We have tried, for instance, to establish a more precise set of hypotheses to be tested by future research. And we have also sought to develop new critical insights into the theoretical traditions in which we work as anthropologists.

At the same time, these chapters offer important corrections to certain features of the modes theory, resulting in a number of refinements to its original predictions. Competing theoretical perspectives have also been presented, but it seems to me that this exercise has done more to promote productive syntheses rather than to create intractable divisions among alternative approaches. This extends also to the ways in which we have all looked back to much older traditions of scholarship, particularly the works of Durkheim and Weber, and the twentieth-century modernist theories they have inspired. What we select, and what we discard, must always be determined by the most basic and pragmatic of scientific principles: economy, empirical productivity, and falsifiability. Such simple principles make all the difference between "paradigms" and "agendas," between knowledge and fashion, and between regeneration and decay. At least we can say that we have an increasingly detailed set of plans and some reliable foundations on which to build.

Notes

1. There is a risk here, however, of falling into the trap of thinking that one element in the nexus of doctrinal or imagistic modes is sufficient to characterize a "mode of religiosity." In suggesting that a certain kind of reflexive discourse on modes of religiosity, on the part of religious adherents themselves, constitutes, in and of itself, a "third mode of religiosity," I think Bayly and I may be at cross purposes on matters of terminology. True, doctrinal revelations are verbalized and imagistic ones are not (or not to any great extent), but while these are necessary features, they are not sufficient to characterize a "mode." Modes, in the sense I've intended at least, are composed of entire suites of mutually reinforcing features. If, following Bayly, we were to characterize modes of religiosity as "modes of experience" or "modes of talking about religion," then I suspect we would end up not with three but with scores (indeed, potentially hundreds) of modes of religiosity.

2. Moreover, Boyer's corpus of research in this area has received some interesting embellishment in a recent book by Scott Atran (2002).

3. Bekah Richert is currently working on a series of experimental studies in Northern Ireland, designed to test the extent to which frequency of repetition influences the nature, rate, and volume of exegetical thinking with regard to ritual procedures. This follows a series of pilot studies on the topic, reported in Whitehouse 2004.

4. For a discussion of the historical emergence of these domains and the differences between religion and the arts/sciences, see Whitehouse 2004; see also McCauley 2000.

References

Atran, Scott. 2002. *In Gods We Trust*. New York: Oxford University Press.
Barkow, Jerome H., Leda Cosmides, and John Tooby, eds. 1992. *The Adapted Mind: Evolutionary Psychology and the Generation of Culture*. Oxford: Oxford University Press.
Barrett, Justin L. 1999. "Theological Correctness: Cognitive Constraint and the Study of Religion." *Method and Theory in the Study of Religion* 11: 325–39.
Barrett, Justin L., and Frank C. Keil. 1996. "Anthropomorphism and God Concepts: Conceptualizing a Non-natural Entity." *Cognitive Psychology* 31: 219–47.
Bossy, John. 1985. *Christianity in the West, 1400–1700*. Oxford: Oxford University Press.
Boyer, Pascal. 2001. *Religion Explained: The Evolutionary Origins of Religious Thought*. New York: Basic Books.
———. 2002. "Review of *Arguments and Icons*." *Journal of Ritual Studies* 16: 8–13.
D'Andrade, Roy G. 1995. *The Development of Cognitive Anthropology*. Cambridge: Cambridge University Press.
Fiske, A. P. and N. Haslam. 1997. "Is Obsessive-Compulsive Disorder a Pathology of the Human Disposition to Perform Socially Meaningful Rituals? Evidence of Similar Content." *Journal of Nervous and Mental Disease* 185: 211–22.

Guthrie, Stewart. 1993. *Faces in the Clouds: A New Theory of Religion.* Oxford: Oxford University Press.

Hirschfeld, Lawrence A. 1996. *Race in the Making: Cognition, Culture, and the Child's Construction of Human Kinds.* Cambridge, Mass.: MIT Press.

Humphrey, Caroline, and James Laidlaw. 1994. *The Archetypal Actions of Ritual: A Theory of Ritual Illustrated by the Jain Rite of Worship.* Oxford: Oxford University Press.

Lawson, E. Thomas, and Robert N. McCauley. 1990. *Rethinking Religion: Connecting Cognition and Culture.* Cambridge: Cambridge University Press.

McCauley, Robert N. 2000. "The Naturalness of Religion and the Unnaturalness of Science." In F. Keil and R. Wilson (eds.), *Explanation and Cognition.* Cambridge, Mass.: MIT Press.

McCauley, Robert N., and E. Thomas Lawson. 2002. *Bringing Ritual to Mind: Psychological Foundations of Cultural Forms.* New York: Cambridge University Press.

Sperber, Dan. 1996. *Explaining Culture: A Naturalistic Approach.* Oxford: Blackwell.

Turner, Mark. 1996. *The Literary Mind: The Origins of Thought and Language.* Oxford: Oxford University Press.

Whitehouse, Harvey. 1995. *Inside the Cult: Religious Innovation and Transmission in Papua New Guinea.* Oxford: Oxford University Press.

———. 2000. *Arguments and Icons: Divergent Modes of Religiosity.* Oxford: Oxford University Press

———. 2004. *Modes of Religiosity: A Cognitive Theory of Religious Transmission.* Walnut Creek, Calif.: AltaMira Press.

Whitehouse, Harvey, and Luther H. Martin, eds. 2004. *Theorizing Religions Past: Archaeology, History, and Cognition.* Walnut Creek, Calif.: AltaMira Press.

Wilson, Bryan R. 1970. *Rationality.* Oxford: Blackwell.

Index

Adeboye, E. A., 28
Advaita Venanta school. *See* Hinduism
African/Aladura church, 19–20
African independent churches (AIG), 19–20
African Political Systems (Evans-Pritchard; Fortes), 34
agnosticism, 60
AIG. *See* African independent churches
Akan, 17
Akhenaten. *See* Amenophis IV
the Aladura: prayer v. sacrifice for, 20; religious approach of, 20–21, 23; religious revival by, 20, 26–27
Alevis: conversion to Sunni Islam, 36–37; as imagistic mode, 31, 35–36, 39, 44; patron saint of, 40; religion/social order for, 39, 43–44; ritual by, 38–39; social order of, 41–42; spiritual stages of, 36; in Turkish census, 46; twelve duties of, 40
Ali, 40
Allah, 41
alufa, 18. *See also* Islam
Amenophis IV, 56
Amun, 56, 58
the Anang, 25

ancestor worship: Balinese form of, 145; deference to, 75–76; LoDagaa and, 55; relationship to, 62; rules pertaining to, 164
Anglican Church Missionary Society (CMS), 24
anthropology, study of, 2, 11, 66–67, 89
anthropomorphism, 54, 190. *See also* religion
Apostolic Church, 20
Apostolic Pentecostal, 22–23
Arguments and Icons (Whitehouse), 1, 12, 33–34, 69, 187, 199
Arianism. *See* heresy
Arya Samaj, 111, 112, 113, 114, 116–17; as cow protectors, 119–20; as modernists, 117–19; teachings of, 116–17, 130n3, 132n19; transmission of, 119
Assembly of God, 22–23
Aten, 56
Atran, Scott, 3

Ba, Amhate, 55
Babalawo: Christianity and, 18; divination by, 17. *See also* Ifa; *orisa*; the Yoruba
Babb, Lawrence, 94

Bach Ma temple, 115
the Bagre, 51, 53
Baktaman people, 13, 96
Bali: Hinduism in, 144–50, 198; Sri Sathya Sai Baba, 146–47, 148–50, 188, 200
Bamiloye, Mike, 28
Barkow, Jerome H., 3
Barrett, Justin, 189
Barth, Fredrik, 89
Bateson, George, 46, 167
Bayly, Susan, 187, 199
the Bektashis, 35
belief, shared body of, 5
Benedict, Ruth, 12, 89
the Berbers, 34
Bhagavad Gita, 146. *See also* Hinduism
the Bible: evangelical interpretation of, 81–84; inspiration/authority of, 79; ritualized illumination of, 195
Big Bang theory, 51
Bill, Samuel, 25
binarism, 2
Bloch, Maurice, 3, 187, 192–95, 199
Blombos caves, 49, 63n3
body movements, ceremonies with, 4–5
Book of the Dead, 58
Bossy, John, 138, 141
Bourkina Faso, 55
Boyer, Pascal, 3, 11, 96, 190
Brahmanism, 54, 90
Brazil, 22
British Academy, 1
Buddhism: anthropology of, 92; communication with absent by, 62n1; development of Sri Lankan, 105–6, 113; doctrinal for, 93; local cults/imagism in, 54, 92, 93; Pali canon for, 92; Protestant, 105–6; reform/accommodation in, 94–95; Reformed, 121; renunciation in, 90; representation of, 114; Sri Lankan, 105–6, 113; teachings of, 54, 92. *See also* Theravada Buddhism

Burge, T., 75
burial customs, 63n2
Bwiti cult, 22

CAC. *See* Christ Apostolic Church
calligraphy, imagistic use of, 54
Cambridge conference, 1–2
Cameron, Euan, 137
canon, 55
Cao Dai: colonialism and, 127–28; as modernists, 111, 112, 117, 118–19, 121; organization of, 125; Reformed Buddhism as, 121; regimen of, 124–25; spiritual messengers for, 125–26, 128, 131n14; Tay Ninh site for, 119, 124, 126–27; transmission of, 124–25; as universal faith, 124, 130
Catholicism. *See* Roman Catholicism
cave art, 49
Celestial Church of Christ, 22–23, 27
cem, 40–41
ceremony, style of, 1
charity, notion of, 140–41
Cherubim and Seraphim (C&S), 20–21
Chisungu (Richards), 162
Chomsky, Noam, 60
Christ Apostolic Church (CAC), 20–21
Christian Association of Nigeria, 23
Christianity, 18, 54; African practices within, 14, 15–16, 19–20, 26; Aladura similarity to, 26–27; *babalawo* and, 11; Born-again, 22, 23, 26–28; DMR modes in, 28; DMR within evangelical branch, 23–24, 84–85, 200; doctrinal mode as evangelical, 79; electronic media and, 28; Eucharist in, 142–44; Judaism, Islam and, 53; missionary tradition of, 11; PNG, 135; Protestant, 79–80; U.S. fundamentalism, 199. *See also* pre-Reformation Christianity; Redeemed Christian Church of God;

Reformation, European; Roman Catholicism
Christianity in the West, 1400–1700 (Bossy), 138
church: authority of, 140; reinforcement of, 84–86
Church of the Lord, 23
circumcision, ceremony for, 66, 67, 170n3
CMS. *See* Anglican Church Missionary Society
codification of doctrinal mode', 13–14, 80
cognitive mechanisms, 3
cognitive optimum position, 189–91, 195–203. *See also* divergent modes of religiosity; religion
colonialism: Cao Dai and, 127–28; religious response during, 20, 25, 119; social change through, 14
communalism, 114, 119, 121
communication: gesture v. oral, 49, 50; quotation/deference in, 71
confraternity, 140
Confucianism, 52, 54, 114
conscience collective, 14
conventions, internalization of, 71
conversion, experience of, 13
Cort, John E., 94–95
cosmology, 53, 63n8
cow protection, 119–20, 131n9
creation, 51–52
Creekside Baptist Church, 79–80
crucifixion, 54
C&S. *See* Cherubim and Seraphim
cults: ancestor v. nature, 15; ancestor worship in, 16; as doctrinal, 5, 11–14; forces of society v. forces of nature, 12; as imagistic, 5, 13–14; microcosmic v. macrocosmic, 15; revival/survival of, 13, 17; in West Africa, 15–17
culture: concept of, 2; differences in, 202–3; elements of, 3; literate v. oral,
53, 55; memory and, 3; religious orientation to, 3, 20, 38, 39, 113

D'Andrade, Roy, 197
Darwin, Charles, 13
Day of Pentecost, 25
Deeper Life, 23, 27
deference: ancestor worship, 75–76; authority of, 69–73, 77; clarity in, 71; communication for, 71; compulsion for, 70–71; consciousness of, 71; exegesis and, 71; origin of, 75; quotation and, 69–70; in ritual, 77; tradition as, 73
developmentalism, 59
divergent modes of religiosity (DMR): cognitive optimum position and, 195–203; embedding of, 188; empirical verification of, 196; historical basis for, 17, 111; integration of, 14, 105, 188, 198; neo-Pentecostalism and, 26; reflection process in, 111–12; reformulation of, 89–90, 97, 187; refutation of, 102–3; scope of, 196; survival of, 17; theory emphasis of, 13, 90, 151
the divine, human contact with, 14
The Division of Labour (Durkheim), 14
DMR. *See* divergent modes of religiosity
Docetism. *See* heresy
doctrinal mode: complexity of, 195; imagism in, 107n10; imagistic v., 122, 135–36, 151; social structure of, 80; splintering of, 106, 111; spread of, 92, 135; tedium of, 84–86, 104, 135, 199, 200, 201
Doctrinal Mode of Religiosity, 6–7
doctrine: access to, 168; body of, 5–6; content of, 12, 13; dogma v., 52; repetition of, 83; spread of, 5, 13
dogma: doctrine v., 52; role of, 53
Drewal, Margaret Thompson, 16

Duffy, Eamon, 136–37
Dumont, Louis, 91–92, 104
Durkheim, Emile, 11–12, 14, 34, 46, 200, 203

eboga, 22
ecstatic practice, 96, 123
Egungun, 16. *See also* the Yoruba
Egypt, 55, 201
The Elementary Forms (Durkheim), 14
Emory University Conferences Subvention Fund, 1, 9n1
empowerment, 26
End-Time Army (Ojo), 27
the Enlightenment, 60
essentialism, 2
Eternal Sacred Order of Cherubim and Seraphim, 23
ethics, doctrinal control of, 83
Ethiopian/Zionist church, 19–20
ethnography, 8, 195
the Eucharist. *See* Christianity; pre-Reformation Christianity
evangelism: beliefs in God, 82; characteristics of, 80, 84–85; doctrinal/imagistic, 23–24, 201; Evangelical Christianity, 84, 85, 200; identification of, 86n2
Evans-Pritchard, E. E., 34, 61
evolution: of brain/language, 63n4; doctrine of, 51
exegesis: deference and, 71; ritual and, 66

Faces in the Clouds (Guthrie), 190
Faith Tabernacle, 20, 27
Fang of Gabon, 22
fasting: before the Eucharist, 144; religious emotion by, 137; renunciation by, 97, 100–102, 104
Fernandez, James W., 22
Fiske, A. P., 191
flashbulb memory, 4
Forge, Anthony, 167

forms, doctrine of (Plato), 55
Fortes, Meyer, 34
Foursquare Gospel, 22–23
French Congo, 22
Freud, Sigmund, 59
functionalism, 75

Gaurakshini Sabhas, 119–20
Gellner, Ernest, 3, 4, 32, 39, 45–46, 89, 94, 199
Ghana, 53
ghosts, 59–60, 62, 96, 139, 191
Gia Long, 115
globalization of religion, 22, 149
the Gnau, 164–67, 197
Gnosticism. *See* heresy
God: communion with, 85–86; evangelical beliefs in, 82; submission to, 83–84. *See also* the divine
Gombrich, Richard, 94, 95
Goody, Jack, 89, 167, 170n6, 187, 199, 201
görgü, 41
the Great Awakening, 24
Gricean principles, 69
Guthrie, Stewart, 190

Haci Bektash, 40
Hafiz, 35
Hasan, 40
Haslam, N., 191
hedonism, 59
heresy: Gnosticism, Docetism, Arianism as, 83; orthodox deviation as, 81
hieroglyphics, development of, 55
Hinde, R., 60, 163
Hindi, 123
Hinduism: Advaita Vedanta school of, 116; Arya Samaj revivalists of, 111, 112–14, 116–20; Balinese doctrinal forms of, 144–50, 198; imagism of, 54; Islam *v.*, 123; renunciation in, 90; representation of, 114; *sramana*

movement in, 91; Sri Sathya Sai Baba, 146–47, 148–50, 188, 200
Højbjerg, Christian K., 187, 199, 201–2
holiness, 26, 27
Holy Ghost Night, 27, 28. *See also* Redeemed Christian Church of God
Holy Spirit, 20, 26, 27
Holy Trinity, 192
Horemheb, 58
Horton, Robin, 15
Howe, Leo, 187, 198, 199, 200
Hume, David, 89
Humphrey, Caroline, 68, 192, 195
Hüseyin, 40
hymns, ceremonies with, 4–5

Ibadan, 22
Ibn Khaldoun, 33
icon: imagery/ritual meaning of, 137; as object of worship, 54
iconophobia, 57, 122
Ifa, 17–19. *See also* orisa
images. *See* icon
images, prohibition on, 55
imagistic mode: as aid to doctrine, 96, 103; complexity of, 195; definition of, 107n8; doctrinal *v.*, 122, 135–36, 151; historicity of, 111; spread of, 92; stigma of, 114, 116, 121, 122
Imam Cafer, 42
inculturation, Vatican II, 23
Indic renouncer religions, 89–106
initiation, 13, 49, 65, 173–76
inspiration, personal, 5
institutional devices, 70
intentionality, search for, 74
Islam: Cham practice of, 115; Christianity, Judaism and, 53; concepts of, 42; doctrinal mode in, 31, 32–33; education in, 72; face-to-face collective ritual under, 32; Hinduism *v.*, 123; Jainism influenced by, 105; religious life in, 32; spread/stability of, 33, 91; stigma of, 122; as theocracy, 33; Turkey and, 46–47, 196–97, 201; Yoruba and, 19. *See also* the Koran

Jackson, Michael, 168
Jainism: anthropology of, 94–95, 106n2; austerity in, 91, 92–93; division of, 93–94; doctrinal in, 93, 188; fasting and, 97, 100–102, 104; Jinas worship, 105; Kanji Swami Panth within, 105–6; local cults/imagistic in, 93, 94, 200; Mahavira, 91, 92; Muslim influence in, 105; ordination ceremony into, 99–102, 107n12; reform/accommodation in, 93–95; renunciation in, 90, 97
Jesus Christ, 18, 79
Jinas. *See* Jainism
Johnson, W. A. B., 25
Judaism, Christianity, Islam and, 53

Kanji Swami Panth, 105–6. *See also* Jainism
Keane, Webb, 68
Keesing, Roger M., 164
Kemal, Mustafa, 42. *See also* Turkey
Keswick Convention, 24–25
Khayyam, Omar, 35
King's College Research Centre, 9n1
kinship, 139
Kongo, 17
the Koran, 19, 53, 72
Korea, 22

labor, division of, 14
Laidlaw, James, 68, 187, 188, 192, 195, 199, 200
language: advent of, 49; symbolism of, 49, 60
Last Judgment, 139. *See also* pre-Reformation Christianity
Lawson, E. Thomas, 3, 191
leaders, religious, 5
Lewis, Gilbert, 187, 193, 196

life after death, 62
Lijadu, E. M., 18
the Lobi, 55
the LoDagaa, 51, 53, 55, 170n6
Lonka Shah, 105. *See also* Jainism
Lord, Albert, 52
Luther, Martin, 58, 138, 141

Madagascar, 18
Magic and the Millennium (Wilson), 12
Mahavira, 91. *See also* Jainism
Maimonides, 54
Malley, Brian, 187, 194–95, 199, 200–201
Marxism, 20
McCauley, Robert N., 3, 191
media, religious coverage by, 28
meditation: as dependent on language, 63n10; experimentation with, 91; foci for, 96
Meeker, M., 47n8
Melanesia, ethnography of, 11, 13
memory: effect of, on culture, 3; episodic/autobiographical (imagistic), 3, 4, 5, 11–12, 13; forms of, 13; mechanisms of long-term, 1; representation of semantic (doctrinal), 3, 4, 11–12, 13; ritual and, 65
metarepresentation, 69
mind, theory of, 69, 76
Minh Mang, 115
the Mishnah, 158–59, 170n1
mnemonics, 162, 202
modes of religiosity, 2, 4; cognitively optimal in, 189–93; comparative analysis as, 112, 113–14; distinctions of, 1, 8, 11–12, 35, 66; establishment of, 8, 11–12, 13–14; interaction of, 93, 173
mode *v.* style, 33
Mohamed, 72
morality, 59
Mount Zion Faith Ministries, 28

music, religious *v.* secular life in, 45
Muslim Society (Gellner), 32, 34
Myths of the Bagre, 51
myth *v.* mythology, 52–53

nagas, 93
A Nation of Empire (Meeker), 47n8
natural *v.* supernatural, 59–61
Naupad Oli Puja, 107n9. *See also* Jainism
Neanderthals, 49, 62, 63n2
neo-Pentecostal. *See* Christianity
the Noise, 24

Obeyesekere, Gananath, 94
objectivism, 2
Obsessive Compulsive Disorder (OCD), 191
Ogun, 17
Ojo, Matthews, 27
Olodumare, 18. *See also* Ifa; *orisa*; the Yoruba
oracles, guidance of, 18
order of natural life, 46
Origgi, Gloria, 69–70
origin stories. *See* creation
orisa: Ifa system for, 17–18; motivation by, 16; Orisa Oko devotee, 17; revelation through, 16, 18; symbols/images of, 16–17. *See also* the Yoruba
Orokaiva people, 13
orthodoxy: attention to, 157; elements of, 81; heresy and, 81; maintenance of, 51; reestablishment of, 58
orthopraxy, 157, 168
Orunmila, 18
Osiris, 58
Osun, 17
Ottoman Empire, 36

Paliau movement, 24
Pali canon. *See* Buddhism
Papua New Guinea (PNG): cults/messianic movements in, 95,

135, 138, 144–45, 151; introduction of Christianity to, 135; religious movements in, 2, 96; taboos in, 102
parables, 192
Peel, J. D. Y., 187, 199
Pentecostalism, 20, 22–25
Plato, 55
Plough, Sword and Book (Gellner), 33
PNG. *See* Papua New Guinea
Poro: initiation cult of, 173–76; intuitive assumption of, 201–2
positivism, 2
possession, 17, 18, 93, 96
Praying Band, 27
pre-Reformation Christianity: charity in, 141; Eucharist in, 142–44; Last Judgment in, 139; medieval practice of, 23, 136–39; saints/relics in, 137
Prey into Hunter (Bloch), 77
Primitive Culture (Tylor), 61–62
Protestant Buddhism, 105–6
Protestant Christianity, 79–80
psychotropic drug, 22. *See also* eboga
purgatory, 139–40. *See also* pre-Reformation Christianity
Puritanism, 23–24

Qua Iboe Mission, 25
quotation: deference and, 69–70; in ritual, 68

Ra, 56
Radcliffe-Brown, A. R., 161
Rappaport, Roy A., 11
rasas, 114
rationalists *v.* relativists, 202
Re, 58
readings, ceremonies with, 4–5
Redeemed Christian Church of God, 23, 27, 28
Redemption Camp, 27. *See also* Redeemed Christian Church of God
reductionism, 2

Reformation, European: grace/salvation under, 141; imagistic reform under, 23–24, 54, 136; practices of, 197; scriptural authority during, 141, 198
reformism, 19, 117–18
relativists *v.* rationalists, 202
religion: anthropology of, 136; anthropomorphism in, 190; Apollonian/Dionysian studies of, 12; the Bible, 79, 81–84, 195; birth/origin of, 13–14, 49, 51; changes in, 58; characteristics of, 59; cognitively optimal aspects of, 189–92, 202; complexity of, 195; divine revelation in, 15; hierarchy of, 54; as intuitive, 104, 189; isolation of, 112; language as precursor to, 50; pedagogy of, 203; perpetuation of, 13; practice of, 167, 170; response to life by, 169, 200; revival showbiz and, 28; salvation in, 12, 82, 141; sect *v.* church, 12; small-scale *v.* world, 12; social change and, 12; social order and, 11–12, 32, 164; survival/vitality of, 13–14; symbolization in, 49, 60; theory of, 11; tradition of, 192
Religion of the Semites (Smith), 50
religiosity: characterization of, 1, 6. *See also* modes of religiosity
renunciation, religions of, 90–106
revelation: content of, 12; individual instance of, 5, 15, 66; through *orisa*, 16, 18; through religion, 15; during ritual, 194; transmission of, 13. *See also* doctrine; modes of religiosity
revivals, 24, 28
Richards, Audrey, 162, 169
rites, liturgical, 5
ritual: alerting quality of, 159; decoding of, 66–67, 71; deference in, 77; empirical verification of, 196; initiation, 13, 49, 65, 173–76; interpretation of, 194–95; memory

and, 65; narratives in, 192; origin of, 193; quotation in, 68; repetition in, 67–69; restrictions in, 164–67; revelation during, 194; routine of, 13, 193–94; style of, 1, 159–60, 170n4, 192; supernatural in, 191; timing of, 163; transmission of, 65, 170, 196, 201; violence in, 77
Roman Catholicism, 23, 54, 137
routinization, 193
Rubayyat (Khayyam), 35

sacrifice: imagistic in, 158; language in, 49; requirement of, 16, 18; self-discipline for, 26. *See also* the Aladura; *orisa*
salvation, 12, 82, 141
Sankara, 116. *See also* Hinduism
Sanskrit, 54, 123
schema theory, 65
schismogenesis, 106
scientism, 2
Second Cult, 24
sermon: ceremony with, 4–5; function of, 84; themes of, 83
Shankland, David, 187, 196–97, 199, 201
Smenkhhare, 57
Smith, Robertson, 50, 51
solidarity, impact of, 5, 14
sorcery. *See* witchcraft
Sperber, Dan, 3, 73, 97
Spirit Movement, 25
spirit possession, 72, 123
splintering of religious forms, 105, 106, 111
sramana doctrine, 91, 95, 104, 106
Sri Lankan Buddhism, 105–6, 113
Sri Sathya Sai Baba, 146–47, 148–50, 188, 200
Sthanakvasis, 105. *See also* Jainism
style *v.* mode, 33
Sufi mysticism, 22, 35, 118, 121, 123–24, 197
Sunni movement, 31, 34

supernatural: natural *v.*, 59–61; in ritual, 191
survival of cult/religion, 13
Swami Dayananda Saraswati, 113, 120. *See also* Arya Samaj
symbolism, language as, 49, 60

taboos, 102, 161–62
Tambiah, S. J., 94
Taoism, 114
Tarkan, 35
Taro Cult, 96
Tay Ninh, 119, 124, 126–27, 128–29. *See also* Cao Dai
TC. *See* Theologically Correct discourse
Templeton Foundation, 9n1
testimony, personal, 85
Theologically Correct discourse (TC), 189
Theosophy, 113
Theravada Buddhism: anthropology of, 106n2; doctrinal/imagistic in, 94; *sramana* origins in, 91; stigma of, 128. *See also* Buddhism
Thomas, Keith, 136–37, 140
Time of Troubles, 58
tongues, speaking in, 20, 26
tooth filing, 148
tradition, 73, 76
trance. *See* possession
transubstantiation, dogma of, 142–43
Trinity, doctrine of the, 59
Turkey: consumerism in, 34; Islam in, 46–47, 196–97, 201; Kemal Ataturk as father of, 42; migration in, 42; secular state of, 35
Turner, Victor, 12
Tutankhamun, 57
Tuzin, Donald F., 167
Tylor, E. B., 49, 50, 61–62

Ulster Evangelicals, 25
Ulster revival, 25
Urdu, 123

Vatican II, inculturation by, 23
the Vedas, 54, 117, 120

Weber, Max, 3, 4, 11–12, 21, 24, 89, 168, 203
Welsh revival, 25
Wesley, John, 24
West Africa: Christian missions in, 14, 15–16; colonialism in, 14; cults in, 15; Islam in, 15; societal hierarchy in, 15; tradition v. world religions in, 15
Whitehouse, Harvey: imagism for, 95, 97; individual experience emphasized, 169; originality of, 89; theories of, 1, 3, 6, 11, 31–32, 79

Wilberforce, Bishop, 52
Wilson, Bryan, 12
Winners' Chapel. *See* Redeemed Christian Church of God
witchcraft, 61, 140
Word of God, 54

the Yoruba: Christianity/Islam for, 18; collective ancestors of, 16; cults of, 16; gods of, 17; holiness/empowerment for, 26. *See also* the Aladura; Ifa; *orisa*

zeitgeist, 27
Zen, 54. *See also* Buddhism

About the Contributors

Susan Bayly is a lecturer in the Cambridge University Department of Social Anthropology and is editor of the *Journal of the Royal Anthropological Institute* (formerly *Man*). Her main research interest is the experience and cultural legacy of colonialism. Her publications include *Caste, Politics and Society in India from the Eighteenth Century to the Modern Age* (1999) and *Saints, Goddesses and Kings: Muslims and Christians in South Indian Society* (1989; second edition, 1992). She has recently done fieldwork in Hanoi and is completing a study of the colonial encounter and its aftermath in Indochina.

Maurice Bloch is professor of anthropology at the London School of Economics. Two of his recent books are *Prey into Hunter* (1992) and *How We Think They Think* (1998).

Jack Goody is a fellow of St. John's College, Cambridge, and formerly William Wyse Professor of Social Anthropology at the University of Cambridge (1973–1984). His most recent books include *The Culture of Flowers* (1993), *The Expansive Moment* (1995), *The East in the West* (1996), *Representations and Contradictions* (1997), *Food and Love: A Cultural History of East and West* (1999), *The European Family* (2000), *The Power of the Written Tradition* (2000), and (with S. W. D. K. Gandah) *The Third Bagre: A Myth Revisited* (2002).

Christian K. Højbjerg is senior research fellow at the Centre of African Studies, University of Copenhagen. He received his Ph.D. at the Institute of Anthropology, University of Copenhagen, where he has also held an appointment as assistant professor. His regional area of specialization is West Africa, and he has carried out fieldwork in Guinea and Mauritania and has worked as a consultant on environmental issues in Senegal. His main interests are in ritual, religion, and politics. He has also specialized in environmental anthropology. He has published many articles on the Loma people in Guinea and Liberia and is currently completing a monograph on Loma religion and political culture.

Leo Howe is a senior lecturer in social anthropology at Cambridge University and the dean of Darwin College. He has published widely on many aspects of Balinese society and culture, and on issues of unemployment, sectarianism, and the politics of work and social security in Northern Ireland. His most recent book is *Hinduism and Hierarchy in Bali* (2001). He may be contacted at leh1000@cam.ac.uk.

James Laidlaw studied social anthropology at King's College, Cambridge, with Caroline Humphrey as supervisor for his doctoral fieldwork in western India, between 1984 and 1990. He is now a university lecturer in social anthropology and a fellow of King's College, Cambridge. More recent fieldwork has been in Taiwan and Inner Mongolia. Publications include *The Archetypal Actions of Ritual* (1994, with Caroline Humphrey), *Riches and Renunciation* (1995), and *The Essential Edmund Leach* (2000, with Stephen Hugh-Jones).

Gilbert Lewis first qualified in medicine at Oxford and then studied anthropology at the London School of Economics, with Anthony Forge as supervisor for his doctoral fieldwork in the West Sepik, New Guinea, from 1967 to 1969. A fellow of St. John's College, Cambridge, and formerly a university lecturer in social anthropology at Cambridge University, his main interests have been in medical anthropology and ritual. He has done shorter fieldwork in the Gambia and Guinea Bissau, West Africa, as well as made further visits to the West Sepik, Papua New Guinea. His books include *Knowledge of Illness in a Sepik Society* (1975), *Day of Shining Red* (1980), and *A Failure of Treatment* (2000).

Brian Malley studied comparative religion at Western Michigan University (M.A., 1994) and anthropology at the University of Michigan (Ph.D., 2002). He currently lectures in psychology at the University of Michigan. His main interests are religion and the intersection of culture and cognition. He is the author of *How the Bible Works: An Anthropological Study of Evangelical Biblicism* (2004).

J. D. Y. Peel is professor of anthropology and sociology with reference to Africa, at the School of Oriental and African Studies, University of London. He has also held appointments at the London School of Economics and at the Universities of Nottingham, Ife (in Nigeria), Liverpool, and Chicago. His principal works have focused on religious, cultural, and political change in West Africa, especially among the Yoruba of Nigeria—*Aladura* (1968), *Ijeshas and Nigerians* (1983), and *Religious Encounter and the Making of the Yoruba* (2000)—but he also has an interest in the history of social thought and wrote *Herbert Spencer: The Evolution of a Sociologist* (1971). He was the editor of *Africa: Journal of the International African Institute* from 1979 to 1986, and was elected as a fellow of the British Academy in 1991.

David Shankland studied social anthropology at Edinburgh, and then moved to Cambridge in 1986 to study with Ernest Gellner. His doctoral fieldwork took place in Turkey between 1988 and 1990, mainly among the Turkish Alevi community. He returned to Turkey between 1992 and 1995 as the assistant, then acting director of the British Institute of Archaeology at Ankara. At present, he is senior lecturer at Bristol University. He has conducted further fieldwork in Anatolia on questions of religion, heritage, and archaeology, and also amongst the Turkish migrant community in Germany. Among his publications are *Religion and Society in Turkey* (1999) and *The Alevis in Turkey: The Emergence of a Secular Islamic Tradition* (2003).

Harvey Whitehouse is professor of anthropology and director of postgraduate studies in the Faculty of Humanities at Queen's University Belfast. A specialist in Melanesian religion, he carried out two years of field research on a "cargo cult" in New Britain, Papua New Guinea, in the late 1980s. In recent years, he has focused his energies on the development of collaborative programs of research on cognition and culture. He is currently the principal grant holder of a British Academy Networks Project on "modes of religiosity" and, in 2003, was appointed to a British Academy Research Readership. He is also coeditor, with Luther H. Martin, of the AltaMira Press Cognitive Science of Religion Series. His previous books include *Inside the Cult: Religious Innovation and Transmission in Papua New Guinea* (1995), *Arguments and Icons: Divergent Modes of Religiosity* (2000), *The Debated Mind: Evolutionary Psychology Versus Ethnography* (2001), and *Modes of Religiosity: A Cognitive Theory of Religious Transmission* (2004).

Made in the USA
Lexington, KY
13 June 2013